GIVE US BACK OUR COUNTRY

Other books by David Flint

The Cane Toad Republic (1999)
The Twilight of the Elites (2003)
Malice in Media Land (2005)
Her Majesty at 80 (2006)

(For a complete list of David Flint's publications see page 383)

GIVE US BACK OUR COUNTRY

David Flint & Jai Martinkovits

Connor Court Publishing
Ballarat

Published in 2013 by Connor Court Publishing Pty Ltd

Connor Court Publishing Pty Ltd.
PO Box 224W
Ballarat VIC 3350
sales@connorcourt.com
www.connorcourt.com

ISBN: 978-1-922168-69-6 (pbk.)

Cover design: Jeff Gollin

The image on the cover is of the superb re-enactment in 2007 of the charge of the 4th Australian Light Horse Brigade in the Battle of Beersheba in 1917. In terms of courage and bravery this has been compared with the Charge of the Light Brigade at Balaklava in 1854. The victory secured at Beersheba was followed by the capture of Jerusalem and the ultimate collapse of the Ottoman Empire. The authors wish to thank Eman for his general permission to use his photograph.

Printed in Australia

CONTENTS

Authors

David Flint was educated at the Universities of Sydney, London and Paris. He is an emeritus professor of law and was chairman of the Australian Broadcasting Authority and the Australian Press Council, president of the National Federation of the English Speaking Union, Associate Commissioner with the Australian Competition and Consumer Commission and convenor of the Committee of Australian Law Deans. He has been National Convenor of Australians for Constitutional Monarchy since the 1999 referendum campaign. The author of several books, he has published widely on topics such as the media, international economic law and on the Constitution. At Barcelona in 1991, he received a World Jurist Association award as World Outstanding Legal Scholar. He was made a Member of the Order of Australia in 1995.

Jai Martinkovits was born and raised in Sydney. His formal training has been primarily in the Information Technology sector, graduating in 2008 with a Bachelor of Computing, majoring in e-Business and Business Information Systems. He has a wide range of interests and is a Red Belt in Taekwondo. He is Executive Director of CANdo.org.au, an organisation dedicated to preserving, protecting, and defending our individual rights, freedoms and traditional values. A strong supporter of Australia's constitutional system and the Australian Flag, he is also Executive Director of Australians for Constitutional Monarchy, an office first held by Tony Abbott. Jai's views have been frequently sought by the television, radio and print media. Most recently Jai featured in a six-part ABC series exploring contemporary issues facing Australia.

Foreword

Our system of government is not working as well as it once did. There has been a serious decline and this must be corrected.

When assessing the work of governments, federal and state, the authors of this book rely on a simple but effective method, which they attribute to me.

This is the "pub test". They say this is no more than shorthand for the common sense, good judgement and the decency of everyday Australians – the rank-and-file who are in the tradition of those who built, fought for and died for this country.

The authors ask whether governments, state and federal, have passed the pub test on a series of burning issues. The sad fact is that far too often they have failed, sometimes miserably.

The book opens with many examples which support the conclusion I hear everywhere: the Rudd and Gillard governments have been the most incompetent, wasteful and deceitful in the history of the nation. Everywhere, property rights of Australians are under threat. Despite the mantra about Australia becoming the food bowl of Asia, our prime agricultural land is being raped and people's lives destroyed, all with the complicity of governments everywhere.

The authors argue that all this is the result of a fundamental problem which, if not solved, will inevitably doom us to being ruled again by similar governments – or even worse.

The problem, they say, is that the institutions of our representative democracy have been seriously compromised and our system of government corrupted. They attribute this to the shady alliance which has emerged between the "faceless men" – the factional powerbrokers who dominate the major political parties – and the "intellectual elites" who have marched through so many of our institutions.

The authors ask one question about this ruling class, as do many of my listeners. Why do they so hate Australia? Little wonder then that the authors describe this alliance of convenience between the powerbrokers and the elites as an Anti Australia Axis.

In a second part, they recall the principles on which Australia was established and developed and for which our soldiers, sailors and airmen fought and died. This part is important; the elites are in the process, through the attempted federal takeover of education, of removing the study of our history from the curriculum. The result is that our young people – and those new to the country – are barely aware of our unique Federation story and of that golden thread that goes back through the Glorious Revolution to the Magna Carta.

In the third part, the authors propose a solution – a reset, if you will – of our Australian democracy. This is to empower the Australian people, who may be trusted more than the politicians to apply common sense, good judgement and decency to the national agenda.

They say the politicians must be made accountable on every day, of every week, of every month and of every year – as is every Australian employee, professional, businessperson, farmer or athlete.

The authors say the solution is through grafting onto our constitutional system the tools of direct democracy. This, they stress, is not the total direct democracy as once existed in Athens. Representative democracy did not exist there. This solution would retain our stable Westminster system, but add onto it tools which would make the politicians truly accountable. They provide valuable evidence from the experience of other countries, principally Switzerland and the United States, which shows that direct democracy does not result in instability or cater for special interests. Instead, it has resulted in lower taxation, and higher standards of government. They say that just the knowledge that the people can use the tools of direct democracy – even without their use – encourages politicians to act in the public interest.

The authors sensibly stress that we should not rush into this. Instead they say there should be an elected convention, similar to the Federation Convention and the 1998 Republic Convention.

To be effective, they argue the Convention should operate under the 1893 Corowa Plan through which federation was achieved. They say that without Corowa we could easily have turned out to be six separate countries. Under this plan, when the convention produces its draft conclusions on, say, the right of recall, or vetoing laws or treaties, or citizens initiating new laws, the parliament and anyone interested should have the opportunity to comment. After the Convention considers these, its final conclusions should be put to the people without being amended by the politicians, or torn apart, diluted or worse, shelved.

This is, I believe, a carefully considered and sensible approach. The process should produce well considered proposals to improve the governance of Australia.

The point is we just cannot go on as we are. This is the 21st century, but we still live under this shady AAA regime – the alliance between powerbrokers and the elites. No other democracy as old as Australia would tolerate something so intrinsically undemocratic. On this the authors also call for the major parties to be finally dragged into the 21st century and be made open, transparent and democratic. And not only as regards their preselections but also as regards their management. They also suggest that as in the USA, citizen judges be able to initiate inquiries into corruption and maladministration. This would also be behind closed doors so the presumption of innocence would be preserved.

I commend this work to all Australians, and I support the proposal that a convention be held to prepare detailed proposals for change for the decision of those who should once again be the masters of the nation, the Australian people.

Further, I would encourage all Australians who support the authors' proposal to make our politicians accountable 24/7, to join the organisation advancing this agenda – www.CANdo.org.au.

Alan Jones, AO

Preface

There is widespread feeling among Australians that their country has been taken away from them and that there is something very wrong in the way in which the country is governed.

Across the country, in our towns, cities and suburbs, on our farms and in our mines, in our pubs and clubs, Australians are asking how this happened and what they can do. They are intensely dissatisfied with their politicians. They want something more than being compelled to vote every three or four years, effectively signing a blank cheque in favour of one of two teams. They increasingly realise that candidates are rarely chosen openly and democratically, and not necessarily on merit but for their loyalty to one or other of the "faceless men". These are the factional powerbrokers who exercise inordinate and undeserved power and authority in modern Australia.

We must never forget that when our forefathers and mothers decided to come together as one people, this continent was already home to some of the most advanced democracies in the world. They achieved federation not through our politicians taking the decision for us, but by the people deciding how it would be done. Once they set their mind to this at Corowa in 1893, this was achieved – with the full co-operation of the British – in a remarkably short period of time.

And let's not forget – this was done without modern communications and transport. When we did come together as one nation, we continued to be an exciting laboratory of new ideas empowering the people.

As with any other human venture, the model we chose is not perfect. Perhaps the greatest weakness was in only partially empowering the people in elections and by ensuring that their consent was only necessary for constitutional change.

What the founding fathers did not know was that our representative democracy would become more and more dominated by a rigorous two-party system controlled essentially by cabals of "faceless men", the factional powerbrokers. They were not aware that these powerbrokers would work arm in arm with the radical elites. Realising that an unachievable revolution was not necessary to deliver their radical and unpopular agendas, the elites soon learned these could be realised behind the scenes via their long march through our key institutions. This would be aided by activist judges and by means of international treaties which are only taken seriously by governments controlled by Western elites.

These elite agendas have led to a number of governments, state and federal, leaving a trail of mounting debt. The governments have also simultaneously demonstrated increasing incompetence and deceit.

Recognising that the people are aware of the decline in the quality of governance, the perpetrators have from time to time unashamedly proposed a series of false "reforms", to use one of their favourite words. This is of course often done to distract the electorate from real reform.

These "reforms" have included fixed terms, longer terms, new methods of voting, making it easier to vote when no one has complained that it was difficult, abolishing one tier of government, introducing a new tier of government, introducing a politicians' republic, increased pay for politicians, increased staff, advisers, even something as obviously transparently useless as community cabinets, etc.

Not one of those actually introduced has improved government. And Australians must be assured that none can. If it is not to increase power it is a camouflage and a distraction. Sometimes it is both.

In summarising what is wrong, we had to be brief – had we written about everything we have been told, Part 1 would have turned into a multi-volume thesis.

Then in Part 2 we recall the institutions on which our country was built and the principles on which the country should be governed. We believe it is important that all Australians, and particularly the young and the new, know these. The observer will have noted an increasing and probably deliberate failure to teach our children about the story of Australia, going back, as it does, through the wonderful story of our Federation through the Glorious Revolution and back to the Magna Carta. This is important as there is a concerted effort to hide this from our children, from new arrivals and even from us.

Finally, in Part 3, we propose a tried and tested solution based on the experience of the most advanced and successful democracies. We argue that while retaining our representative democracy under our federal Westminster system, we, the people, must make our politicians truly accountable. This should be more than in elections every three or four years too often between candidates chosen for factional loyalty rather than merit. The answer is to make the politicians accountable – just as rank-and-file Australians are – on every day, of every week, of every month and of every year.

This can be done by introducing into Australia the tools of direct democracy, tools which have worked and are working well in Switzerland and over 20 American states.

We propose that a convention of delegates be elected by the voting population to work out a series of proposals to be considered by the Australian people in referendums. We believe that delegates should not be paid to ensure and to demonstrate that their only concern is only about the future of Australia.

Their function would be to produce proposals for referendums about the right of the people to petition for a national vote on the recall of a government, for the repeal of an unpalatable new piece of legislation (for example a new tax) or a treaty, and for the introduction of new legislation enjoying popular support but in which the politicians lack interest.

Another issue is whether the major political parties, in return for the massive legal, financial and policy advantages their agents have voted themselves, should be required to come into the 21st century, and to be like parties in other advanced countries – open, transparent and democratic, especially as regards preselections and in relation to their management.

Or are they to remain a national disgrace, remaining under the thumb of a cabal of factional powerbrokers, more often than not selecting candidates not on merit but on factional loyalty and advancing their own power and wealth to the detriment of the national interest?

The convention would also consider whether machinery should be established for citizens themselves to initiate enquiries into corruption and crime without a government having to establish a royal commission, as in the United States.

We realise that such a convention will only be held if the politicians decide on it. And the politicians will only do so if there is enormous pressure from the public for a convention to at least consider these important issues.

In our final chapter we ask you to join with us in achieving this solution. We believe that united the Australian people can force the powerbrokers and the elites to give us back our country, just as the Australian people in 1893 directed and guided politicians in adopting a process to make us one people in one nation with one destiny.

We believe we should do this not only for ourselves but out of honour for those who made and fought for this country, and for future generations to whom we owe the duty of passing on what we have inherited.

David Flint

Jai Martinkovits

You may follow David Flint on Twitter at **@profdavidflint** and Jai Martinkovits at **@jaimartinkovits**

Acknowledgement

The authors wish to acknowledge the valuable work in the field of direct democracy of Professor de Q. Walker, Dr. Joseph Poprzeczny, Ted Mack and the Hon. Peter Reith, as well as the invaluable support of Alan Jones AO. David Flint especially pays tribute to Amy Brooke for providing a forum for the exchange of ideas at her Summer Sounds Symposium in New Zealand and for her role in leading the 100 Days movement which had inspired him to work on developing a similar movement in Australia.

CHAPTER 1

Stop giving the politicians a blank cheque

1.1 Introduction: The emergence of an Anti-Australian Axis (AAA)

The theme of this book is that the advanced democracy which our forefathers bequeathed to us – and for which our armed forces fought and died – has been seriously corrupted.

An Australian version of a guided or managed democracy is being surreptitiously imposed on the people. This does not augur well for the future of our nation.[1]

We all know that some countries are very successful – as measured in terms of the health, wealth and education of its people. Others are not.

What are the reasons for this?

There is strong and growing evidence that the success of a particular country cannot be explained by the race or colour of its people, nor even its natural endowments.[2] Rather its success can be traced directly back to the quality of its institutions.

Australia, as one of the world's oldest representative democracies, was once endowed with very sound institutions – ones based on our ancient traditions and values. But in recent years those institutions have been more and more compromised. This can be traced directly to the takeover of significant parts of the major political parties by a new brand of "faceless men", the factional powerbrokers.

From this base they have gradually compromised many of the institutions of our representative democracy, while awarding themselves

1

ever increasing power and wealth. A series of scandals concerning the powerbrokers has revealed a world far removed from that of ordinary Australians, one where premiers and even a prime minister can be brought down, and where the faceless men reward one another with millions of dollars of other people's money.

Just as bad money drives out good money under Gresham's Law, so the rule of the "faceless men" in the Labor Party has led to the rise of similar gangs of powerbrokers in some parts of the Liberal Party.

Political power is more and more exercised in the interests of the faction first and then the party, rather than the public interest or any decent regard for the views of the members of the party. They are reduced to making tea and scones, paying subscriptions, raising money, doing unpaid office work, delivering brochures and being the hard working foot soldiers in each and every election campaign. Threatened with penalties, even expulsion, if they dare step out of line, they know they are taken for granted by the party hierarchy.

In the meantime, the intellectual elites who have marched through so many of our institutions find it convenient to tolerate and support the rule of the powerbrokers. In return, the powerbrokers are quite willing to advance the elites' agenda to dismantle our traditional values and institutions, providing this does not compromise their personal interests.

They, the faceless men and the elites, are bound together in an alliance or axis of convenience, united against the people of Australia. The Australian rank-and-file are bewildered by their agenda. A question about their agenda often heard on commercial talkback radio is to the point: "Why do they hate Australia?" These policies are the results of this alliance of convenience, a veritable Anti-Australia Axis between the faceless men, the factional powerbrokers and the elites.

And who are these elites in this Anti-Australia Axis? They were first identified by the American author Christopher Lasch.[3] He described elite opinion as opinion typical of today's upper and middle-class liberals, that is 'liberal' in the American sense, left-wing on social and cultural issues.

As with their Australian equivalents, their opinions and agenda are to be contrasted with the traditional and pragmatic view of the vast majority, who are above all endowed with common sense, good judgement and decency.[4]

The elites are prominent in the universities, especially the humanities faculties, the mainstream media, politics and the higher bureaucracy.

Their views on a wide range of issues typically do not pass the common sense test, or as the nation's highest rating radio commentator Alan Jones succinctly put it, "the pub test." As Nick Cater argues in a recently published book, they have a right to rule mentality.[5] But from their strategic positions in our institutions and with generously rewarded associates in key international organisations, they have been successful in making it difficult for any but the strongest willed and most courageous to speak out against vast parts of their agenda.

Should anyone do so, and their views reach the mainstream media, they are rarely answered by reasoned argument, but more often than not, by ridicule and contempt. The purpose is obvious; it is a brutal way to silence them. This can result in what is sometimes referred to as the spiral of silence.[6] This describes the phenomenon where the more an individual suspects his view on some important issue is losing ground, the more uncertain he may become of himself and the less he may be inclined to express his opinion. The scarcity of contrary views in the media thus can help reinforce the elites' view.

But whatever happens in the debate, the direct result of the adoption of the elite agenda has been disastrous.

How else can we explain the loss of control of our borders, the extraordinary winding down of the defence of this country, the massive increases in foreign aid principally for the benefit of corrupt governments and elite consultants, the limitations on the freedom of speech of critics, the spectacular decline in law and order, the policy of abandoning the mentally ill to the streets, the denigration of religion, the massive increase in the number of unborn children whose lives are terminated, the adoption of a carbon dioxide tax which cannot possibly affect the climate and the adoption of fashionable and passing theories which have resulted in our children being less educated and at a greater cost than ever before?

No wonder people ask of this Anti-Australia Axis, "Why do they hate Australia?"

The elite's endorsement of theories which fail the common sense "pub test" and are clearly not in the national interest can perhaps be explained by the celebrated paraphrase of the teachings of G.K. Chesterton. This is that when a man stops believing in God, it is not that he believes in nothing. He then believes in anything. Government in Australia for some time seems to have involved the endorsement of a continuing parade of curious and fashionable ideologies and beliefs, all imported, and all with disastrous consequences.

The dominant theory at the time of writing is the absolutist endorsement of a three part infallible almost religious dogma.[7] There is an insistence that this must be taught in the schools, relayed by the media and unconditionally believed by all. It is even supported by a liturgy. This is an annual candlelit dinner in an inner city luxury restaurant during Earth Hour.

The first part of the theory is that human sourced carbon dioxide emissions are having such an immediate and catastrophic impact on climate, that they are the cause of all so-called "extreme weather" events. So all hot and cold weather, floods and droughts, are now held to be the direct result of those emissions.[8]

The second part of this absolutist theory is that nothing else is making any discernible impact on the climate. So those factors which must have caused long periods of global warming and ice ages are now, if not inoperative, of little significance.

The third part of the theory is even more curious. This is that governments have the ability to change the climate. This is to be done in two ways. First, the lives of the ordinary Australians, including their standard of living, are to be significantly curtailed. Ordinary Australians are to be moved away from the country and separate suburban houses and herded into high-rise agglomerations with reduced access to motor cars, minimal electricity and little or no air-conditioning.

In the meantime the elites are to continue to emit vast amounts of carbon dioxide as they fly across the country and around the world in anything but economy class to attend a never ending succession of liturgical celebrations called earth summits, held in air-conditioned luxury offices and hotels in magnificent resorts. There the elites pay homage to their Primate, Al Gore, and spend their time decrying the incidence of global warming caused by the rank-and-file – but only those in Western democracies; and not only through massive subsidies for uneconomic solar power and wind turbines. Hence the eagerness of the righteous trio, Julia Gillard, Kevin Rudd and Malcolm Turnbull for Australians to do serious penance, through the most burdensome of carbon dioxide reduction.

The second way governments will change the climate is through an alliance with merchant banks across the world, to establish artificial carbon markets which will produce unbelievable wealth for the bankers, the powerbrokers and the elites. The entry into the carbon market may be preceded – as in Australia – by a carbon dioxide tax. While making life more expensive for Australians and driving jobs offshore, the tax is not imposed on the massive amount of coal exported with government encouragement to foreign countries, which then has the advantage of having cheaper energy than Australia.

To do this indicates a complete absence of common sense. This is demonstrated by the fact that the carbon dioxide tax was levied at \$23 a tonne increasing to \$24.15 in July 2013. Originally, the Australian tax was to turn into a floating carbon price with a \$15 a tonne floor, but in August 2012 the government decided that Australia would adopt the EU system in 2015-2016 at an estimated price of $29 a tonne.[9] Not only is this economic madness, it will not change the climate and was levied in breach of a very clear promise not to do so in the 2010 election.

That Australian business is grossly disadvantaged is demonstrated by the fact that there is no national carbon tax in the US, Canada, China or India and that after a market crash in April 2013, the carbon price is less than $4 in Europe.[10] On a per capita basis, the EU is the second most burdensome in the world, raising just over $1 per person per year. The Australian is the world's most expensive carbon dioxide tax raising almost $400 per person per year.[11]

But to soften up the population which may be harbouring doubts about the theory and government policy to answer it, especially the carbon dioxide tax, we are assured by politicians that "the" science is settled, and that there is a consensus among scientists. Scientists and intellectuals who dare to dissent are ridiculed and denounced in a mild version of Lysenkoism. This was unleashed by Soviet dictator Joseph Stalin, with the result that hundreds of Russian scientists were dismissed, imprisoned and killed for daring to go against the theories of genetics and agriculture propounded by a communist charlatan, Lysenko.

The application and enforcement of the extreme theory of man-made global warming, as well as other unlikely theories, can best be achieved when the institutions of democracy have been compromised, as they have been in modern Australia.

So the last thing the Anti-Australia Axis of faceless men and the elites would want is for our institutions to become as democratic as they were intended by our founders and by the people. They will therefore advance all manner of arguments ridiculing and deriding any proposal to bring to Australia the tools of direct democracy such as the recall of governments, the people being able to block taxes the politicians promised never to impose or the people being able to introduce legislation the country is calling out for.

In the lead up to the 2011 New South Wales election, the Liberal Party, then in opposition, promised to convene a panel of constitutional experts to conduct a review into recall elections.[12]

Once in government, the enquiry was established. However, one could assume that the government was surprised when it reported in favour, after, it would seem, having arranged it to report negatively from the beginning.

When a senior minister in the O'Farrell government was asked why they had been sitting on the proposal for 18 months, the minister replied "well now that we're in government, there is no incentive to do anything about it."[13]

Despite the honesty of this admission, it reinforces the need for the people to be empowered between elections. As they are powerless, unlike the situation in Switzerland,[14] the mainstream media are more concerned with the personalities of the contenders for political office, with many spending their time and their efforts barracking for their preferred team.

Whenever there is a rising concern about our corrupted system, the public indicate they are losing confidence in the politicians, a solution will be proposed by the elites which they claim will resolve this.[15]

Thus we have seen the argument that if parliaments only moved from three to four year fixed terms, governments will miraculously be improved. We have been told that they would then have the time to govern properly without thinking of the next election. This was pushed by the media and by politicians. The public were persuaded to accept what was a fraudulent manoeuvre to make the lives of politicians easier. That was the only advantage from this move. Nobody seriously would argue that government in the states has been improved because of this change.

The public may at times accept the solution suggested, for example, four year terms. They soon see this is no solution at all and government does not improve. Indeed, it is hard to recall a time at which there has been more dissatisfaction with the political system, the politicians and the media commentariat.

The public lives in a state of perpetual hope that a new team will repair the system, but they are reluctant to expect too much.

In what is laughingly called a representative democracy, our members of parliament are minutely controlled not only in the way they vote but even when they may speak and what they may say. This has in no way been changed either by any solutions from the elites or changes of government. The most extreme form of control is through the Labor Party's caucus pledge. This evolved into its most extreme form under the Rudd government, recalling almost the so called democratic centralism which Lenin introduced to control the Bolshevik Party. Under Kevin Rudd, a "kitchen cabinet" of senior ministers effectively displaced the caucus of all MPs as the power centre within the Parliamentary Labor Party.

To understand why this could happen, it is necessary to recall that a significant number of Labor MPs come directly or indirectly from the unions. But these are no longer led by proud workers who have risen from the shop floor, as they were in Labor's golden age. Today they come from a new class of university trained elites who are free from the rigorous standards of financial propriety required of company directors. Ambitious for safe seats and other cosy appointments, and owing allegiance to some or other powerbroker they are more compliant than their predecessors.

And as governments have fallen under the control of the powerbrokers and the influence of the elites, the restraints which were once considered normal no longer seem to apply. As a result, governments at all levels – federal, state and local – have increased their share of the Australian Gross Domestic Product (GDP) from about 20% in the 1960s, to around 35% or almost half a trillion dollars today.[16]

Governments now waste money in a way no prudent citizen or business person would. With the indulgence of too many High Court judges with a centralist agenda and the weakness of some but not all state politicians, federal governments have led the way with their excesses, restricting themselves neither to their core duties, nor to the powers granted to them under the Constitution.

Using the word "reform" as a cloak of infallibility, governments are increasingly moving beyond what has been traditionally thought of as their proper areas. One example was the Rudd government's disastrous $2.8 billion home insulation plan, to which we shall return.[17]

While governments have been intent on accumulating new powers, they have been at times indifferent and at other times grossly negligent in the exercise of their core duties. Just take the approach of government to their duties to defend the realm, to control our borders, and ensure that law and order prevails across the nation.

Electing a government in the 21st century is tantamount to signing a blank cheque on your bank account, guaranteed by your home, your assets, and your income. Worse, it is also tantamount to signing a blank cheque on your children's and your grandchildren's bank accounts, guaranteed by their homes, their assets, and their incomes.

You are giving this blank cheque to people not really chosen by you, but where your choice is restricted to those candidates too often selected by the powerbrokers not on merit but on their willingness to obey.

Is this the way our founders intended the country to be run? Is this the Australia the pioneers slaved to build? Is this the country that our servicemen and women fought for and too often died for? Is this why people go off to work every day and children study? Do they only do this to see their country dominated by self-interested cliques?

Politicians and governments are surely the servants of the people. They were never intended to be the preserve and puppets of the powerbrokers and the elites.

To restore good government in Australia and, even more importantly, to ensure we never again fall into the situation where government is incompetent, wasteful and deceitful, the solution is not in some new fix proposed by the elites. They are, after all, part of the problem.

Instead, the Australian people, endowed as they are with great common sense, good judgement and decency, must take charge. They must no longer be reduced to choosing between candidates preselected by the powerbrokers every three or four years. For the sake of the nation, the politicians – those who govern us – must be made accountable on every day, in every week, in every month, just as the Australian people are in their employment and in business relations.

This book proposes a way in which we can restore Australia as a democratic country, while preserving stable government under the constitution.

1.2 Institutions of a successful representative democracy

Australia is indeed a fortunate country. Over two decades, she has been among those countries at the top of the United Nations Human Development Index, a formula which ranks countries across the globe according to the health, wealth and education of their people.[18]

Along with other countries in the Commonwealth and indeed the whole English speaking world – the Anglosphere – Australia has inherited essentially British institutions. Not perfect, they perform well – indeed, in comparison with most others, very well. The countries of the Anglosphere were among the very few in the world which showed no interest at all in communism, in distinct contrast with most of the Latin, Germanic and Slav world. And Australians took these British institutions, Australianised them, building our own unique federation.

Ironically, the British had, from the very beginning, endowed the bleak and unpromising penal colony they established at Botany Bay in 1788 with sound institutions.[19] And, within a surprisingly short period of time, they granted the colonists self-government under the Westminster system. From about this time, Australia became one of the world's richest countries and, unusually, has maintained this since.[20]

In the mid-19th century the British even tried to rush their reluctant colonies into a continental federation. This was unusual, as imperial powers did not normally seek to strengthen local power.

The first recorded statement of the case for Australian union, with "a central legislative authority", was not made by an Australian, but by the Colonial Secretary, Earl Grey, in a despatch of 31 July 1847. This was greeted with a "storm of indignation", with Earl Grey responding that he had no wish to impose unwelcome constitutional change.[21]

Only later did Australians realise the good sense in the British suggestion, timing their union into a Federal Commonwealth to coincide with the first day of the 20th century. Australia's founding fathers were to demonstrate superb good sense in grafting onto the Westminster system aspects of both American federalism and Swiss direct democracy. They wisely declared that the federal package which they had designed should only proceed with the agreement of the people in the self-governing colonies, the future states of the federation.

The institutions which had emerged over the period 1788 to 1901 were those of a robust and mainly representative democracy. Although not emphasised in our schools, this fact – more than any other – explains Australia's success as a nation. As Professor Niall Ferguson pointed out in the 2012 BBC Reith Lectures, what is crucial to the success of nations is their institutions, rather than the genetic make-up of their populations, their geography or even their natural wealth.[22]

Professor Ferguson points to the distinction made in the academic literature between two phases or patterns of human organisation.[23] The first is what can be called the natural state or the "limited access pattern". This is characterised by a slow-growing economy, relatively few non-state organisations, a small and quite centralised government operating without the consent of the governed and social relationships organised along personal and dynastic lines, which result in laws that are enforced unequally.

By way of contrast the second is the "open access pattern",

characterised by a faster growing economy, a rich and vibrant civil society with numerous organisations, a bigger, but decentralised government and social relationships governed by impersonal forces like the rule of law, involving secure property rights, fairness, and, at least in theory, equality.

As we point out in Chapter 13, England was the first country to make the transition from "limited access" to "open access". This was in the Glorious Revolution of 1688, the most important beneficial political event in the history of the world since the Magna Carta.[24]

It is sad that few Australians today – except for the old – know anything about this. Elderly Australians are more likely to be informed on our roots – their education although shorter and usually in larger classes was, frankly, far more rigorous. Today, even students in university law schools and departments of politics more often than not are unaware not only of the importance of the Glorious Revolution, but even of the event itself.

The Glorious Revolution strongly influenced the American Revolution, hence an understanding of what was achieved by the former is essential to an understanding of our institutions and those of the entire English-speaking world. It explains why we and similar countries have been so successful in freeing the talents and skills of our people to make a more prosperous and happy society. An understanding of those institutions also explains why we must be on our guard concerning any proposal which will diminish them. In particular we must be on our guard against the whittling away of what has been achieved.

If our children are deprived of knowledge about this, it will be so much easier to undermine our heritage.

Professor Ferguson's opinion on the crucial importance of institutions in human development is attracting increasing support in leading academic circles.

In a recently published study, Massachusetts Institute of Technology and Harvard Professors Daron Acemoglu and James A. Robinson pose the crucial question as to why some nations are rich and others poor, and why they are divided by wealth and poverty, health and sickness, food and famine.[25] They ask whether any one of a range of factors – culture, race, weather, geography, natural wealth or even an ignorance of what the right policies should be – is crucial.

They conclude that none of these factors is definitive. Otherwise, they ask, how can we explain why Botswana has become one of the fastest growing countries in the world, while other African nations, such as Zimbabwe, the Congo, and Sierra Leone, are mired in poverty and violence?

They conclude that it is man-made political and economic institutions that underpin economic success, or indeed, the lack of it.

Among many examples which they believe prove their theory is one which stands out – Korea, or rather the two Koreas. A better example could not have been designed in a laboratory, if experiments on this scale were possible.

Korea was once an homogeneous nation. It was divided into two states at the end of the Second World War and endowed with institutions appropriate to the sphere of influence into which they fell – communist or Western. As a result the North Koreans are now among the poorest on earth, and the South Koreans among the richest. The reason cannot be their race or origin. It is the institutional basis of each state.

The authors reiterate their conclusion that the reason for success does not lie in geography or in the race of the people, whether or not they have a work ethic or any other considerations, save for one. That is whether the country has "extractive" political institutions which concentrate power in the hands of a narrow elite and which arrange governance to suit that elite. Or are the institutions "inclusive", that is, pluralistic, democratic and open and thus offering what they describe as engines of prosperity to the people?

The truth of their thesis can be illustrated by recalling that at the birth of the Commonwealth of Australia in 1901, Australia and Argentina were the world's richest countries and both inherited Judeo-Christian values.[26]

At that time, Argentina was effectively a part of the extended British economic sphere; it was never a British colony and therefore did not inherit British institutions.

There were significant differences between Australia and Argentina. Australia was at that time a recently federated group of self-governing, democratic, and practically independent British colonies under the rule of law. She had inherited her institutions from Britain and had Australianised them, drawing also on Canadian, American and Swiss experience.

Argentina had declared her independence in 1816, and she had to fight Spain to realise it. The institutions of the two countries in the 19th and 20th centuries were strikingly different. Spain had not granted inclusive institutions to her colonies, as the British had even to their thirteen American colonies. The reason was simple, Spain did not have them at home – how could she give them to her colonies even if she wanted to? The same was true of the other European imperial powers. The one other country which had inclusive institutions at home, the Netherlands, was not prepared to apply them to the jewel in their Crown, the Dutch East Indies. This was to have unfortunate results when Indonesia successfully took her independence. She could not draw on a successful model of self-governance, as Australia did.

The 20th century history of Argentina has been one of instability, periods of brutal dictatorship, and economic decline. Apart from her unwise war against Britain in 1982 over the Falklands, the Argentinean military was not involved in combat even in the two World Wars. As a result, she did not suffer the enormous losses both in terms of human potential and wealth that Australia did. Just this fact should have put her well ahead of Australia economically. But the Argentinean military seemed to prefer to interfere in government. Their worst involvement was in the military dictatorship which seized power in 1976, when the junta murdered around 13,000 political prisoners, some by being forced out of aeroplanes over the sea. It was only their defeat in the Falklands war which led to the overthrow of the junta in 1983.

As a former minister in Argentina's Menem government observed on the ABC's *Four Corners* program in 2002, the two countries do have some similarities. But, he said, there is one important difference: "Australia has British institutions. If Argentina had such strong institutions she would be like Australia in ten or twenty years."[27]

Readers may wonder why the strength of the institutions of our unique representative democracy is not sufficiently recognised in our schools and universities, in our parliaments and media and in the instruction of new citizens.

1.3 Declining standards

The theme of this book is that in recent years, our foundation institutions have been seriously compromised and corrupted by the factional powerbrokers who control the major political parties, and that this is the reason why the standard of public administration has so declined.

The overwhelming majority of Australians, however they vote, will normally accept the government in power as legitimate and entitled to serve its term. However, at the time of writing, a number of Australians, it would seem larger than usual, are questioning the competence of the Gillard government and whether it should remain in office.

Labor historian Professor Ross Fitzgerald has described the legacy of the Gillard and Rudd governments as one of "wasted opportunities, flawed judgment, poor policy implementation and ugly and divisive politicking. Worse still is that her government's handling of our nation's finances will adversely impact on future generations in the form of higher taxes and reduced services".[28]

Such a lack of confidence in an elected government has only occurred once before, at least in recent times. This was in relation to the Whitlam government in 1975. Indeed, had the people been empowered to recall that government, the nation might not have seen the divisions and bitterness which occurred when the opposition withheld supply in order to bring down the government. The fact that the governing party, when in opposition, had adopted precisely the same tactic on 170 occasions for the specific purpose of bringing down the government is usually ignored by commentators.[29] The only difference between those 170 occasions and 1975 was that they were unsuccessful.

Although the people will eventually remove a government they have judged to have failed, any government can do enormous damage while in office. Dismissed by the profligate as a truism, we must always remember there is no such thing as a free lunch. The debts and the mess they leave behind may take years, decades and even generations to cure.

Australians must bear in mind that it is not just possible, but highly likely that at some time in the future other governments will be elected which are subsequently found by most Australians to be incompetent, wasteful and deceitful. And it should not be assumed that these will always come under the Labor brand.

The emergence of such a government is a likely consequence of the close control the powerbrokers have secured over the major political parties, and their implementing the elites' agenda.

With their dwindling membership and centralised control, the major political parties can hardly be said to represent the nation. This is particularly true of the Labor Party, which unfortunately encourages a degree of competitive imitation by some within the Liberal Party.

Denying the states their intended constitutional role and denying the people the freedom to make their decisions and lead their lives as they wish, the powerbrokers seek to exercise more and more power over the affairs of the nation and the lives of its citizens.

We have seen this in such matters as the Rudd government's decision to install pink batts in people's roofs, hardly a matter for any government, much less the federal government. As a result, four people died, well over 200 houses were destroyed in fires and vast amounts of money wasted. After spending $2.45 billion on ceiling insulations, a third of which appear to be faulty or dangerous according to a review of almost 14,000 homes earlier in 2012, taxpayers would be forced to pay another $424 million, if not more, to sort out the dangers.[30]

Another was the move into the state area of education with the $16.2 billion spent in the Building the Education Revolution, and involving the loss of several billion dollars.[31]

Then there was the technological equivalent of the pink batts – a prime example of old world socialism – the National Broadband Network. When the initial proposal failed, Prime Minister Rudd and Communications Minister Stephen Conroy roughed out a plan at an April 2009 meeting on the Prime Minister's VIP jet. This was to involve splitting Telstra and replacing its copper network with a shorter life fibre network. And not just to the node, but to homes and businesses across the nation, which opposition communications spokesman, Malcolm Turnbull, estimated would cost approximately 3-4 times as much.[32]

The government committed $43 billion dollars to the project without a cost benefit analysis and by selecting the applicable technology. Declaring it would be an investment with private backers, they decided that the commitment should be off-budget.[33] According to the Coalition, relying on an assessment from the Macquarie Bank, the final cost of the NBN rollout could more than double and exceed $90 billion by the time it is finished.

It is "off budget" because it is apparently seen as an investment. As sales of assets are included in income, why is not investment treated as government budget expenditure, especially an investment for which there is no cost benefit analysis?[34]

Then a tender for the $223 million Australia Network, the overseas television service, was the subject of political interference. There was a report by the Auditor-General.[35] Twice the independent evaluation panel recommended the contract be handed to the commercial entity Sky News. Sky News is partially owned by the seven and nine television networks and through Sky, News Corporation. On the second occasion, the government cited media leaks, called on the Federal police and then awarded the contract to the ABC. It went further and although not envisaged in the tender, made the allocation of the service to the ABC permanent.

The pink batts scheme and the NBN are two examples of the government moving outside of its areas of responsibility and against the original constitutional intention. Both the NBN and the Australian Network are examples of the government using unbusinesslike and questionable processes concerning large amounts of public money.

But, at the same time, the federal government has proved to be singularly deficient in fulfilling its core responsibilities, in particular the following:

- the defence of the nation,
- the protection of the borders,
- the protection of the interests of Australia and Australians beyond our borders,
- the careful and prudent supervision of federal government expenditure,
- the provision of a safety net for only those in genuine need,
- the health system,
- the provision of infrastructure of national importance, and
- the governance of the territories.

The states share some of these responsibilities in a supporting role, but have primary responsibility for the following:

- the careful and prudent supervision of state government expenditure,
- education, especially public education,
- law and order,
- the provision of infrastructure of state importance,
- hospitals, and
- local government.

A full examination of the way in which governments, federal and state, have acquitted themselves in these fields would require a major treatise. Most Australians old enough to remember tell how standards have fallen over the years. So in the following chapter, we propose to examine briefly how governments, dominated by the powerbrokers and the elites, are managing – or rather mismanaging – their responsibilities.

This leads through to our conclusion in Part 3: Australians must stop giving the politicians a blank cheque every three or four years.

Endnotes

1 Believing that Western style democracy was inappropriate for Indonesia, President Suharto introduced a form of autocratic government in 1957 offering a blend of nationalism, religion and communism. This ended in bloodshed 1966 with a failed coup *d'état*. See also Sheldon S. Weldon, *Democracy Incorporated: Managed Democracy and the Specter of Inverted Totalitarianism*, Princeton University Press, Princeton, 2008.

2 While highly critical of the elites, *The Australian*'s senior editor Nick Cater argues that our success comes from the Australian character: Cater, Nick, *The Lucky Culture*, Collins, Pymble, 2013.

3 Christopher Lasch, *The Revolt of the Elites*, W.W. Norton, New York, London, 1995; David Flint, *The Twilight of the Elites*, Freedom Publishing, North Melbourne, 2003; N. Cater, Top of the class and looking down on the nation, *The Australian*, 4 February 2013. http://www.theaustralian.com.au/national-affairs/opinion/top-of-the-class-and-looking-down-on-the-nation/story-e6frgd0x-1226567729242 (retrieved 09.02.2013).

4 Carl J. Friedrich, *The New Belief in The Common Man*, Little, Brown and Company, Boston, 1942.

5 Cater, op.cit.

6 David Flint, op. cit., 2003.

7 A recent NASA report finds that CO_2 is actually cooling the earth: http://principia-scientific.org/supportnews/latest-news/163-new-discovery-nasa-study-proves-carbon-dioxide-cools-atmosphere.html (retrieved 97.05.2013).

8 See e.g., Australian summer lurches from fire to flood, *The Australian*, 30 January 2013, http://www.thenational.ae/news/world/asia-pacific/australian-summer-lurches-from-fire-to-floods

9 Professor Henry Ergas says the government has misrepresented Treasury modelling on the EU carbon price. He says it does not forecast a $29 per tonne price in 2015-16 as Minister Combet claims; it is the minimum price needed for deep global emissions reductions to occur: Ergas, Henry, Show us the models, *The Australian*, 22 April 2013. http://www.theaustralian.com.au/opinion/columnists/honesty-would-prove-priceless/story-fn7078da-1226625436024 (retrieved 22.04.2013).

10 Sid Maher, "EU carbon crash to dog $10bn budget hole", *The Australian*, 18 April 2013. http://www.theaustralian.com.au/national-affairs/treasury/eu-carbon-crash-to-dig-10bn-budget-hole/story-fn59nsif-1226623027747 (retrieved 18.04.2013).

11 Piers Akerman, "Julia Gillard's carbon tax is hurting families and must be scrapped", *Daily Telegraph*, 21 April 2013. http://www.dailytelegraph.com.au/news/opinion/julia-gillards-carbon-tax-is-hurting-families-ans-must-be-scrapped/story-e6frezz0-1226625112520 (retrieved 21.04.2013).

12 http://www.dpc.nsw.gov.au/__data/assets/pdf_file/0013/134221/Panel_of_Constitutional_Experts_-_Review_into_Recall_Elections.pdf (retrieved 22.03.2013).

13 See Chapter 18.

14 See Part 3.

15 See Chapter 12.

16 Leading economist Professor Judith Sloan pointed out that in the early 1960s, the share of all government spending was just over 20% of GDP; by 2012, it was 35%: http://www.theaustralian.com.au/opinion/increasing-taxes-not-the-answer-try-smart-spending/story-e6frg6zo-1226536279614 (retrieved 14.12.2012); see the national debt clocks http://www.australiandebtclock.com.au/clocks (retrieved 8.01.2012).

17 See Audit Report, *Home Insulation Programme*, 2110-2011 http://www.anao.gov.au/~/media/Uploads/Documents/2010%2011_audit_report_no_12.pdf (retrieved 28.01.13)

18 http://hdr.undp.org/en/statistics/hdi/(retrieved 31.07.2012).

19 See chapter 4.

20 Ian W. McLean, *Why Australia Prospered*, Princeton University Press, Princeton, 2012, pp. 1-10.

21 John Quick, and Robert Garran, (1901), *The Annotated Constitution of the Australian Commonwealth*, reprinted by Legal Books, Sydney, 1995, p. 83.

22 http://www.bbc.co.uk/programs/b01jmx0p/features/transcript (retrieved 20.07.2012).

23 Douglass C. North, John Joseph Wallis, &. Barry R. Weingast, "A Conceptual Framework for Interpreting Recorded Human History", *NBER Working Paper No. 12795*, December 2006.

24 Extended by a Convention of the Scottish Estates and the Scottish Parliament to the then separate Kingdom of Scotland by the *Claim of Right*, 1689. The two kingdoms were united by the *Treaty of Union*, 1707.

25 Daron Acemoglu and Jim Robinson, *Why Nations Fail*, Profile Books, London, 2012.

26 In *Why Australia Prospered*, Princeton University Press, Princeton, 2012. Ian W. McLean argues against there being a single dominant influence explaining Australia's success. Nevertheless he recognises the strong influence at time sof institutional quality.

27 David Flint, op. cit., pp. 42-45.

28 Ross Fitzgerald, 5 January 2013. http://www.rossfitzgerald.com/2013/01/generations-will-reap-brutal-legacy/(retrieved 6.01.2013).

29 Sir David Smith, *Head of State*, McLeay Press, Paddington, 2005, pp 264-266.

30 http://www.theaustralian.com.au/news/opinion/pink-batts-debacle-teaches-government-costly-lessons/story-e6frg71x-1225939909818 (retrieved 20.07.12).

31 http://www.deewr.gov.au/Schooling/BuildingTheEducationRevolution/Pages/default.aspx (retrieved 20.07.2012); see Chapter 3.

32 http://www.smh.com.au/it-pro/government-it/nbn-alternative-a-huge-saving-says-turnbull-20120417-1x5nt.html

33 Simon Benson, "The Ninety Billion Nightmare – the real cost of the NBN rollout", *Daily Telegraph*, 8 April 2013. http://www.dailytelegraph.com.au/news/the-ninety-billion-nightmare-the-real-cost-of-the-nbn-rollout/story-e6freuy9-1226614471419 (retrieved 08.042013).

34 Both a $30 million implementation study and modelling have been kept secret: Henry Ergas, "Show us the models", *The Australian*, 22 April 2013. http://www.theaustralian.com.au/opinion/columnists/honesty-would-prove-priceless/story-fn7078da-1226625436024 (retrieved 22.04.2013).

35 Auditor-General, Audit Report No. 29 2011-12 Performance Audit, *Administration of the Australia Network Tender Process*, http://www.anao.gov.au/~/media/Uploads/Audit%20Reports/2011%20

CHAPTER 2

Defenceless, a mosque-driven foreign policy and crime ridden

In the previous chapter we set out the core responsibilities of government, federal and state. We argued that under the influence of the AAA, the alliance or axis between the powerbrokers – the faceless men – and the elites, there had been a significant decline in the performance of these functions. At the same time the federal government was attempting to interfere in purely state responsibilities and also in matters the province of the citizen and not that of a bloated and inefficient government. Here, we look at what the AAA has given us in three core areas – defence, foreign policy and law and order. The result would dismay those who built, fought and died for this country

2.1 Defence

The ambitious 2009 Rudd government Defence White Paper has been abandoned by the Gillard government. In 2010-11 defence spending was cut by 5.4%, in 2011-12 by another 5.1%, and in 2012-13 by a further 10.5%.

In the meantime, China spends 10 times as much on defence as it did in 1990. "Australia's defence budget is inadequate," US Richard Armitage, former Deputy Secretary of State and a great friend of Australia told Fairfax's Peter Hartcher.[1]

"It's about Australia's ability to work as an ally of the US," he said. "I would say you've got to look at 2% of GDP", that is an extra $6 billion in spending annually (planned spending in 2012-2013 is $24 billion).

"A large island nation like Australia, rich in resources, needs a robust military capability," he added.

This is free loading on the US which, even after recent cuts, will still spend 3.5% of GDP.

The Rudd-Gillard governments have taken up to $24 billion out of defence, but ridiculously claim this has no impact on the security of the nation.[2] Instead, Retired Major General Jim Molan says they "have accepted an increase in strategic risk to Australia, in order to lessen their own political risk". While Asian defence spending is rising significantly, Australia's is falling. General Molan warns that the threat to Australian values, interests and prosperity is higher than we have seen for decades. He believes that a direct threat to Australia is least possible in the medium to long term. But the Gillard government's policy of reducing defence expenditure to 1.5% of GDP is putting our defence forces into terminal decline. It will be very difficult to correct this.

The defence budget should not be turned on and off as if it were no more than a matter of discretionary spending. Defence needs long lead times and a seriousness beyond party politics.

The result is that there are no submarines to replace the decrepit and always inadequate Collins Class ones. The original acquisition of these by the Hawke government was guided more for trade union and electoral reasons than by a proper consideration of national defence needs.

When a decision is taken about their replacement, ideology and politics are likely to preclude the leasing or purchase of nuclear powered submarines. In the meantime we have no replacement fighters for the RAAF, nor the latest artillery for the Army.

Further, we are letting our troops down. Men and women going in to battle to defend our way of life are inadequately equipped, and are issued with inferior safety equipment.[3]

Professor Alan Dupont of the University NSW, a former analyst with the Defence Department, says: "The best time to invade Australia will be around 2028-30. That's a serious comment."[4]

The release of a Defence White paper[5] in May 2013 did not hide the fact that, as Peter Hartcher puts it, by cutting defence to its smallest since before World War II, we are now freeloading on the implicit guarantee of US protection, at a time when "the US's relative power is at its feeblest since World War I."[6]

Director of Military Prosecutions

In addition, the government has not yet proposed the repeal of the legislation adopted unanimously, but against basic common sense, to centralise all military prosecutions in the hands of a Canberra based official, the Director of Military Prosecutions.[7] It should be noted that the controversial first incumbent, Brigadier Lyn McDade, had no combat experience.

Her decision in 2010 to charge three Australian special force soldiers was received with surprise, incredulity and outrage.

It was fortunate that after a long delay, the charges were dismissed by the Chief Judge Advocate (CJA) Brigadier Ian Westwood at a pre-trial hearing on 20 May 2011.[8] It is not obvious under the legislation that the pre-trial hearing should function this way. It was later revealed that Brigadier McDade considered the CJA had made new law, and lamented the fact that she could not appeal and was not funded for this. The Minister for Defence surprisingly said he was confident that funding would have been granted had Brigadier McDade asked. Ominously a spokesman told *The Sydney Morning Herald*'s Tom Hyland that some of the issues raised by Brigadier McDade would be "remedied" under new legislation setting up a new military court.[9]

The sense of outrage about this case demonstrates that, in the ultimate analysis, no prosecution should ever be launched unless this course is approved by the soldiers' peers – those who have combat experience.

It is completely unacceptable that the DMP should have the sole discretion to launch a prosecution.

Just imagine if such a position had existed in World War II. Had prosecutions been launched whenever civilians were inadvertently killed, the AIF, the RAN and the RAAF would have been rendered impotent.

The Menzies and Curtin governments would never have proposed such a position over the armed forces as the DMP. They had too much common sense.

If there is to be a central Office of Military Prosecutions, any proposed prosecution should have the support of the relevant commanding officer. This could be reviewable at the next level and/or by a tribunal composed of serving officers.

In just about all respects the government has clearly failed in this crucial core duty of defending the Australian nation.

2.2 Foreign affairs

Another core duty of the federal government is the protection of the interests of Australia and Australians beyond our borders – foreign affairs, or as the Constitution describes them, "external affairs."

A key exercise of this power has involved the borrowing of billions to buy what was to be a vanity pulpit for the former Prime Minister then Foreign Minister, Kevin Rudd. This was a temporary seat on the UN Security Council.[10]

But it is not going to be occupied by him – unless of course there is another coup by the faceless men and the ALP decides after all the nasty things they said they want him back.

Until then Prime Minister Julia Gillard and Foreign Minister Bob Carr will use their very expensive new toy, the vanity pulpit, to bore us with endless "initiatives" on world issues. The fact is the Russians and Chinese who actually run the Security Council will ignore each of them.

And that is not all. They have to borrow billions more to pay the balance of the price. They claim it cost "only" $26 million. It was a bargain, they say.

But as with the Building the Education Revolution (the BER), the pink batts and the NBN, the government specialises in hiding the real cost of its projects from prying eyes.

To buy the temporary seat on the UN Security Council, the foreign aid budget was increased to $5.2 billion in the 2013 financial year.[11]

Foreign aid has been aptly described as poor people in rich countries subsidising rich people in poor countries.

Apart from a band of well paid consultants enjoying their carbon emitting business class air travel and five star hotels, this observation is a reasonable description of a significant amount of foreign aid. It is even used for politicians to attend conferences with politicians of like-minded parties.[12]

In the period leading up to the 2012 Security Council election, much of our foreign aid was targeted to countries well away from our region.

Australia is not, after all, a power with worldwide interests to protect, and with what the government has done to our defence forces, will have great difficulty defending our coastline. With the navy now acting as a welcoming force for illegal immigrants their hands are full anyway.

We have bought a seat in a club, the majority of whose members are authoritarian, dictatorial and corrupt. We have done it by paying those same members with money we don't actually have. The Australian taxpayer will have to pay the interest and eventually find the money to repay the principal.

The vanity pulpit is a useless trinket. Worse, it means we are even more involved in an organisation which has shown itself often to be of limited use, not to mention an avenue for the massive and continuing fraudulent transfer of wealth from the taxpayers of Australia and other Western countries to corrupt authoritarian politicians in poor countries.

A report by US Reserve Bank chairman, Paul Volcker, found billions of dollars had been swindled from the UN.[13] The resulting body established to fight corruption was far too effective for the UN and was wound up. Investigative bodies were either neutralised or removed.

The fact is the corrupt members of the UN who profit from the fraudulent diversion of funds ensure that any attempt to clean up the UN and its many agencies will not be successful. If the government wants to do anything useful with its vanity pulpit it should lead the push to reform the UN. Unfortunately that won't happen.

Expect all sorts of spin coming out of Canberra about very important initiatives in the Security Council. No doubt the many gullible members of the press gallery will recirculate the press releases they receive, thus ensuring there is less reporting of the government's continuing financial excesses and policy failures.

2.3 Minister for Foreign Affairs

In the meantime, the jubilation in the press gallery about the appointment of Bob Carr as Senator and Foreign Minister was to be short-lived. Their reaction was predictable: after all, he is one of them.[14]

This demonstrated once again how much the gallery has abandoned the sceptical principle crucial to good journalism. If you doubt that, recall how *The Australian*'s Hedley Thomas was almost alone among journalists in applying that principle to the Queensland floods enquiry, and then with Michael Smith, Alan Jones and Andrew Bolt on the Prime Minister and the AWU "election slush fund".

The press gallery was dazzled by the Carr appointment. They saw it as a coup by a prime minister who had earlier been rolled by her cabinet colleagues. Some even suggested it might be the silver bullet that would turn the tide of public opinion in favour of the government.

It took only one day for Senator Carr to demonstrate his weakness for the grand theatrical gesture, and for the most transparent spin. Having unwisely decided that his tête-à-tête with Graham Richardson should be broadcast, and on the basis of musings by one Papua New

Guinea minister about a possible delay in the elections there, he said he would consider the most powerful attack on a foreign country short of a declaration of war – international sanctions. But it wasn't Iran or Syria; it was a friendly country, Papua New Guinea.

Sounding like a comedy spoof on Neville Chamberlain in 1939, he declared that if the Papua New Guinean Prime Minister did not commit unequivocally to a June polling date, Australia would have no alternative but to organise the world to condemn and isolate it. "We'd be in a position of having to consider sanctions."

Those who have any understanding of foreign affairs cringed. The threat of sanctions should only be undertaken after a careful appraisal of the situation, not on live television and on the basis of one vague report. Where was the gravitas and wisdom about which the press gallery had waxed so lyrical?

In this Senator Carr had gone even further than his predecessors, who have too often thrown their weight around in relation to small Pacific countries.

We have already scored an own goal because of our attempts to direct the Fijians on how to run their internal affairs. Prime Minister Frank Bainimarama, in balancing Indian human rights with Fijian nationalism, is steering a course between Scylla and Charybdis. Yet the former foreign minister Kevin Rudd even attempted to block the employment of those magnificent Fijian troops in UN peacekeeping operations, something at which they have been so successful. All of this has only driven the Fijians closer to other powers, including China.

On the next day, when reality dawned, the minister must have imagined he was back in Macquarie Street. Instead of admitting his faux pas, and apologising, he decided to shoot the messenger. He claimed his words had been "misunderstood and used out of context."

That only compounded the original sin. Did he really think readers, viewers and above all the Papua New Guineans were so naive as to believe this?

Apart from this totally unnecessary diplomatic incident, the Foreign Minister decided that, having expressed his concern over the massacre of Afghans by an American soldier, he would offer a gratuitous, convoluted and obviously rehearsed comment on the latest Newspoll, the opinion poll used by *The Australian*.[15]

"Tony Abbott is like a cheapskate hypnotist in a rundown circus. He's saying to the electorate, 'Look into my eyes, you are growing weaker: no more boats. Look into my eyes, you are growing weaker: end Labor's big bad tax. Look into my eyes, you're growing weaker: debt and deficit'. He's trying to hypnotise the electorate with these slogans. It's a very cheap performance. And if you paid five bucks to get into Wirth's Circus and that's all you got from the hypnotists, you'd ask for your money back."

This was so infantile and embarrassing it sounded as if it had been written by a teenage apparatchik. Why did our Foreign Minister memorise such rubbish and deliver it in a press conference about Afghanistan?

Then in an interview on the ABC's *7:30* program, Carr told Chris Uhlmann he had offered his condolences through the Brazilian ambassador to the parents of the young Brazilian killed in a confrontation with the police in Sydney. Yet the fact that the victim's parents were already dead had been reported on the ABC's *AM* that morning. It was yet another unfortunate gaffe.[16]

Senator Carr has long been given to the grand theatrical gesture. Without thinking of all the disadvantages – including the fact that no governor could be appointed from country NSW or interstate – he decided, in sole consultation with the then editor of *The Sydney Morning Herald*, to expel the Governor of NSW from Government House.

This decision horrified the caucus and the cabinet. Paul Keating said it was the reason why he lost the 1996 election. This led to one of the largest and most peaceful non-political and non-union demonstrations seen in Sydney, where Macquarie Street was filled with over 20,000 protesters.

He has also sought to demonstrate to all and sundry his personal brilliance, learning and erudition.

One was when he was parading his knowledge of US history and praising the Supreme Court's decisions about race on the ABC's panel on the presidential election on 8 November 2008, when British author and journalist Christopher Hitchens interjected "like Dred Scott."[17]

"Yes, a great decision," enthused Carr.

In that decision in 1857, *Dred Scott* v. *Sandford*,[18] the US Supreme Court held that the Constitution guarantees property rights over runaway slaves – even in a state that had abolished slavery. Slaves could never become US citizens and were denied constitutional protection. This decision featured in the seven debates in Abraham Lincoln's presidential campaign. Some even say it caused the Civil War. If Senator Carr didn't know this why did he rush in to praise it?

A Foreign Minister of Australia cannot afford to make grand theatrical gestures or substituting demonstrations of his personal brilliance for diplomacy. This may impress the Canberra press gallery but it can do great damage to our foreign policy.

Many had hoped that Senator Carr would be a calming influence in the cabinet, warning the ministers that their profligacy, incompetence and untruths would lead to defeat and damage Labor for a very long time.

There were even those who thought that he could turn around the fortunes of the government, perhaps assume the leadership.

Nothing has changed in a government which has handed our borders over to people smuggler management. Through their negligence they have also allowed corruption and mismanagement to flourish in the customs department.

One result is the vast number of semi automatic pistols used in the crime wave which has become a feature of Sydney night life.

Exposed on this, the government has devised a response which only the highest paid spin doctors could devise. As with the Building the Education Revolution (BER) scandal, the government has avoided a real Royal Commission by an independent and qualified jurist with powers to compel witnesses to appear and for documents to be produced. The revelations would be too hot in an election year. Instead a board has been appointed to advise the government on anti-corruption measures.

Veteran detective, Tim Priest, wonders why the government has concentrated more than 25% of its staff based in an area that has one airport, no sea ports and one railway station – Canberra.[19]

He says systemic failings in Customs have been well known for years, e.g., a "staggering" 53 freight containers laden with drugs, which passed through the screening procedures at Botany Bay terminal undetected, found their way across NSW and had to be tracked down by NSW police.

Again, he says, the NSW police came to the rescue when they discovered boxes of semi-automatic Glock pistols passing freely through our air-freight system undetected by Customs and making their way to a small suburban Sydney post office, where they disappeared into the criminal market place.

In the meantime, when Baroness Margaret Thatcher died, and before she was buried, the foreign Minister used a TV interview to condemn the former prime minister of a major ally as "unabashedly racist".[20]

2.4 Foreign policy now determined from the steps of the Lakemba mosque

After spending billions to acquire a temporary seat on the UN Security Council, the government was unable to take a position on the first important question to come before the UN. The issue was whether Palestine should be accorded observer status..

This was one of those occasions where the government had an opportunity to take a stand on principle, even if it was unlikely to make a difference to the outcome. But they lacked the political spine to do so.

Initially the Prime Minister decided that Australia should oppose the motion. According to the prominent Labor MP, Michael Danby, Foreign Minister Carr broke cabinet solidarity by betraying the Prime Minister in a numbers campaign behind her back.[21]

He says Senator Carr pleaded to caucus members, "How will I explain this on the steps of the mosque at Lakemba?"

This move against the Prime Minister was designed to force a change of the long standing bipartisan policy supporting Israel and about Palestinian statehood.

Mr. Danby said this was "unforgivable" and "unacceptable" behaviour.

The Foreign Minister's action forced Ms Gillard to change her position and announce Australia would abstain from the UN vote on according observer status as a non-member state.

Mr. Danby suggests that a principal reason for the change was the potential impact of a No vote on Muslim voters in Western Sydney.

So is Australian foreign policy to be determined not in the interests of this nation, or on principle, but by a minority of voters?

2.5 Border Control

In the meantime, the government has outsourced the selection of increasing numbers of illegal immigrants to the people smugglers based in Indonesia, a subject we return to in Chapter 10.

Their illegality is confirmed by their doing deals with criminals, involving the payment of money and the hiding or destruction of the passports they needed to enter Indonesia as tourists.

Most remain welfare dependent even after five years and in due course invite three more to join them, according to one report.[22]

2.6 State government responsibility

But while its performance in fulfilling its core duties has been at best inadequate, the federal government has followed a long tradition of Canberra moving into areas intended by the constitution to be the preserve of the states, or which are properly matters for decision by individuals, families and business rather than government. This is costly – in 2007, federal duplication of state responsibilities was estimated to cost $20 billion.[23] Worse, perhaps, the government is not so good that it can afford to be distracted from its core duties.

This duplication achieves few concrete results for the nation. Both federal and state governments seem to have abandoned building up essential infrastructure in major areas. There has long been a ban on new dams, notwithstanding the population increase and government's glib mantra that Australia must become the food bowl of Asia. The Rudd government was accused of stacking a Northern Australia Land and Water Taskforce with people opposed to the harvesting of water.[24] Their conclusion was that Northern Australia could never be a food bowl for Southeast Asia or anywhere else because, as one member said, "we just don't have enough water".

The Taskforce relied on the work done by the CSIRO's Northern Australia Sustainable Yields project, whose scientists were told not to worry about investigating dams. *The Australian* revealed that the Taskforce had misquoted the CSIRO in reporting that one billion litres of rainfall fell across the north each year. The CSIRO had found that this was one million billion litres.

This quite irrational long term ban on new dams complies with fashionable theories concerning the environment which are propounded in the elite salons of the inner cities. It has suited governments under the influence of factional powerbrokers to apply this agenda in order to maintain key elite support. Why coalition governments have also gone along with this is not clear, unless their powerbrokers want to enjoy elite support too. The leaking in early 2013 of a coalition discussion paper for Northern development seems to represent a welcome break from this.[25] Other important infrastructure, considered normal in many other countries, is too often absent in Australia.

This should be contrasted with what was achieved by a succession of state governments when the population was smaller. Most of Sydney's railway system, including the underground network, and many of the dams were completed before the Second World War. Sydney depends on a major dam built decades ago for a city one quarter of the size. Sydney had one of the largest tramway systems in the world before this was unwisely pulled out in the 1960s.

These are essentially State government responsibilities. But given the way in which the federal government has cornered taxation income in Australia, the states are now dependent on federal largesse to achieve this.

That so little important infrastructure has been completed can best be explained by the serious decline in the quality of representative government brought on by the rule of the factional powerbrokers in their axis with the elites.

Let us return then, to the situation following the 2010 election.

The Gillard government suffered a serious loss of confidence when it clung to power after the 2010 election by entering into an alliance with the Greens. To do this, the Prime Minister and Treasurer broke a significant election promise that they would not introduce a carbon dioxide tax.

Later the Prime Minister reinforced an impression that she takes her commitments lightly when she broke her promise to Independent MP Andrew Wilkie to introduce gambling legislation. This was when she was able to secure an additional vote in the House by removing Labor Speaker Harry Jenkins and offering the position to coalition renegade, Peter Slipper. However Mr. Wilkie did not proceed with his often repeated threats to withdraw support from the government.[26]

To many people, the Prime Minister should not have been allowed to break her promise with impunity. This has contributed to a growing dissatisfaction concerning the inability of the people to exercise control over the politicians. All of this has coincided with the compromise of our system of representative democracy by the powerbrokers, and the increased control governments impose over us.

Government control is not a recent development. As the leading business man and former Chairman of the ABC Maurice Newman argues, there has been a surreptitious forty year trend in which governments of different colours, federal, state and local, have tightened their grip over our lives.[27]

One of warning signs of such further intrusion is when politicians describe some measure as a "reform", a term which our media thoughtlessly adopt.

"The bigger the self-styled reform, the more there is to celebrate," writes Mr. Newman. "Leaders want to show they are 'doing something'."

He warns that the increasingly complex regimes require more bureaucrats to administer them, entrenching a master/servant relationship between the politicians and the people. At the same time these complex regimes offer the politicians more opportunities to dispense patronage to rent-seekers and special-interest groups.

As a result the balance of power has tipped inexorably in favour of the political elites. Like the boiling frog, he says, older Australians have watched the slow attrition of their democratic rights "without any sense of what was happening to them".

In the meantime a massive attempt has been undertaken to indoctrinate children to believe that government is the solution to all problems.

This, he declares, is the road to serfdom, a serfdom in which the people serve the politicians and the bureaucrats – the antithesis of representative democracy.

2.7 Law and Order

The maintenance of law and order, referred to once as The Queen's Peace, is a fundamental duty of government. The primary responsibility lies with state governments, but the federal government also has a role and can have a major impact.

On several occasions, both have seriously mismanaged this. If there were only one argument for making our politicians more accountable, it would be in their failure to maintain law and order at a level Australians expect.

Australians could be forgiven for believing that a succession of governments, state and federal, has adopted the following 10 point plan to empower the criminal classes. This has of course not been their intention. But the cumulative effect of the following policies, adopted by government on the advice of the elites, has been to achieve precisely this – to empower the criminal classes.

The Australian people would not have adopted any of these policies had they been asked – they have far too much common sense.

1. Tolerate petty crime. This can be achieved by abolishing, for example, summary offences. As crime increases, people will soon realise that it is pointless to report many burglaries and assaults, which does wonders for the statistics.

2. Undermine the family and create welfare dependency. Thus ensure there is a significant number of healthy and able taxpayer young men and women with nothing to do..

3. Introduce discriminatory policing. Especially avoid confrontations with youth from certain ethnic communities.

4. Make serious policing difficult or impossible. Make police selection politically correct by reducing standards, tie the police up in paperwork and make them subject to complaints to politically correct bureaucracies, thus subjecting them to endless internal and external enquiries.

5. Undermine both the jury and trial judges. Lessening their role, keep them in the dark, subject trial judges to minuscule controls on their ability to instruct the jury or their discretion on sentencing, and encourage taxpayer-funded appeals even on the most technical matters.

6. Always show more concern for the accused and less concern for the victim. Make trials longer and more technical, concentrating inordinately on whether evidence should be seen or heard by the jury. Increase possible defences and ways to avoid or diminish responsibility, and restrict evidence which may be considered by the jury.

7. Lower or remove quality controls on immigration by, for example, abdicating control over the borders, reducing security checks and by outsourcing immigration administration to people smugglers.

8. Remove discipline from the schools and in its place insist on the self-esteem of all students.

9. Arm the criminals by abandoning serious control of the borders and allowing an influx of weapons.

10. Make criminals understand that even if they caught and convicted, and the conviction and sentence is upheld on the inevitable appeal, punishment is likely to be light. Above all, denounce zero tolerance and mandatory sentencing, keep juries in the dark, ensure sentences are low or nominal and encourage generous parole.

Older Australians will have seen a significant decline in the standard of law and order in the country. By comparison with the United States, Australia's crime rate is now 43% higher.[28]

Proportionately, there were 100% more assaults and 150% more rapes in Australia than in the United States. There are 31% more bribery offences in Australia than America. On other measures Australia is better than the United States which has, for example, 150 times more murders with firearms than Australia.

Whether it be because of the neutering of the police, negligence in the administration of immigration, the release of the dangerously medically ill into the community, the moving of the pendulum in criminal trials significantly towards the accused and away from the victim, or the imposition of grossly inadequate punishment, the decisions or lack of them have been made by the politicians.

Each of the following examples indicates an absence of down-to-earth common sense. Had they been left to rank-and-file Australians, a sensible decision would have been taken. The important question is how do the people control the politicians and ensure sensible decisions are taken.

First, our police forces have been neutered. They are subject to over-regulation and required to respond to complaints to a number of institutions. Their reporting requirements are so demanding and heavy, there is a distinct disincentive to their taking action in relation to crimes. Because of their bureaucratic obligations, far less time is spent on the streets on their fundamental duties.

In addition, recruiting has been subject to criteria which are strongly politically correct. And above all there just are not enough police. There are 217 police per 100,000 people in Australia. In New Zealand there are 247, in the United States 256 and in the United Kingdom 307.

Then there is the problem with the methods of policing. More and more this has involved a "softly softly" approach to criminals, based on the belief that by going hard on criminals who already have a dislike of authority, it will only reinforce that dislike. The criminal classes treat this with the contempt it deserves and do not, of course, reform their behaviour. The "softly softly" approach only results in the criminal elements not respecting authority and being encouraged to go further.

One notable example of the selective application of the "softly softly" approach was after the Cronulla riots, when heavily armed men formed a revenge motorcade outside of a mosque. (Bear in mind that traditional methods of tough policing were used against the rioting youths on the beach at Cronulla). The police were instructed to keep away from them.

Another was on Australia Day 2012 when there was a race riot provoked by a prime ministerial advisor. The riot took place outside a restaurant in Canberra where the Prime Minister and the Leader of opposition were speaking. Rather than confronting the rioters, the police rushed the Prime Minister and the Leader of the Opposition to their cars. The Prime Minister was carried bodily, her face almost scraping the ground. Video news reports of this went round the world. Had this happened decades ago, the police would have warned the rioters and ordered them to disperse. That would probably have resolved the issue.

What is needed in Australia is a return to the doctrine of zero tolerance of crime, no matter how small. When this approach was followed in New York under Commissioner Bratton and Mayor Rudy Giuliani, the murder rate fell by three-quarters.

The second failure has been in relation to immigration policy. Too often, the federal government has failed to select immigrants carefully on the basis of merit, and in particular on being satisfied that the immigrant will observe Australian laws, adopt our fundamental values and make a positive contribution to society. The result has been the formation of ethnic gangs who terrorise the suburbs and towns.

Adopting a correct immigration policy has absolutely nothing to do with race or colour; it has to do with quality. It was the way in which the post-war immigrants were chosen.

The first glimmer of the failure to apply this rigorous test was under the Fraser government in the 70s. Gerard Henderson, who was then working for Prime Minister Malcolm Fraser, recalls that prominent members of the Australian Maronite community approached the government during the Lebanese civil war to allow some Lebanese Christians, who had close relatives in Australia, to settle here.[29]

Malcolm Fraser decided, against advice, that this should be done by relaxing the rules regarding refugees. But rather than admitting Lebanese Christians in need, visas were granted to Muslims – often on the flimsiest evidence they had close relatives or, indeed, any relative in Australia.

According to Gerard Henderson, the program soon became known as "the Lebanese concession". Although they were admitted as refugees, they were not fleeing persecution but rather the impact of a civil war. With the generous family reunion that was then allowed, more than

25,000 Muslim immigrants soon came to Australia, settling mainly in south-western Sydney, around the Arncliffe and Lakemba mosques.

Christian Lebanese leaders warned the government that allowing in large numbers of poorly educated Lebanese Muslims, ill-equipped to enter the workforce and with a number being fundamental Islamists, would be a disaster. Under the next government, this community was identified by the Labor Party as likely to be its constituency. This apparently led to the then Prime Minister, Paul Keating, overruling his immigration Minister, Chris Hurford, who had decided to expel the controversial cleric Sheik Taj el-Din al Hilaly.

Malcolm Fraser also failed in not applying a rigorous test for immigration in relation to some of the Vietnamese immigrants who slipped in during his administration.

And now, with the collapse of border control under the Rudd and Gillard governments, we are seeing this problem being repeated.

Whenever the immigration program is mismanaged by the federal politicians, the burden is then on the state authorities to respond to the problem. As the veteran Sydney detective Tim Priest observes, each new wave of racial gangs has been more violent and more dangerous. He was one of the front-line policemen who led the war against the Vietnamese drug lords in Cabramatta, a Sydney suburb. But then he found his biggest battle was to be not against the criminals, but against politicians, police bosses and bureaucrats. He was forced out, only to be vindicated later by parliamentary enquiries.[30]

In 2003 he predicted that the Sydney beachside suburb Cronulla would be a flashpoint – there were riots there in 2005. He said that within the decade, the Lebanese Muslim gangs would spread rapidly across Australia to expand their enterprises and no-go areas would develop in south-western Sydney.

He also predicted there would be a dramatic rise in gang shootings in Sydney.

All of that has come to pass. His fundamental warning was that if action were not taken soon (that was in 2003) it might be impossible to bring the problem under control, and that the costs of attempting to do so later would be enormous, indeed "unimaginable."

He also foresaw the "serious possibility" that some of the Middle Eastern elements would go a step further and "engage in terrorist acts against Australia". He believed, correctly, that the ingredients for this were already there. He warned that overseas experience indicates that it is it is a small step "from urban terrorism to religious and political terrorism".

He expressed the hope – which in retrospect must be seen to be a vain hope – that people in government and the police would ensure that "we don't lose the values and the rights we have received from past generations".

The third area of policy failure relates to mental health, a problem which has been increased by the use of what are so innocuously described as "recreational" drugs. Some say the problem is exacerbated by the over-prescription of medicinal drugs, now even used for behavioural problems in children which are sometimes no more than the result of a lack of discipline in the schools. This in turn results from the adoption of official policies that have led to that state of affairs.

Claiming there were weaknesses with mental health institutions, the politicians accepted that the answer was not to improve the institutions. Instead, the politicians were advised to close down the institutions and to move the mentally ill "into the community". This had two advantages for state governments. The mentally ill were moved from state to federal budget responsibility. The buildings in which the mental health institutions were located were sold off and the proceeds immediately spent. (It is a truly remarkable aspect of government finances that unlike ordinary people, governments sell off the people's assets and spend the price gained immediately on day-to-day living).

The result is that some of those suffering from mental health problems, who are released "into the community", end up homeless and on the streets.[31] Some have proved dangerous, particularly when they get their hands on weapons, including knives. They are often said to be safe if they take their medication. In a decision devoid of any common sense, the responsibility for taking the medication is left to the mentally ill.

A judge told one of the authors about a case which he heard concerning a bus driver. As soon as he opened the doors at a particular bus stop, an insane person rushed in with a knife and began slashing the driver's face. On hearing the plea that the insane person was quite safe provided he took his medication, the judge suggested to the prosecution that the public official and / or medical practitioner who took this decision should be brought before the court. The crown prosecutor decided that the best answer was to attempt to humour the judge.

The fourth and fifth policy areas relate to the often grossly inadequate punishment of the guilty, but also in the conduct of criminal trials. In these, the pendulum has been in recent times so moved that is excessively protects the accused, rather than the victim.[32]

Under the influence of a coalition of defence lawyers and psychiatrists – and in the absence not only of any lobby to act on behalf of the general public and with the common sense with which the average Australian is endowed – more and more information is withheld from the jury and trials are excessively delayed, longer and more technical. Appeals on all manner of grounds, even the most ridiculously technical, are publicly funded and far too prevalent.

Trials are now essentially about the defence trying to keep the jury in the dark. So trial judges are fearful that their decisions concerning the admission of evidence, and their instructions to the jury, will justify grounds for some appeal, however technical. On every piece of evidence defence lawyers can argue that it is unfair to admit it, that it was illegally or improperly obtained or that its "probative value" outweighs the danger of unfair prejudice to the accused. When there is more than one accused, objection may be made about evidence against one being prejudicial against the others. Whatever ruling the trial judge makes – and there will be many – can be a ground for appeal.

Given the public funding of appeals, and the resources put into them, it is rare that a jury's decision and a judge's sentence is final. Too often, for relatively trivial reasons, a new trial is ordered. Imagine the stress for, say, a rape victim.

The jury should not be treated as composed of near idiots, but allowed a certain amount of discretion. The scope for technical objections to the admission of evidence should be significantly limited. Rather the jury should, with the assistance of the judge, decide what weight they consider appropriate in relation to evidence which is hidden from them but which is really relevant. Their decision should normally be final.

Our criminal justice system at work

Let us look at a recent example of the workings of our criminal justice system. Most Australians would be surprised to know that being involved in a drive-by shooting is in itself no evidence of any intention to harm anyone inside.[33]

Australians may also be surprised to know that it is wrong to tell a jury that the prisoner they are trying had absconded while on bail and run off to Lebanon. He was arrested and gaoled there on local charges. When he served his Lebanese sentence he was extradited back to Australia.

But an Australian jury couldn't be trusted with such information.

That prisoner was Saleh Jamal.[34] And thanks to Australian taxpayers funding his defence and appeals – and our gold plated criminal justice system – he is now free.

He belonged to a Kings Cross cocaine gang, "DK's boys". The DK stands for triple convicted murderer Danny Karam, now serving three life sentences plus 50 years and four months.

In 1998 the gang planned the notorious drive-by shooting of the

Lakemba police station, shattering its plate-glass doors with sixteen bullets. A get-away car was stolen, with weapons ammunition and stockings at the ready. Four men did the shooting, with Jamal on the outside listening to the police scanner and ensuring the get-away. The stolen car was destroyed.

Jamal was arrested for his role in this in 2004. While on bail he absconded to Lebanon on a false passport.

On his extradition in 2006, he was tried and sentenced to nine years on an unrelated charge – the 1998 kneecapping of a rival drug dealer.

He was found guilty over the drive-by shooting and sentenced to a maximum of 12 years' gaol.

On appeal last year, the Court actually acquitted him on the charge of intending to shoot policemen – "maliciously discharging a firearm with intent to do grievous bodily harm". So merely being involved in a drive-by shooting of a police station is no evidence of an intention to shoot those within.

Apart from letting the jury into the secret that Jamal had skipped bail, the unfortunate trial judge was rapped over the knuckles for not making sure Jamal was present when the court went to see the police station.

Understandably the police weren't going to take any chances. He would be in orange overalls, shackled and restrained and in a cage within a police van. The judge was worried that if the jury peered into the van they would see this and be prejudiced against him. Anyway his counsel would be present and nothing was to be said at the inspection.

Although Jamal was not obviously disadvantaged by this – indeed he was helped by it – the Court of Criminal Appeal concluded that the trial was flawed.

They ordered a new trial on the lesser charge of firing a firearm in or near a public place.

At the end of the resulting twelve day retrial before a District Court Judge sitting without a jury, Jamal was found not guilty.

In the meantime, two other members of the gang were also acquitted. Two turned Crown witnesses and were granted immunity.

And Jamal is now free to walk the streets.

Other examples of the working of our judicial system relate to the lenient sentences imposed for child offenders.[35]

We once had an effective and fair criminal justice system. What do we have now? It is certainly gold plated. But for whom?

Common sense proposal

It was a breath of fresh air to read that the Chief Justice of Queensland, Paul de Jersey, argued that the criminal histories of defendants should be revealed to juries.[36] He said that the public is smart enough to hear the truth in court about relevant past offences.

"Why," he asks, "should a jury be denied knowledge that an alleged rapist committed another rape six months earlier ... or that an accused charged with fraud has a string of convictions for dishonesty?"

In the meantime, even when an accused is found guilty of some appalling offence, the penalty is too often inadequate, and even then subject to remission.

The old adage that it is better 100 guilty men go free than one innocent man go to gaol has been used to redesign our criminal justice system. This has been to the great advantage of the defence lawyers, to those who practise in the field of psychology and, of course, to the criminal class. Insufficient attention is paid to the need for a reasonably speedy justice, the interests of the victims and the general state of law and order which ensues from the laxity of present system of criminal justice.

A serious return to zero tolerance, speedy but fair trials, a decent respect for the role and function of the jury, and serious punishment for serious crimes would go a long way to reducing crime in Australia. The mentally ill who are dangerous should not be left to control themselves by prescription drugs. And federal governments should stop importing those who are likely to form the nexus of the next racially based criminal gangs.

The average Australian knows all this. Why don't the politicians? Since they have demonstrated themselves incapable of exercising proper control, the only answer is to make them accountable.

Endnotes

1 http://www.smh.com.au/opinion/politics/toothless-among-asian-tigers-20120720 -22fc8.html#ixzz21DQVDWlp (retrieved 20.07.2012).

2 Jim Molan, "Why our defence forces face terminal decline", *Quadrant*, March 2013, No. 494, volume LVII, No. 3.

3 http://www.smh.com.au/national/letting-the-troops-down-20100507- ujoj.html

4 Loc.cit.

5 http://www.defence.gov.au/WhitePaper2013/docs/WP_2013_web.pdf (retrieved 07.05.2013).

6 Peter Hartcher, "We rely on the US at our peril", *Sydney Morning Herald*, 7 May 2013 http://www.smh.com.au/comment/we-rely-on-the-us-at-our-peril-20130506-2j3ds. html#ixzz2SXe3TOyv (retrieved 07.05.2013).

7 David Flint, "Military prosecutions: Parliament must act now". On Line Opinion, 8 October 2010. http://www.onlineopinion.com.au/view.asp?article=11070&page=0 (retrieved 02.03.2013)

8 Transcript of Proceedings, Sergeant J and Lance Corporal D (Australian Military Court, Pre-Trial Directions Hearing, Chief Judge Advocate Westwood, 20 May 2011); *Yearbook of International Humanitarian Law*, Vol 14, 2011, Correspondents Reports, http://www.asser.nl/upload/documents/20121018T042513-Australia%20YIHL%20 14%202011.pdf (retrieved 04.05.2013).

9 Director of Military Prosecutions, Annual Report 2011, p. 13; Tom Hyland, "Military prosecutor slams judges ruling", *The Sydney Morning Herald*, 8 July 2012. http:// www.smh.com.au/opinion/political-news/military-prosecutor-slams-judges-ruling-20120707-21o26.html#ixzz2PWpe6DIk.(retrieved 05.04.2013).

10 David Flint, "Congratulations on your useless billion dollar seat", *The Punch*, 24 October 2012. http://www.thepunch.com.au/articles/Congrats-on-your-useless-billion-dollar-seat/ (retrieved 24.10.2012).

11 $375 million was diverted to onshore asylum seeker processing in December 2012, 18 December 2012 *ABC*. http://www.abc.net.au/news/2012-12-17/australia-to-cut-aid-to-fund-asylum-seeker-costs/4432606 (retrieved 28.04.2013).

12 Ean Higgins, "Poor miss out as pollies live large", *The Australian*, 26 April 2013. http://www.theaustralian.com.au/national-affairs/foreign-affairs/poor-miss-out-as-pollies-live-large/story-fn59nm2j-1226629607150 (retrieved 28April 2013).

13 Independent Inquiry Committee, *Report on the Manipulation of the Oil-for-Food Programme* (27 October 2005). http://www.iic-offp.org/story27oct05.htm (retrieved 28.04.2013).

14 David Flint, "Grand theatrical gestures are no way to conduct foreign policy", *The Australian*, 26 March 2012. http://www.theaustralian.com.au/national-affairs/opinion/grand-theatrical-gestures-are-no-way-to-conduct-foreign-policy/comments-e6frgd0x-1226309690606 (retrieved 20.01.2013).

15 http://www.news.com.au/breaking-news/bob-carr-starts-fast-tony-abbotts-a-cheaps-circus-act/story-e6frfku0-1226298019230 (retrieved 07.05.2013).

16 http://www.theaustralian.com.au/national-affairs/opinion/grand-theatrical-gestures- are-no-way-to-conduct-foreign-policy/story-e6frgd0x-1226309690606 (retrieved 28.04.2013).

17 http://www.theaustralian.com.au/national-affairs/opinion/grand-theatrical-gestures-are-no-way-to-conduct-foreign-policy/story-e6frgd0x-1226309690606 (retrieved 28.04.2013).

18 60 U.S. 393 (1857)

19 Tim Priest, "It appears Customs failures threaten security", *The Australian*, 28 December 2012.   http://www.theaustralian.com.au/national-affairs/opinion/customs-failures-threaten-security/story-e6frgd0x-1226544300327 (retrieved 28.12.2012).

20 http://www.smh.com.au/comment/thatchers-critics-neither-balanced-nor-respectful-20130415-2hw1j.html#ixzz2QcxuUpfz (retrieved 28.04.2013).

21 http://www.dailytelegraph.com.au/news/opinion/doing-the-right-thing-is-no-longer-an-option/story-e6frezz0-1226534754391(retrieved 28.01.2013).

22 See chapter 10.

23 Professor George Williams, "So much government, so little done", *The Sydney Morning Herald*, 13 March 2007. http://www.smh.com.au/news/opinion/so-much-government-so-little-done/2007/03/12/1173548110245.html?page=fullpage (retrieved 19.01.2013).

24 Asa Wahlquist, and Lenore Taylor, "Dams not an option in Labor food plan", *The Australian*, 9 February 2010. http://www.theaustralian.com.au/archive/business-old/dams-not-an-option-in-labor-food-plan/story-e6frg95o-1225828061772   (retrieved 30.03.2013).

25 http://www.abc.net.au/news/2013-02-08/supersized-vision-for-northern-australia-stirs-pot/4509466

26 Piers Akerman, "Wilkie-Gillard to dump pokie pledges", *Perth Now*, 18 January 2013. http://www.perthnow.com.au/wilkie-gillard-to-dump-pokie-pledges/story-fn-6mhct1-1226247467721(retrieved 19.01.2013.)

27 http://www.theaustralian.com.au/national-affairs/opinion/sound-of-silence-kills-free-speech/story-e6frgd0x-1226432218279 (retrieved 23.07.2012).

28 http://www.nationmaster.com/compare/Australia/United-States/Crime (retrieved 07.05.2103)

29 Gerard Henderson, "Immigration mistakes return to haunt us", *Sydney Morning Herald*, 31 October 2006. http://www.smh.com.au/news/opinion/immigration-mistakes-return-to-haunt-us/2006/10/30/1162056925283.html? (retrieved 27.01.2013).

30 Priest, Tim, "The rise of Middle Eastern crime in Australia", *Quadrant*, January 2004; see also Tim Priest, Richard Basham, *To Protect and To Serve: the untold truth about the New South Wales Police Service*, New Holland, Sydney, 2003.

31 "Over 100,000 Australians are homeless, the Rudd government planning to halve this by 2020: Rudd's 2020 homeless pledge welcomed", *Sydney Morning Herald*, 21 December 2008. http://news.smh.com.au/national/rudds-2020-homeless-pledge-welcomed-20081221-72rw.html (retrieved 15.03.2013).

32 Margaret Cuneen, *Sir Ninian Stephen Lecture*, University of Newcastle, 2005. http://www.smh.com.au/news/national/margaret-cunneens-lecture/2005/09/23/1126982234942.html

33 *Jamal* v R [2012] NSWCCA 198 (8 June 2012). http://www.austlii.edu.au/cgi-bin/sinodisp/au/cases/nsw/NSWCCA/2012/198.html?stem=0&synonyms=0&query=Jamal (retrieved 16.03.2013) .

34 http://www.smh.com.au/nsw/brutal-story-ends-as-kneecapper-freed-20130314- 2g384.html#ixzz2Nf5wui52 (retrieved 16.03.2013).

35 E.g., "Six years for fatally bashing girl friend's son", *CANdo*, 26 April 2013. http://www.cando.org.au/updates/296-six-years-for-fatally-bashing-girlfriend-s-four-year-old-son; Fife-Yeomans, Janet, "Paedophiles walk as their victims suffer", *Daily Telegraph*, 29 April 2013. http://www.dailytelegraph.com.au/news/paedophiles-walk-as-victims-suffer/story-e6freuy9-1226631175281, Case Studies, *Daily Telegraph*, 29 April 2013. http://resources.news.com.au/files/2013/04/28/1226631/190273-case-studies.pdf (retrieved 29.04.2013).

36 Renee Viellaris, "Queensland Chief Justice Paul de Jersey wants criminal pasts revealed", *Courier-Mail*, 15 March 2013. http://www.couriermail.com.au/national-news/queensland/queensland-chief-justice-paul-de-jersey-wants-criminal-pasts-revealed/story-fndo4ckr-1226597690808#ixzz2NYm7wMkY(retrieved 07.05.2013).

CHAPTER 3

Schools in decline

In recent years, successive federal governments have tried to take control of education, notwithstanding that, constitutionally, this is clearly a state responsibility. They have set up their own bureaucracy, and spent vast amounts of the taxpayers' funds. In the meantime, educational standards in Australia have fallen and are falling further.

In a series of media releases and interviews in January 2013, the Federal Minister of Education, Peter Garrett, unsurprisingly extolled the government's initiatives for the year. These included a new funding model from the Gonski report, as well as a national plan for school improvement.[1]

Welcomed by the teachers' unions, this was criticised by some as merely a continuation of the failed "Education Revolution" announced by Prime Minister Kevin Rudd and administered by his then Minister for Education, Julia Gillard. A key element was the BER, the Building the Education Revolution. This was a financial disaster which resulted in billions of dollars of waste.[2]

The government's critics were under-reported in the media, while a major advertising program supporting the government was undertaken by the unions.

In a bizarre move which is redolent more of an authoritarian country or even a dictatorship, schools with recently finished BER buildings have been required to hold election year "recognition ceremonies" during the 2013 year. They are to praise the government and to invite federal Employment Minister Bill Shorten to speak.[3]

Education spending over the last ten years has increased by $13.5 billion, says Ben Jensen, director of the Grattan Institute's school education program.[4] But Australia is one of just four OECD countries in which 15-year-olds actually went backwards on international assessments between 2000 and 2009.

He says that the principal driver of spending increases in this period, promoted by the teachers' unions and by both sides of politics, has been to reduce class sizes. This he says is "incredibly expensive". At best it results in only marginal improvements in student learning. It is, he concludes, a "huge waste of money".

Citing international evidence, he argues that the best schools and the best school systems focus single-mindedly on children's learning. And to improve learning there is a need to improve teaching. The Federal government's Gonski proposal for the states and the Commonwealth to spend $6.5 billion extra each year is more of the same policy to increase funding without attending to improved teaching.

Professor Henry Ergas observes that the Gonski report significantly makes no mention of one crucial finding in the modelling it commissioned.[5] This is that poor school performance is not due to insufficient funding.

As we note below, this is what all the critics are saying and the federal government is ignoring. Throwing money at education won't improve standards. It will probably increase bureaucratic waste.

But this finding, which, as Professor Ergas says, "cuts at the heart of the government's rhetoric and that of the teachers' union", is not mentioned in the Gonski report.

The problem in education is that too many politicians have approved or tolerated the adoption here of the demands of the teachers trade union, including a series of new radical fashions in education – just as they were being found to be unworkable in their country of origin.

Michael Gove, the British education minister, recently pointed out that progressive educational theory stresses the importance of children following their own instincts, instead of being taught.[6] This can even be seen in the design of the modern classroom which takes away the authority of the teacher. The children are arranged almost as if they are in a restaurant, with the intent that they engage in sophisticated after dinner discussions about what they may choose to learn.

In the modern classroom the children are effectively expected to teach themselves. They go where they want to. Michael Gove says this was not always the favoured theory of the left. He points to the view of the father of Euro-Communism, Antonio Gramsci, that the working class should be liberated through the power of traditional education.

But since then we have seen much of education fall under the control of the elites who endorse "progressive "education and reject and ridicule the traditional approach. But as Michael Gove points out, despite the more than abundant proof everywhere that children perform better when taught according to the principles of traditional education, there is still a dogmatic resistance from the elites to any reversion to tried and tested methods.

There is one famous exception to this. This is when the elites decide what schooling should be arranged for their own children. In other countries and in Australia there are numerous examples of the prominent people on the left, who publicly endorse the need for progressive education, but who ensure that their children are taught according to traditional methods.

Nevertheless, these new radical fashions have been adopted not only in the schools but also in teacher education where the performance of graduates is controversial. When Professor Rob Tierney, the Dean of Education and Social Work at the University of Sydney, recently argued that "poor performing students" do not graduate from teaching courses, Paul Koff of Glenhaven in New South Wales responded in a letter to *The Sydney Morning Herald* with the observation, "If only this were true."[7]

He said that in the recent past at his local school, they were sent student teachers of English who had managed to reach their final year of university with "little mastery of spelling or grammar." Many, he said, were "unable to write cogent essays". One student teacher said she had never studied Shakespeare at school or tertiary level. He said another student teacher was unable to read a simple passage out to a class, openly stating that he was "no good at reading".

When the university was contacted regarding this "rather huge impediment" to English teaching, the student teacher was moved to another school. The explanation was that there was a "personality clash" with the supervising teacher.

This example further illustrates that the fundamental problem in education is not funding as such. Instead, sound standards should be restored both in teaching and in teacher education. In addition, more funding should be allocated to the classroom rather than funding so generously the state bureaucracies and the parallel federal bureaucracy.

Education, under the Australian Constitution, is a state responsibility. In the view of the founders, this was best administered locally, not centrally as we would the defence of the nation. This has the control in essentially state areas of responsibility is that the lowest common denominator will tend to apply – that is what has happened in other areas. It is now happening in education, which has nothing to do with the Canberra politicians, who have great difficulty in handling their core functions.

All of this has developed from a decision which was made under the Menzies government decades ago to grant financial assistance for science laboratories in the Catholic system and other private schools. This was not about running education but rather addressing the anomaly that Catholic parents were funding both state schools and the Catholic parochial schools. Unlike similar Protestant schools, Catholic parochial schools had not been absorbed into the state system in the 19th century.

In recent years, the federal government has sought an increased role in managing the school system. As a consequence taxpayer funds are being wasted on bureaucratic duplication for no good purpose.

Alongside the eight state and territory departments of education, we now have a Federal Department of Education, Employment and Workplace Relations (DEEWR).

One of the ways the politicians waste our money is in their constantly changing the names of departments and programs and moving them around, even ones which have nothing to do with federal government responsibilities.

Until 2007 this department was known as the Department of Education, Science and Training (DEST). Before that it was the Department of Education, Training and Youth Affairs which traded under the ugly acronym, DETYA.

Contrast that with Canada, which has no federal department of education. Canada has a high performing schools system, a fact acknowledged in the Gonski report.[8]

Peter Garrett, the Federal Minister for School Education, claims that the government's 2013 proposals will result in a dramatic improvement. He says: "Students starting their education journey this year will be part of an education system that will be in the top five in the world by the time they leave Year 12 by 2025."

Education expert Dr. Kevin Donnelly dismisses this claim. He says it is as empty as former Prime Minister Bob Hawke's celebrated promise, "By 1990 no Australian child will be living in poverty."[9]

Donnelly points out that we only have to look at the Rudd and Gillard governments' record to date and the flaws in proposed initiatives to realise Australian students will never be among the top five. Donnelly lists three:

- Providing a computer for every Year 9 to 12 student across Australia. The program did not take into account inadequate internet connections, lack of teacher profess-ional development and suitable software and that computers would be superseded by new technologies such as tablets and e-readers. (The computers were also significantly over priced).[10]

- The $16.5 billion Building the Education Revolution, which has proved to be a casebook example of financial mismanagement and waste.
- The Gillard-inspired national curriculum, beginning with history, English, mathematics and science, and compulsory for all Australian schools.

Let us examine the history curriculum. It ignores the fact that Australia is, as former Prime Minister John Howard says, a product of Western civilisation.[11] The curriculum is slanted to the progressive left view of the world prepared to replace fact with myth. One example is the claim that Gough Whitlam and not Harold Holt abolished the White Australia policy.

British history is completely purged from the curriculum. John Howard points out that the "influence of British institutions on Australia is a fact not nostalgia: Magna Carta, parliamentary democracy, the language we speak, which, need I remind you, is now the lingua franca of Asia, much of the literature we imbibe, a free and irreverent media, a relatively simple system of political discourse, the rule of law and trial by jury; indeed many of the sports we play; these are all owed in one form or another to the British."[12]

Mr. Howard argues that we cannot know modern Australia well without understanding the British story. He asks: "How can young Australians ever be expected to understand how fragile and hard-won the rule of law is, without knowing a little about the English Civil War?"

Once again we can see the wisdom of our founding fathers – and the generation which approved the constitution – in deciding that education was to be a state responsibility, and not something which should be added to the already large number of issues for the federal authorities.

Dr. Donnelly refers to another problem, that of teaching reading in the early years. This is obviously an essential foundation to any education system. He says that while the minister claimed that the more effective phonics and phonemic awareness method is included in the national English curriculum, the reality proves otherwise.

With the traditional teaching of phonics, children are taught the relationship between letters and groups of letters and sounds. But the preferred approach of those responsible for the English curriculum is the failed "whole-language" approach.

Under this failed approach children are told to look and work out the meaning of words by their context.

This has been the prevailing orthodoxy in Australian schools for many years. Does it work? Well, the proof of the pudding is, as they say, in the eating.

Australian Year 4 students are ranked 27th in the world in the Progress in International Reading Literacy Study. Australian students are outperformed by all other English-speaking nations, for example, England, the US and New Zealand.

Our primary school students are the lowest performing of any English-speaking nation, just above the world's lowest-performing developed nations, according to Ben Jensen, director of the Grattan Institute's school education program.[13]

He argues that to improve student learning, there must be a strong link between design and implementation. But the current education system actually separates the responsibilities for what we teach (the design of the curriculum) from how we teach it (implementation in schools). The first is now federal; the second is a state responsibility. No-one with common sense would tolerate such a system. Ben Jensen contrasts this with Hong Kong. There, the reform of the curriculum was designed to improve teaching. It was to change how students learned to read and how reading was taught through improved teaching practices. In just five years, Hong Kong moved from 17th to second in world rankings of primary students' reading literacy – Australia sits in the 27th position.[14]

Donnelly says the government is running out of time to finalise a new funding regime as the current socioeconomic status model expires at the end of the year. Peter Garrett's media release promises that the ALP government is committed to "delivering a fairer funding system" and, as a result, will "deliver better results for our students".

The minister is wrong on both counts, according to Donnelly, as the government-endorsed Gonski report discriminates against non-government schools.

"Parents who send their children to Catholic and independent schools, in addition to paying taxes for a system they do not use, face the prospect of fees escalating as non-government schools will be denied the same minimum level of funding guaranteed to government schools", he says.

What we are seeing is an undermining of the constitution, as Canberra seizes powers it was never intended to have and which the people never granted. This goes against the common sense, good judgement and sense of decency of rank-and-file Australians. The federal government is abusing the power of the purse – a power seized in breach of the clear original constitutional intention and against all the principles of federalism to do something far beyond its competence – run Australia's school system.

The result will be a further lowering of standards of literacy and numeracy, together with achieving a sinister political agenda. This is to ensure that young Australians are ignorant of our history, including the reasons why we are one of the world's oldest continuing democracies.

Endnotes

1 http://ministers.deewr.gov.au/garrett

2 See Chapter 1.

3 Schools benefitting from the Building the Education Revolution were required to hold election year "recognition ceremonies" during the 2013 year. They are to praise the government and invite federal Employment Minister Bill Shorten to speak, see Gemma Jones, "Schools used as election fodder", *Daily Telegraph*, 24 January 2013. http://www.dailytelegraph.com.au/news/schools-used-as-election-pr-fodder/story-e6freuy9-1226560422676 (retrieved 12.02.2013).

4 Ben Jensen, "Wrong fix for failing schools", *The Australian*, 23-24 February 2013. http://www.theaustralian.com.au/national-affairs/spending-billions-is-the-wrong-fix-for-our-failing-schools/story-fn59niix-1226583841041 (retrieved 23.02. 2013); Devine, Miranda, "Literacy? Read this and weep", *Daily Telegraph*, 3 April, 2013, http://www.dailytelegraph.com.au/news/opinion/literacy-read-this-and-weep/story-e6frezz0-1226611182944 (retrieved 05.04.2013).

5 Henry Ergas, "Show us the models", *The Australian*, 22 April 2013. http://www.theaustralian.com.au/opinion/columnists/honesty-would-prove-priceless/story-fn7078da-1226625436024 (retrieved 22.04.2013).

6 Michael Gove, *The Progressive Betrayal*, 5 February 2013. http://www.newsweekly.com.au/article.php?id=5496 http://www.smf.co.uk/media/news/michael-gove-speaks-smf/ (retrieved 15.03.2013).

7 http://www.smh.com.au/national/letters/rudd-too-smart-to-go-after-the-poisoned-chalice-20130219-2ephf.html#ixzz2LOBgc0Ff (retrieved 20.02.2013).

8 Ben Jensen, "Feds could save education by staying out of it," *The Australian*, 2-3 February, 2013. http://www.theaustralian.com.au/national-affairs/opinion/feds-could-save-education-by-staying-out-of-it/story-e6frgd0x-1226566878920 (retrieved 02.02.2013); he argues for voucher funding, autonomy, competition, choice, discipline and education in the classical and liberal sense, see Donnelly, Kevin, "Education hijacked by PC left", *The Australian*, 16-17 February 2013. http://www.theaustralian.com.au/national-affairs/education/education-hijacked-by-pc-left/story-fn59nlz9-1226579053605, (retrieved 16.02.2013).

9 "Shades of Hawke as Garrett rides out on his schools crusade", *The Australian*, 29 January 2013. http://www.theaustralian.com.au/national-affairs/opinion/shades-of-hawke-as-garret13).

10 Minister Peter Garrett claimed the program had been delivered on time and within budget, with 957,805 computers being purchased at a cost of $2.4 billion, which is $2505 per computer. But as Catallaxy Files points out, the retail outlet Harvey Norman was at the same time selling Toshiba Satellite C850/05D Laptops for $698

each, and obviously at a lower price for a bulk purchase, see Government Purchasing, *Callaxy Files*, 3 February 2013. http://catallaxyfiles.com/2013/02/03/government-purchasing/ (retrieved 12.02.2013).

11 John Howard, *Sir Paul Hasluck Foundation Inaugural Lecture*, December 2012, No. 492, Volume LVI, Number 12. http://resources.news.com.au/files/2012/09/27/1226482/801957-sir-paul-hasluck-foundation-inaugural-lecture.pdf (retrieved 05.05.2013).

12 Ibid.

13 "Feds could save education by staying out of it", *The Australian*, 2-3 February 2013. http://www.theaustralian.com.au/national-affairs/opinion/feds-could-save-education-by-staying-out-of-it/story-e6frgd0x-1226566878920 (retrieved 02.02.2013).

14 Ibid.

CHAPTER 4

They are stealing your property

4.1 Governments can steal your property – and they do

You think you own the dream property you scrimped to buy? That if it has to be taken for some public purpose, at least you will get fair compensation. Only Marxist, communist states take property without compensation. And that doesn't happen in Australia. Not in our representative democracy.

Well, the fact is, they can. And it can happen under governments of all persuasions and across the nation, with two exceptions.

So beware – governments can effectively steal your property, and give you nothing in return. Not only can they do this, they are doing it now.

In recent years there has been an intellectual softening up by the elites of Australians' traditional rights to their property, especially their homes and their farms, namely the idea that an Australian's home is his or her castle. This has resulted in "a gradual, but significant, erosion of traditional protections for private property rights".[1] To most, this has gone unnoticed, at least until they have been personally affected. This has been done without the approval of the Australian people. Had they been asked, they would have never agreed. This is yet another example of the crying need to empower the people against the machinations of the elites and the party powerbrokers before it is too late.

Louise Staley points out that the disregard for and lack of interest that is shown in property rights is somewhat unusual given the highly fashionable status of human rights in elite circles. She warns that property rights in Australia are being attacked simultaneously on a number of fronts, and that the existing protections we take for granted are insufficient and largely symbolic.

Section 51(xxxi) of the Australian Constitution provides that:

> The Parliament shall, subject to this Constitution, have power to make laws for the peace, order, and good government of the Commonwealth with respect to ... the acquisition of property on just terms from any State or person for any purpose in respect of which the Parliament has power to make laws.

But this does not apply to the states, and even then the High Court has read down the meaning of the provision. In practice it is not too difficult for the federal government to devalue property significantly without there being an "acquisition".[2]

From the very settlement itself in 1788, when the rule of law was introduced, Australia has enjoyed a respect for property rights. Indeed the first civil case was brought by convicts who were awarded damages for the loss of private property.[3]

But in recent years there has been an increasing disregard by politicians for private property. Just as representative democracy was being compromised by the major political parties, the idea has emerged that property rights are outdated. As long ago as 1975, High Court Justice Lionel Murphy declared that "[t]he exaltation of property rights over civic and political rights is a reflection of the values of a bygone era".[4]

This would have been seen as an elitist minority view in the 70s. But with the ascent rule of the powerbrokers and the elites in their AA Axis, this view has infected government practice. The right of Australians to enjoy their property is now under attack.

As we mentioned above, there are two exceptions from this, both in relation to mining. One is native title, where potential miners must negotiate generously with the indigenous owners, assisted by the National Native Title Tribunal. Native Title is a curious collectivist title invented by the High Court and codified by the Federal Parliament.[5]

The indigenous owners have a statutory Right To Negotiate, with most negotiations ending in the conclusion of an apparently mutually beneficial Indigenous Land Use Agreement (ILUA). Proposed legislation would strengthen the right of indigenous parties.[6]

The other exception is in Western Australia, where the law provides better protection for private landholders than in most states, including the need for the landholder's written consent for a mining tenement over the surface of the land and to within a depth of 30 metres.[7] The federal coalition has indicated that they support the principle that miners should not enter on land where the landowner is opposed, a matter which we return to below.

These exceptions apart, the sweeping disregard for property rights particularly affects the nation's primary producers and those with tracts of non urban land. Indeed it seems especially aimed at them. In any event we are seeing a wave of effective expropriation across the land where formal ownership remains vested in the victims, but where this formal ownership is rendered partially or totally useless.

This was the claim that the farmer Peter Spencer made when his land was declared to be part of a carbon sink by the NSW state government to assist the Commonwealth to comply with carbon emission restrictions under the Kyoto Protocol. At the time the government would not ratify the Protocol, but wanted to show it was reducing Australia's carbon dioxide emissions.

After a legal action seemed unsuccessful, Mr. Spencer began a hunger strike to publicise what had happened to him and to many other farmers. The media took notice, and eventually Mr. Spencer was persuaded to give up his hunger strike. On 1 September 2010, he persuaded the High Court to require the Federal Court to hear his case.[8] Peter Spencer is one of thousands of farmers who are the victims of a war waged on them. Their properties have been neutralised by state governments without any right to compensation.[9]

In a number of other ways, legislation has been introduced which renders private property less useful and less valuable than it otherwise would have been. Examples include the loss relating to the protection of native vegetation, the allocation of water rights, carbon sinks, wind farms, and so-called environmental planning.

Add to this the gross negligence of governments in, for example, bowing to fashionable green demands in not undertaking prudent program of back burning on state controlled land leading to the massive fuelling of bushfires, as in the devastating bushfires in Tasmania in January 2013.[10]

The fact is that governments across Australia have, against all common sense and previous experience, inserted "a fire-vulnerable society" into a "fire-prone environment".[11]

Roger Underwood, a retired forester and chairman of The Bushfire Front, a volunteer organisation dedicated to getting bushfire management in WA back on the rails, warns that national parks and "conservation reserves" are being neglected and are accumulating "combustible bushfire fuels year by year".

This is being done by politicians, many of whom are selected by the factional powerbrokers, and who act in accordance with the agenda of the elites who hold fashionable ideas about how farmers have despoiled the land and how it can be returned to their idea of a pristine condition.

As for "climate change", Roger Underwood explains that this is only a "gutless excuse" for what he identifies as failed land management by our authorities and their green supporters. Australia, he reminds the elites, has always been a hot, windy and dry country experiencing periodic droughts.

The point is that many of the severe bushfires – and the consequential loss of property and the loss of life – are the direct result of gross negligence by governments.

Let us now consider one example of the way in which government is seriously devaluing the property of ordinary Australians.

In 2012, Miranda Devine wrote about Bernard and Rikki Grinberg, who run a caravan park on eight pretty hectares behind South Ballina Beach.[12] They had invested their retirement savings into restoring what was an old camping ground into a low-key, affordable, family-friendly eco-resort, the Ballina Beach Village.

But their investment was threatened by a green-dominated council which rezoned this from a recreational zone to the environmentally sensitive category of E2, which Miranda Devine notes is the next stage down from a national park, and forbids tourist activity.

They are allowed to continue with their eco-resort under an "existing uses" provision, but whenever they want to change anything, they have to submit a development application and prove to Ballina Shire Council they are not "intensifying" the use of their land. Miranda Devine gives some extraordinary examples.

"Now, every time they want to change anything, whether it is to use crockery at their kiosk, hire a singer to play in their piano bar, renovate the interior of an old shed to turn it into a yoga studio, even trim a branch off a termite-infested tree that might fall on a tent, they have to submit a development application and prove to Ballina Shire Council they are not 'intensifying' the use of their land."

As Rikki Greenberg explained in an interview recorded online, the effect of these planning changes was to make their business unviable.[13]

What is happening to the Greenbergs is not an isolated instance. The property rights of people across NSW and beyond are being attacked by politicians acting under various laws.

Landowners who find their property rezoned to some zone from which humans are to be eventually exiled have found their property values slashed overnight, leaving them unable to improve their land, farm it effectively or sell it to recover their investment which may well be mortgaged.

Miranda Devine says that in Ballina and Byron shires as much as one third of agricultural land has been rezoned.

She points to the case of a macadamia farmer leaving a paddock fallow for a year, a standard farming practice to rest the soil. If next year he decides to replant macadamias on that paddock, or even switch to mangoes, he has to apply for a DA, a development application, a time-consuming and expensive process.

Rezoning land to a more restrictive regime is known as "dezoning", but the Greenbergs with justification see this as "land theft". They have spent $150,000 just in trying to operate their business.

They told Miranda Devine that the E2 and E3 zonings are "the exocet missile of green bureaucracy". Planning laws have "given very powerful weapons to very misguided people", they say. One farmer was advised by professional valuers that the E2 dezoning had more than halved the value of his land from $5.6 million to $2.6 million.

When the people of New South Wales voted to change the government in 2011, they thought the new Coalition government would restore their rights. But all they have done, say the Greenbergs, is to "rejig" the planning template which gives extraordinary powers to councils.

Miranda Devine says this is why the NSW economy is still on its knees. "The O'Farrell government is squandering a huge mandate with its timid and ineffectual approach. It is more determined to be loved by everyone than to do the tough job it was elected to do: fix 11 years of Labor mismanagement."

"We have an insane planning regime which is cutting the value of people's property in half", she writes. "Just fix it."

Julia Patrick contrasts the situation in Australia with that of Alabama which has become the state in the USA where "infringement on the property rights of citizens linked to any other international law … is prohibited".[14] She points out that in Australia a plethora of legislation relying on our obligations as signatories to international conventions have made us subservient to the United Nations.[15] She says the push to remake Australia a socialist state under the guise of concern for the environment is emboldened by these obligations. One initiative was announced by the Minister for the Environment, Tony Burke, on 4 November 2012, namely the National Wildlife Corridors Plan. This is to connect habitat patches, protected areas and national parts to allow for the movement adaption and evolution of animals. As these corridors develop the result will be to put productive land out of reach.

People's superannuation plundered

Prime Minister Kevin Rudd promised not to touch the Australian people's superannuation: "Not one jot," he said, "not one tittle."[16]

In fact the Rudd and Gillard governments have raided the Australian people's superannuation – their savings for their retirement – at least nine times. In doing this they have effectively removed $8 billion dollars of retirement savings, thus reducing people's pensions.[17]

The $1.4 trillion Australians currently have in their retirement savings is an attractive target to any government in financial difficulties.

In the 2012-13 financial year the federal government spent $100 billion more than John Howard did in his last year but taking in $70 billion more, and is borrowing heavily. It is not surprising then that Minister Bill Shorten told the superannuation industry on 29 November 2012 that "nothing is off the table" in the pursuit of savings to preserve the government's budget surplus. (The Treasurer Wayne Swan announced over Christmas that the surplus had disappeared).[18]

The attitude of the political elites to the people's savings and their property is illustrated by the language used. Terry McCrann argues that this is demonstrated in the Treasury's 2013 Annual Statement on Tax Expenditures.[19]

This says the "tax expenditures" on superannuation would be $32 billion in 2013 and would reach $45 billion by 2015-16, and these are fiscally "unsustainable".

But these "tax expenditures" are not what the rank-and-file Australian would regard as money actually spent by government. To call these "expenditures" goes against common sense. What they represent is the gracious decision of the politicians not to tax us at the highest rate. Our politicians obviously consider themselves very generous in leaving us some of our savings.

Terry McCrann says this exercise catches Treasury in total intellectual incoherence and exposes their and the politicians' mindset.

They might as well calculate the biggest tax expenditure of all – not taxing all income at the 46.5% top tax rate. Anything less than this is, in the mind of the elites, a gift from them to the people.

They obviously regard all of the people's savings and property as susceptible to their demands, acting of course in the public interest by spending other people's money.

What the people are allowed to keep is a concession, and act of kindness by our masters, the elites acting with the powerbrokers. For which we should be grateful.

But how different is all is when we come to how the political elites treat themselves. It is as if they are to have the privileges the aristocrats enjoyed before the French Revolution.

After the 2013 election, the former Attorney-General Nicola Roxon will receive over $120K a year for life – and she's only 45 and has only worked for 15 years as an MP.

Prime Minister Julia Gillard and Wayne Swan will get more – $170K a year for life. There will be other benefits, especially for the Prime Minister.

Ordinary Australians would have to put around $5 million into their superannuation to equal this – and the politicians can get theirs as soon as they leave Parliament, ordinary people have to wait. (Some reforms were introduced by the Howard government on the demand of the then opposition leader Mark Latham – but not affecting Mr. Latham and all those under the old scheme).

And an increase in the superannuation contributions tax from 15% to 30% applying to other well paid Australians announced in May 2012 has not yet been extended to the politicians, although media criticism encouraged an explanation from the government that they would get around to it.[20]

Coal seam gas mining

In the meantime there is a looming crisis across the country concerning coal seam gas (CSG) mining. This is especially so in New South Wales and Queensland. Most Australians have no objection to CSG mining, provided that it does not take place on prime agricultural and urban land, in catchment areas or damaging to underground water.

Under the law, a property owner will own all of the minerals under the land unless these have been reserved to the Crown, which is the right of the Crown of the particular state. Most minerals are reserved to the Crown.

In the controversy in 2010 concerning the imposition of a federal mining tax and even taking over state mineral taxes, the Rudd government argued that the minerals under the land belonged to the people of Australia. In fact they usually, but not always, belong to the Crown. But rather than the Crown in the right of the Commonwealth, as the Rudd government claimed, they belong to the Crown in the right of the relevant state. As the Crown acts as advised by the relevant state government, and each state as a representative democracy, if the minerals belong to the people, they belong to the people of the relevant state. It is not surprising that the NSW Independent Commission Against Corruption is currently investigating whether certain powerbrokers reaped millions from the peoples' minerals, even arranging senior ministerial changes to achieve this.

Grants of land had at times been made in the past where the minerals were not reserved to the Crown . In two cases in New South Wales, these privately owned rights were expropriated with grossly inadequate or no compensation. This was effected by the Wran Labor government in 1981 and the Greiner Coalition government in 1991.[21]

These seizures bordered on or were legal thefts of private property justified only by the greed of the governments concerned. But apart from these instances it is clear that the property to most onshore minerals and petroleum is vested in the Crown, in the right of the relevant state.

In the majority of cases today, landholders do not own the minerals. This does not justify the state government allowing the extraction of the minerals in such a way that the property and income of landowners, their tenants and those nearby can be seriously and irreparably damaged, their health seriously impaired and water aquifers seriously depleted and damaged.

Australians living on prime agricultural and urban land have rights, including those which caused the revolt of the American colonists, the rights of life, liberty and the pursuit of happiness. The lives of our fellow Australians and whole communities are being damaged and destroyed because of the greed of the politicians who are supposed to represent them.

Just as Shylock in the *Merchant of Venice* was entitled to his pound of flesh, but not entitled to anything more, so the miners should be entitled only to the minerals without destroying the activities of those who own the land.

Antonio promised that if he defaulted on the loan Shylock might take "a pound of flesh". But that was all. There was no mention of blood.

> Then take thy bond, take thou thy pound of flesh;
> But, in the cutting it, if thou dost shed
> One drop of Christian blood, thy lands and goods

Are, by the laws of Venice, confiscate
Unto the state of Venice.

Putting aside the regrettable and wholly unjustified anti-semitism of the time, there is a fine analogy here. If in extracting coal seam gas, lives are seriously damaged or destroyed and communities ravaged, the miners and the politicians should be liable to make massive reparations to those concerned. Of course, this could make some mining unviable. If so, the politicians should never have approved it in the first instance.

There could not be a better example of the need to make all politicians really accountable 24/7 – and not just every three or four years – than what is going on with CSG mining in New South Wales under the O'Farrell Coalition government.

People are discovering to their surprise and their horror that CSG mining is to proceed on prime agricultural and urban land as well as water catchment areas.

Anyone concerned about these issues understood clearly at the last election that CSG mining would not proceed in those areas if a Coalition government were returned. They believed that lines would be drawn on the map of New South Wales which would protect these. "No ifs or buts."

People feel cheated, and there will be growing anger across the state. The argument that the government is bound by licences granted by the previous government does not hold water. New approvals are being granted, and the government says it cannot cancel approvals without being liable to pay massive compensation. Parliament can, as previous parliaments under governments of both sides have.

The citizens of New South Wales or of any shire or municipality in the state should demand the right to be able to petition for a binding vote on CSG on prime agricultural land or urban land and in water catchment areas.

As anti-CSG campaigner Graeme Gibson from the Hunter Valley

Protection Alliance said recently, "We were promised by (Premier) Barry O'Farrell, (Planning Minister) Brad Hazzard, (Resources Minister) Chris Hartcher and George Souris prior to the last election that there would be no CSG mining in the vineyard area."[22]

Mr. Gibson said this as AGL commenced drilling on Pooles Rock Vineyard in the Hunter Valley. This used to belong to former Macquarie Bank chairman David Clarke who, during his life, was vehemently opposed to CSG mining there.

"It appears they were just lies to gain election", Mr. Gibson added.

It is clear that the farmers and other landowners are not going to roll over for the politicians, the lobbyists and the powerbrokers. Twelve people were arrested on 7 January 2013 at a protest against CSG mining in northern NSW where activists locked themselves to trees and trucks.[23]

Home buyers were not told that AGL Energy was proposing a northern expansion of its Camden gas project that would bring coal seam gas wells close to their homes and involve drilling directly underneath them.[24] As a result this was suspended.

But according to the Stop CSG Illawarra campaign, the O'Farrell government seems hell bent on developing CSG in the drinking water catchment, regardless of risk or the level of community opposition.[25]

This is despite the promise by Premier O'Farrell at a rally at Woodbury Park in March 2011, "The next Liberal/National government will ensure mining cannot occur in any water catchment area and that any mining leases and exploration permits will reflect that common sense. No ifs, no buts, a guarantee."

The Stop CSG Illawarra campaign reports that the NSW government has replaced the entire board of the Sydney Catchment Authority. The new chairperson is a former director of two of Australia's largest mining companies, and for the first time in its history there is no public health expert on the board.

They ask "what is going on between the O'Farrell Government and the mining industry?" This was the subject of a powerful interview with Premier O'Farrell by Alan Jones on 12 December 2012.[26]

In the interview, the Premier said he was bound by CSG licences and exploration rights on prime agricultural and urban land and even near major dam catchment areas granted by the previous Labor government.

If he did, he says, the government would be liable to pay massive compensation.

But in a following interview broadcast on 14 December 2012, Alan Jones spoke to one of the authors of this book, who said that there is no constitutional or legal barrier to stop the Premier from acting in the way the voters at the last election expected.[27]

In February 2013, the Premier wrote to the ICAC Commissioner David Ipp asking whether the state government should amend the Mining Act and suspend Bylong Valley exploration licences granted to Cascade Coal, which is related to an ICAC investigation. 2GB's Alan Jones asked, "So what happened to the multi-million dollar compensation claims, bogeyman Premier? Or was that simply always a phoney excuse for you and Chris Hartcher to hide behind?"[28]

Parliament, he says, could stop these activities. It will be said that if such a law empowered the government to act, investors would lose confidence.

Some CSG miners who are lusting after prime agricultural land and urban land will. But this is only because the land is close to infrastructure, which, it will be noted, had been funded by the taxpayers.

Do we really need them?

The country is sitting on a sea of CSG – so why don't they leave prime agricultural land to future generations?

In February 2013, the federal government indicated its concern over the environmental standards required on CSG mining in NSW. Federal Environment Minister Tony Burke said NSW is not "using the best qualified science and the best processes" to consider coal seam gas exploration and mining applications. But as Alan Jones pointed out, his new-found concern had more to do with pressure from independent ally Tony Windsor – whose vote is crucial in the hung Parliament – and his own South Western Sydney seat of Watson, where electors are horrified about AGL's plans to drill 66 more coal seam gas wells around Camden, Campbelltown and Liverpool.[29]

Tony Burke was the minister who ultimately approved coal seam gas mining using fracking, which has devastated some of the nation's best agricultural land in Queensland's Darling Downs.

He says he is particularly concerned about possible subsidence caused by drilling. But, as Alan Jones points out, if he were genuinely concerned about CSG mining he would also be talking about fracking and the hundreds of dangerous chemicals used in fracking and the resulting contamination of the water table and also about protecting prime agricultural land.

In any event, Tony Burke eventually gave federal approval in February 2013 to each of the NSW proposals.[30]

But in March 2013 the Federal Government announced legislation to empower the Minister for the Environment to consider the cumulative impacts on water of new CSG wells and mines under the legislation to be introduced to parliament.[31] At present this is limited to the impact on water in relation to endangered species or on certain wetlands.

Then in the face of massive public resistance to CSG mining on prime agricultural and urban land, the O'Farrell government announced on 19 February a ban on new CSG activity within two kilometres of residential areas and industry clusters across the state.[32] In addition, the chief scientist and engineer Mary O'Kane is to review all such activity in NSW and report on any risks by July.

Opponents greeted the decision as a step in the right direction but emphasised that it only relates to "new" CSG mining. Then in March

2013 there were reports that the Wallarah 2 mine near Wyong would proceed notwithstanding a pre-election commitment delivered to an anti-CSG rally that it would not allow this in government: "No ifs or buts."[33]

There remains an overwhelming view among the public that CSG mining should not be allowed even under existing licences over prime agricultural and urban land and in water catchment areas.

In its Call to Country campaign, the Lock the Gate Alliance has released a resource pack including maps showing where CSG mining is occurring or is planned.[34] The Alliance is calling on the federal government to act including holding a Royal Commission to investigate the management of coal and gas resources by all Australian governments. If one is held it should extend to the role and influence of the powerbrokers in these matters.

The attitude of a future coalition federal government may well differ from those of their state colleagues and from the Gillard government. In response to a question from broadcaster Alan Jones on 2 May 2013, opposition leader Tony Abbott expressed an important principle.

"Miners should not go onto farms, if they're not wanted.

"It's very wrong and they shouldn't be going onto land where the relevant land owners don't want them. And it is as simple as that." [35]

Governments – especially in New South Wales and Queensland – were elected in the strong belief that this would be the result. That the NSW government had to be dragged in this direction by public pressure is clear evidence that the Australian people must now be empowered with the tools of direct democracy.

The people of New South Wales, Queensland and other states should be entitled in a democracy to require the enactment of a *Prime Agricultural and Urban Land and Water Catchment Protection Act*. After all that is precisely what they expected would be the result of the 2011 election.

In a democracy, the people are supposed to be the masters, not the politicians. Should they not be made accountable all of the time, rather than every three or four years?

4.2 Putting housing beyond the reach of so many

Australia still has the most unaffordable housing markets in the world despite two years' of stagnant or falling house prices.[36] This is because of the restrictive land policies the politicians and bureaucrats have imposed for ideological reasons, and in a country which is emptier than most. This has been exacerbated by the current policy following UN Agenda 21 to remove land from farming and return it to the wilderness. This is an example of the elite agenda of authorities following the "soft law" promulgated by some international body.[37] Among international lawyers, "soft law" – some declaration or other instrument which is persuasive but not binding – is likely to morph into binding law. This is done either by the ratification of subsequent international treaties or by governments, local state or federal adopting them.

These restrictive land policies are a tempting target for the powerbrokers who rule with the elites. This is convenient for both the elites and the politicians. The elites can campaign against the farmers whom they hate and whose farms they wish to turn into barren land. The politicians can enjoy enormous power in making decisions in favour of those seeking land rezoning.

According to investigative reporter Deborah Snow, former housing department staff recall that Ian MacDonald, as a minister, was consistently lobbying for housing department land to be made available to developers.[38]

Ian McDonald is at the time of writing being investigated by the NSW Independent Commission Against Corruption.

And in November 2012, the New South Wales Coalition government approved the rezoning of land below the Canberra airport flight path to allow for housing development. The Coalition had strongly opposed the rezoning in opposition. The Minister, Brad Hazzard, described this as a "win-win" decision, saying rezoning would not stop Canberra airport's potential growth or loss of its status as a 24-hour curfew-free passenger and freight hub.[39]

The next generation of young Australians and their children – often referred to as "working families" – are the victims of these restrictive land policies. They are paying through the nose to satisfy the vanity and moral superiority of the politicians and bureaucrats who constantly tell us of their concerns about the warming of the planet, protecting spotted frogs or whatever other craze happens to be fashionable in their inner city salons or at the international conferences in five star hotels to which they fly in business and first class.[40]

Bob Day AO is a very successful businessman and one of the founders of Home Australia. He argues that our planning regulations have the effect of driving home prices up artificially, thus pricing new and low income home buyers out of the market.

He proposes a pragmatic down-to-earth five point plan to ensure that the present and future generations of Australians can buy their own homes.[41] We would add a sixth point. They are:

1. Where they have been applied, urban growth boundaries or zoning restrictions on the urban fringes of our cities need to be removed. Residential development on the urban fringe needs to be made a "permitted use". In other words, there should be no zoning restrictions in turning rural fringe land into residential land.

2. Small players need to be encouraged back into the market by abolishing compulsory "Master Planning". If large developers wish to initiate Master Planned Communities, that's fine, but don't make them compulsory.

3. Allow the development of basic serviced allotments i.e., water, sewer, electricity, storm water, bitumen road,

street lighting and street signage. Additional services and amenities (lakes, entrance walls, childcare centres, bike trails, etc, can be optional extras if the developer wishes to provide them and the buyers are willing to pay for them).

4. Privatise planning approvals. Any qualified town planner should be able to certify that a development application complies with a local government's development plan.

5. No up-front infrastructure charges. All services should be allowed to be paid for through the rates system i.e., pay "as" you use, not "before" you use.

6. Not to proceed with the Gillard government's proposed uniform occupational health and safety law, at least to the extent that it will force the nation's army of volunteers into a highly bureaucratised and expensive system. Common sense would tell the politicians that many people will just give up volunteering. According to a study by the South Australian Housing Industry Association, just in that state the law would add $20,000 to the cost of a new house, cut more than 10,000 jobs, and cut $1.4 billion from the state's economic activity.[42]

If the politicians were made truly accountable to the people, as they ought to be in a democracy and are in countries such as Switzerland, they would know that if they did not act the people could force through sensible laws to cure this artificial barrier to young Australians being able to purchase housing at reasonable prices.

Endnotes

1 Louise Staley, *Reshaping the Landscape: The quiet erosion of property rights in Western Australia*, Institute of Public Affairs & Mannkal Economic Education Foundation, *Project Western Australia* Discussion Paper, December 2007, http://www.mannkal.org/downloads/projectwa/ProjectWA-FINAL.pdf (retrieved 05.05.2013), cited by Lorraine Finlay, "The Attack on Property Rights", *Proceedings of the Twenty-second Conference of The Samuel Griffith Society*, 2010. http://samuelgriffith.org.au/docs/vol22/vol22chap3.pdf (retrieved 8.01.2013).

2 Finlay, op cit. p 5.

3 *Cable* v *Sinclair* [1788] NSWKR7

4 *Attorney-General (Cth); Ex rel Mckinlay* v *Commonwealth* (1975) 135 CLR 1, per Murphy J at 53; Finlay, op cit, p 5.

5 *Native Title Act*, 1993 (Cth).

6 *Native Title Amendment (Reform) Bill (No. 1)* 2012 (Cth).

7 *Mining Act*, 1978 (WA).

8 *Spencer* v *Commonwealth of Australia* [2010] HCA 28.

9 Michael Duffy, "Farmers are pushed beyond limit", *The Sydney Morning Herald*, 18 June 2010. http://www.smh.com.au/news/Opinion/Farmers-are-pushed-beyond-limit/ 2005/06/17/1118869093828.html (retrieved 07.04.2013); Peter Spencer, *Land and Sea-Property: The Institute of Secure Property -the most important human right* , Lecture, Cairns, 27 April 2010. http://sosnews.org/pdf/peter-spencer-cairns.pdf (retrieved 07.04.2013).

10 Miranda Devine, "Green arrogance burns fiercely", *Daily Telegraph*, 9 January 2013. http://blogs.news.com.au/dailytelegraph/mirandadevine/index.php/dailytelegraph/comments/green_arrogance_burns_fiercely/ (retrieved 9.01.2013).

11 Roger Underwood, "Flaming idiocy", *Quadrant On Line*, 31 January 2013. http://www.quadrant.org.au/blogs/doomed-planet/2013/01/flaming-idiocy (retrieved 03.03.2013).

12 Miranda Devine, "We must weed out the councils gone wild green", *Daily Telegraph*, 28 July 2012. http://blogs.news.com.au/dailytelegraph/mirandadevine/index. php/dailytelegraph/comments/we_must_weed_out_the_councils_gone_wild_ green/#.UBR3rO8aCf4.mailto (retrieved 07.05.2013).

13 http://audioboo.fm/boos/973113-governments-effectively-stealing-your-property-and-it-s-australia (retrieved 8.01.2013).

14 Julia Patrick, "Green Dreaming of a human free environment", *Quadrant*, March 2013, Volume LVII, Number 3.

15 E.g., *Environment Protection and Biodiversity Conservation Act*, 1999 (Cth).

16 http://karenandrewsmp.com/2013/02/pm-dodges-question-on-future-changes-to-super/ (retrieved 07.05.2013).

17 Peter van Onselen, "Labor losing edge as champion of superannuation",*The Australian,* 6 October 2012. http://www.theaustralian.com.au/opinion/labor-losing-edge-as-champion-of-superannuation/story-e6frg6zo-1226489311491 (retrieved 21.02,2013).

18 http://www.theaustralian.com.au/national-affairs/treasury/focus-back-on-super-tax-breaks/story-fn59nsif-1226526153194 (retrieved 21.02.2013).

19 Terry McCrann, "Political and bureacratic elite reveals tax-grab tendencies", *The Australian,* 9 February 2013. http://www.theaustralian.com.au/business/opinion/political-and-bureacratic-elite-reveal-tax-grab-tendencies/story-e6frg9k6-1226573909233 (retrieved 21.02.2013) interviewed by Alan Jones at http://www.2gb.com/audioplayer/7336 (retrieved 21.02.2013).

20 http://www.dailytelegraph.com.au/news/high-fliers-get-huge-tax-break/story-e6freuy9-1226575924903 (retrieved 21.02.2013.) http://mfss.treasurer.gov.au/DisplayDocs.aspx?doc=pressreleases/2013/005.htm&pageID=003&min=brs&Year=&DocType= (retrieved 21.02.2013).

21 *Coal Acquisition Act,* 1981, s 6; *Petroleum (Onshore) Act,* 1991 s 6.

22 http://www.news.com.au/national/mining-leaves-a-bitter-taste-winemaker-david-clarkes-anti-coal-seam-gas-crusade-collapses/story-fndo4bst-1226546296316 (retrieved 9.01.2012).

23 http://www.theaustralian.com.au/news/breaking-news/arrested-at-nsw-coal-seam-gas-protest/story-fn3dxiwe-1226548880883 (retrieved 5.01.2013).

24 http://www.illawarramercury.com.au/story/1220063/home-owners-fear-csg-drilling-under-feet/?cs=12 (retrieved 9.01.2013).

25 http://stop-csg-illawarra.org/2012/catchment-csg-plans-revived/

26 Hear a powerful interview with Premier O'Farrell and 2GB's Alan Jones on 16 December, 2012 at http://www.2gb.com/audioplayer/6406 (retrieved 9.01.2013).

27 http://audioboo.fm/boos/1116072-states-can-stop-csg-on-prime-agricultural- urban-land-if-they-want-to

28 http://www.2gb.com/article/phoney-excuses-coal-seam-gas-mining (retrieved 07.02.2013).

29 http://www.2gb.com/article/coal-seam-gas-betrayal (retrieved 19.02.2013).

30 http://www.smh.com.au/opinion/political-news/burke-approves-huge-gas-and-coal-plans-20130211-2e8vh.html

31 http://www.theaustralian.com.au/business/mining-energy/new-environmental-controls-for-coal-seam-gas-projects/story-e6frg9df-1226595523987(retrieved 13.03.2013).

32 http://www.news.com.au/breaking-news/national/nsw-govt-bans-csg-mining-near-homes/story-e6frfku9-1226580728512#ixzz2LHbSMmXT(retrieved 07.05.2013).

33 Sean Nicolls, "O'Farrell silent on mine and its Liberal champion", *The Sydney Morning Herald*, 9 March 2013. http://www.smh.com.au/nsw/ofarrell-stays-silent-on-mine-and-its-liberal-champion-20130308-2fquy.html#ixzz2N6JTHJnt (retrieved 09.03.2013).

34 http://www.lockthegate.org.au/calltocountry (retrieved 02.05.2013).

35 http://www.2gb.com/audioplayer/8802(retrieved 02.05.2013).

36 Simon Johanson, "Australian housing 'severely unaffordable'," *The Sydney Morning Herald*, 22 January 2013. http://www.smh.com.au/business/property/australian-housing-severely-unaffordable-20130121-2d2gk.html#ixzz2IemaVpbU (retrieved 27.04.2013)

37 See chapters 5 & 6

38 Deborah Snow, "A career taken to pieces", *Sydney Morning Herald*, 16-17 February 2013. http://www.smh.com.au/nsw/a-career-taken-to-pieces-20130215-2eijh.html (retrieved 16.02.2013)

39 http://www.canberratimes.com.au/act-news/nod-for-2000-tralee-homes-20121105-28ukb.html (retrieved 16.02.2013); hear Alan Jones http://prod.2gb.com/article/canberra-airport%C2%A0 (retrieved 16.02.2013)

40 Simon Johanson, op. cit. (retrieved 22.01.2013).

41 Bob Day, *Home truths revisited: The politics of home ownership*. http://www.nationbuild.com/docs/pdf/hometruths2.pdf (retrieved 03.02.2013).

42 Chris Kenny, "It's state v commonwealth, with safety the loser", *The Australian*, 23 January 2012. http://www.theaustralian.com.au/national-affairs/opinion/its-state-v-commonwealth-with-safety-the-loser/story-e6frgd0x-1226250752470 (retrieved 29 April 2013).

CHAPTER 5

Why do they hate our farmers?

Farming is a demanding vocation. Not only is the work physically demanding and the hours long, the farmer is at the mercy of the weather. For example, how often have they been in a long drought, only to be followed by heavy rain or even floods which destroyed the first promising crop for years?

To make matters worse, governments and the bureaucracy seem to have declared war on our farmers.

While the powerbrokers are probably indifferent to their plight – and as we are seeing from the 2013 hearings of the ICAC, one is alleged to have been happy to buy their farms to clean up the odd $100 million for inside information on where the mining licences are to be handed out – they have no hesitation in applying the policies of the elites who seem to if not hate, at the very least despise our farmers. This is because the powerbrokers and the elites tolerate one another in that axis of convenience, one which we have christened the AAA, the Anti-Australia Axis.

This is the only conclusion which we can possibly draw from the application of a whole range of policies which are so obviously undermining and destroying so many farmers. None of these policies would have been applied by rank-and-file Australians who are usually endowed with a good portion of common sense, good judgement and decency. Not one of these policies would pass the ubiquitous "pub test".

It is clear that a war is being waged against our farmers with full force of government. With the exception of the weather, the worsening crisis in farming is the direct result of the actions and failure to act of the politicians, and not only those in the Labor Party. The farmers are not rolling over.

There was a major meeting of dairy farmers in south-west Victoria in the middle of January 2013.[1] They were protesting that while the income of dairy farmers and the value of their farms had declined significantly, feed costs were up by 15% and electricity costs were up by a massive 50%. Disappointed with their representative organisations they formed Farmer Power to fight for something eminently reasonable, a fair price for their milk for justice.[2]

They are not asking for some exorbitant price; they are only asking for a price which will enable them to stay on their farms. We would have thought that in the 21st century, the vast political class including their bureaucracy with instrumentalities such as ACCC would have protected them.

The decline in their income to levels below the cost of production was caused by the decision of the duopoly retailers, Coles and Woolworths, to slash the price of their own-brand milk to one dollar per litre. Analysts believe that Coles hopes to extract at least $500 million from the farmers to underwrite the price cuts. If this is achieved, the Coles Chief Executive could qualify for a $38 million bonus.

There is a policy vacuum in our competition law and practice in effectively dealing with the free world's least competitive retail market. It is said that the duopoly controls 92% of the retail food market and growing proportions of the petrol distribution market and the liquor market.

This has continued under both Labor and Coalition governments. A typical example was the introduction in 2006 of a bill for a statutory exemption covering shopper dockets where a retailer provides discounted shopper dockets to a supermarket customer – for, say, petrol or liquor bought at an outlet owned by the retailer.[3]

Surely the politicians knew this would damage and drive out of business independent petrol stations or liquor stores? Indeed, was it not designed to do precisely this? So why was it introduced and passed? Was it incompetence or was it that our politicians wish to destroy small business?

In the meantime governments of both persuasions have been obsessed with applying the most radical free trade policies, which are also espoused by our leading trading partners. But unlike the politicians in most of our leading trading partners, our governments actually apply these free trade policies to agriculture. Nobody else does. Even if some economists say that there is still an advantage in doing this, what person with common sense would apply such policies? Once again we see an example of the politicians failing the "pub test".

The result is that our farmers' access to the markets of most of our leading trading partners is extremely limited or even closed to them. Worse, the local retail duopoly import subsidised produce from overseas against which no farmer could possibly compete.

Governments from both sides do not seem to see the contradiction in failing to deal both with our retail market duopoly and the hypocrisy of the governments of our leading trading partners who tell us to practise free trade but actually practise the most extreme protectionism at home. Australia must be a laughing stock among agricultural ministers in the European Union, the United States and Japan.

Ordinary Australians would never have set up such a trap for our farmers. The politicians did precisely this. So our farmers are squeezed by the retail duopoly of Coles and Woolworths on the one side, and by the protectionists in the European Union, Japan and the United States on the other, while Australian politicians have applied a ruthless and ideological national competition policy which has led to the deregulation of much of the Australian agriculture.[4]

Add to this the cavalier ending of the quarantine which has so long protected us from imported diseases, all done in the name of those same free trade obligations, which other countries observe only when it suits them. Why have the lobbyists been so successful with our politicians?

Then there is the application in Australia of the United Nations Agenda 21 which has as its aim the removal of much land from farming and grazing – not further housing which is forbidden or discouraged.[5] It is to return agricultural land to the wilderness.

At the same time, some state governments and in particular the New South Wales Coalition government are pursuing coal seam gas mining on prime agricultural land, an issue discussed in more detail previously.[6]

The list of attacks on farming does not stop there. In 2012, the Gillard government panicked and without consultation with our trading partners and the industry, and contrary to advice, completely closed down the live cattle export trade industry because of one television program. Our principal trading partner for the trade, Indonesia, has understandably decided that we are not a reliable source.

So when the federal government decided to reopen the trade, the Indonesians set import limits at about one half of what they were. And the result of the government's precipitate action, workers have lost their jobs, including indigenous workers, farmers have been reduced to penury or even bankruptcy, and communities sent into economic decline.[7]

And as Patrick Byrne observed, farmers have taken another hit from the politicians in 2012 and 2013.[8] The new Murray Darling Basin Plan, adopted into law, will mean that around one-third of irrigation water will be taken out of farm production. This will devastate many Basin communities.

He says that the latest blows to farmers come just as they should be enjoying the benefits of emerging from the long drought.

The attack on farmers is coming from all of the arms of government, most of which have long been captured by the elites.[9] The plight of 5,000 farmers in the Goulburn Valley is far too typical. Two neighbours in the Valley, Kieran Grinter and Alison Couston, belong to families who have been running family dairy farms for generations. They decided in 2013 to take a stand against plans by the Victorian government-owned water monopoly, Goulburn-Murray Water, to close down irrigation channels on which the 5,000 farms rely. It is being done to modernise the water network and make it more efficient. Ms. Couston asks how this can happen in Australia.

She says "the government can just come in and say 'tough' because they have a plan which says individuals don't matter but their 2020 food bowl vision does".

If you want to see the face of modern Australian farming, and compare the powerbrokers who run this country, just look at the ABC's *7.30* on a hearing of the Independent Commission Against Corruption (ICAC), in Sydney on 30 January 2013.[10]

Just watch and listen to the fine upstanding young Bylong Valley farmer, Stuart Davies.

He is the salt of the earth. Then watch the report about the multi-millionaire Labor powerbroker and former politician, Eddie Obeid, and his family.

In this hearing, Moses Obeid admitted the family stood to make only $75 million on inside information concerning mining rights. Counsel assisting the commission had estimated that it was $100 million. About $30 million has already been received and invested in waterfront real estate in Sydney and the North Coast.

In the ABC's *7.30*, farmer Stuart Davies asked why the NSW O'Farrell government does not cancel the mining rights over prime agricultural land. Many rank-and-file Australians would join with him in asking that question. Since then the New South Wales Premier has written to the ICAC requesting advice on whether the mining licences should be cancelled, no doubt exercising the power he previously denied the Parliament has.

When the politicians are not actively attacking the farmers, there seems an indifference to the need to maintain a sufficiently large number of Australians in agriculture, and Australian land in Australian hands.

Senator Bill Heffernan frequently complains about the level of foreign sovereign investment in Australia – investment by foreign government owned entities, and the negative impact of tax receipts.[11] No longer do they need an army to take over, he says. There is a growing awareness of this issue. Thus the sale of the large Cubbie Station cotton farm, then in administration, to a joint venture between China's Ruyi and the Melbourne-based Lempriere Capital in 2013 was controversial. According to reports, it is likely to continue to be carved up among foreign investors, with domestic buyers thin on the ground and reluctant to invest in agribusiness.[12] Reports that the owners were considering selling the government some of its considerable water rights which were given without charge were not well received.

In the meantime, farmers are tired of being told that world food security is seriously in issue and they have the potential to be the food bowl of Asia. They are tired of being told to significantly increase production by 2050 to meet the basic food needs of the world's nine billion hungry people, and that the economic prosperity of the country will depend on them after the mining boom is over.[13]

Notwithstanding the fact that this valiant hard working class, the salt of the earth, provide high quality food and food security to Australia they remain the target of the politicians and the elites who administer government at all levels across the nation and who apply a wide ranging and seemingly never ending series of programs and policies against the interests of the farmers, and also the interests of Australia.

Endnotes

1 Patrick J. Byrne, "Dairy crisis part of wider rural malaise", *News Weekly*, 2 February 2013, http://www.newsweekly.com.au/article.php?id=5447 (retrieved 03.02.2013).

2 http://www.farmerpower.com.au/

3 *Trade Practices Legislation Amendment (No 1) Act (Cth) 2006.*

4 Byrne, op. cit.

5 See Chapter 6.

6 See Chapter 4.

7 Clint Peck, "Indonesia continues import cuts from Australia", *Progressive Cattleman*, 24 August 2012. http://www.progressivecattle.com/index.php?option=com_content&view=article&id=5004:indonesia-continues-import-cuts-from-australia&catid=129:clint-peck&Itemid=182 (retrieved 29 April, 2013).

8 Ibid.

9 Sue Neales, "Farmers fight flow-on effect of water row", *The Australian, 23* February 2013. http://www.theaustralian.com.au/news/nation/farmers-fight-flow-on-effect-of-water-row/story-e6frg6nf-1226583914549 (retrieved 24.02.2013).

10 http://www.abc.net.au/7.30/content/2013/s3680693.htm

11 http://www.billheffernan.com.au/Media/LatestNews/tabid/87/articleType/Article View/articleId/313/Senators-up-ante-on-foreign-investment.aspx (retrieved 28.03.2013).

12 http://www.couriermail.com.au/business/farm-investors-slow-to-cotton-on-to-venture/story-fnefl294-1226597635704 (retrieved 28.03.2013).

13 Sue Neales, "Hungry in the food bowl", *The Australian*, 1 February 2013. http://www.theaustralian.com.au/news/features/hungry-in-the-food-bowl/story-e6frg6z6-1226566245920 (retrieved 03.02.2013).

CHAPTER 6

Subjecting us to a foreign agenda

6.1 Our federation compromised

We argue in a subsequent chapter that our Australian federation has been severely compromised by the politicians and the judges.[1] This is the form of a federal compact envisaged by our founding fathers, and approved by the Australian people in the original referendum. Moreover it is the form of federation which the Australian people have repeatedly indicated they prefer in a series of failed referendums to centralise more power in Canberra.

By denying that clear will of the people, a succession of federal governments, with the complicity of some state politicians, have moved into matters which were intended to be reserved for the states. This has led to an expensive and wasteful duplication.

Worse, the federal government has been distracted from and paid insufficient attention to its core duties and responsibilities.

The federal government is now in the unacceptable position that it collects about 80% of all taxes and hands back about 40% to the states with instructions on how to spend it. Referred to as Vertical Fiscal Imbalance, ours is the worst example of a fiscally centralised federation in the world. The consequence is that the states are no longer responsible to the people for properly spending this money.

The federal government tries to control state matters, and thus mismanages its core federal responsibilities. State politicians do not have to explain to their electors how they have managed their finances and responsibilities and invariably blame the federal government for any difficulties. It is not the system the founding fathers designed, the people approved and confirmed whenever they are asked.

After almost a century of this centralist adventure, it is clear that a solution is beyond both the politicians and the judges. They are determined to stay with the mess they created.

Remember that our federation was the work of delegates who in the main were chosen by the people and who, including the politicians, were very much free of factions and parties. They acted on the whole in the best interests of the people and of course the final decision was with the people.

The solution today is most likely to be found by the following process. We propose in this book that a convention consisting of unpaid delegates be elected to resolve this problem which is at the very basis of our constitutional system. In our view they would agree on a series of referendums to be put to the Australian people to clean up the mess made by teams of politicians and judges determined to change the constitutional system without consulting the people.

6.2 Giving up our independence – ceding sovereignty and Agenda 21

In 2012, many Australians were astounded by a speech made by the then leader of the Greens Party, Dr. Bob Brown, who greeted his audience with the opening words "Fellow Earthians ...".[2]

Believing that the absence of any other intelligence in the universe could be because they had "extincted" themselves, he proposed this solution. We should live under a world government with our sovereignty transferred to a global parliament. That we would then be a tiny minority in a vast sea of representatives of mainly corrupt and totalitarian governments did not seem to cause him any concern.

The fact is that one world government means being governed by faceless bureaucrats from the United Nations.

To those of the elites who would dismiss any concern about "one world government" as evidence of paranoia, Dr. Brown's speech and especially the speech delivered on 20 November 2000, by the then conservative French President Jacques Chirac at The Hague celebrating the United Nations Kyoto Protocol should enlighten them as to what is being proposed by very powerful forces across the world.

President Chirac said: "In this, [for] the very first time, humanity is instituting a genuine instrument of global governance ... By acting together, by building this unprecedented instrument, the first component of authentic global governance, we are working for dialogue and peace."[3]

Bob Brown's call was an extreme example of politicians wishing to hand over the independence and the sovereignty of a proud and free nation to international bodies without the approval of the Australian people.

But the fact is that, to an extent, this has already occurred.

In recent years, the elite establishment has found that in international law, as with judge made law, they have a valuable tool through which they can achieve their agenda outside of and in contradiction to the democratic process.

Once they can say that some practice is sanctioned by international law, they can suggest to the layman that this is somehow sanctioned by a higher authority. This is not so. They are not referring to customary international law which emerged from the practice of nations, but to international treaties.

Australia has entered into and continues to enter into a wide range of treaties on all manner of subjects. These are more often than not formulated in the United Nations, the majority of whose delegates represent authoritarian dictatorial and corrupt governments.[4]

This is done by an alliance of Western political and bureaucratic elites with various corrupt dictators. This is done on the basis that the more democratic and law-abiding a country is the more punctilious it will be in respecting its treaty obligations. The more authoritarian and corrupt a government, the less likely it will be to observe its obligations. This does not stop such countries sitting on the UN Human Rights Council and there judging democracies, including Australia.

Agenda 21

A significant development in ceding Australian sovereignty occurred when the Keating government committed Australia to the UN action plan on sustainability, Agenda 21. This was adopted at the UN Conference on Environment and Development (UNCED), the Earth Summit, held in Rio de Janeiro in 1992. This was done without a referendum or even an Act of Parliament.[5]

Identifying man as the problem, this program is designed to end national sovereignty, severely limit private property and even restructure the family. A central goal is a vast population movement away from the country into concentrated, high level cities, and turning vast parts of the country into a wilderness. The media have shown little interest in this extraordinary plan. Sydney radio station 2GB's Brian Wiltshire is a notable exception, for which he has been unfairly ridiculed.

It is hardly surprising that rank-and-file Australians are little aware of the commitment which has been made on their behalf. If they knew this, it would explain a lot – the use of environmental laws to turn farming lands over time into wilderness, the takeover of local government planning powers by the New South Wales state government to cram people into high-rise buildings (e.g., in the garden suburbs on Sydney's North Shore), the introduction of a carbon dioxide tax to make what should be the cheapest electricity in the world one of the planet's most expensive, and the two decade moratorium against new dams

One observer likens this program to collectivisation under communism.[6] Critics in the USA argue that the UN sustainability agenda eventually seeks to lower our standard of living, limiting freedom of choice in terms of food, transportation, housing – and even family size, as in Communist China."[7]

The Australian people have never ever agreed to such an agenda. To most Australians it indicates a complete absence of common sense. However, as we have seen with policies designed to concentrate the population to high-rise buildings with air conditioning too expensive to use, it is already being put into place. It is also demonstrated in NSW legislation authorising Greens dominated local government authorities to take drastic action concerning land use, as well as the campaign of harassment against farmers in the name of environmentalism.

This agenda is greatly assisted by a shadowy entity based in Bonn, the former capital of the Federal Republic of Germany. Innocuously named the International Council for Local Environmental Initiatives (ICLEI), this was founded in 1990 as the precursor for Agenda 21.

ICLEI now coordinates the work of key local government authorities around the world in fulfilling Agenda 21.

Would Australians be surprised to know that our membership is second in size only to the United States? Such is the dominance of the elites over our institutions, Agenda 21 is being applied by the powerbrokers in the major parties. (This is on the proviso that it does not compromise their immediate interests, such as CSG mining on prime agricultural and urban land and in water catchment areas).

Perhaps to allay fears about the medium and long term impact of the program, Agenda 21 began by merely making suggestions to local governments how to develop more "sustainable" communities through zoning and planning laws.[8] Since then, these local government authorities give the impression that they are, if not taking their orders, at least obtaining inspiration from Bonn. This has the result of subverting private property rights in Australia and in continuing to harass and target farmers, eventually driving them from the land.

This is an agenda which most Australians have never heard of. In achieving this result, the politicians have been greatly assisted by the High Court's broad interpretation of the external affairs power under the Constitution.

It is important that Australians understand what is involved in this subtle device invented by calculating lawyers to centralise power in Canberra.

Under the Westminster system, a treaty is made by the Crown, the executive, without the necessary involvement of parliament. (This dates back to the days when diplomacy was conducted by or on behalf Kings or Princes who actually governed. Today a treaty is made by the Australian Crown, acting on the advice of the ministers.)

It is useful to contrast this with the situation in the United States. Unlike the Westminster system, a treaty can only be entered into by the President with the advice and consent of a two-thirds vote in the Senate.[9] When so approved a treaty immediately becomes part of the US law. (An Australian treaty only has internal legal effect when its terms have been adopted in legislation).

When Agenda 21 began to be adopted in the US though sympathetic local governments, this attracted increasing opposition. In June 2012, the State of Alabama enacted legislation protecting private property and due process by prohibiting any government involvement, including that of local government, with or participation in Agenda 21.[10] This remarkable measure was ignored by most of the mainstream media, but it is likely to be followed in other states as Americans come to realise what is involved and how it is contrary to the fundamental principles on which the US was founded. The mainstream media also ignored seminars arranged in Australia in September 2012 by Dr. Amy McGrath where the leaders of the Alabama movement, the Alliance for Citizens Rights, Kenneth Freeman and Don Casey, spoke about their campaign.

It is not surprising then that the work of Agenda 21 sympathisers is made easier in Australia than in the United States. As we have seen, parliamentary approval is not necessary for the Crown to enter into a treaty. However, and unlike the United States, Australian treaties have no internal or domestic legal effect until legislation is passed to apply the treaty. This does not stop Australian authorities from treating international instruments which are not yet treaties, as what is known among international lawyers as "soft law" and applying it in Australia. Some local government councils are doing precisely that. They are imposing what can only be described as a "reign of terror" against the property rights of Australians.[11]

An audacious attempt by the High Court to circumvent the constitutional limitation and hold that treaties entered into could have immediate effect in Australia has not been successful.[12]

At the same time, the making of treaties has had a dramatic effect in expanding the powers of the federal government. This is because one of the powers of the federal parliament is to make laws with respect to "external affairs".[13]

This was never intended to mean that whenever the executive enters into a treaty, parliament may legislate in the areas the subject of the treaty. For example if a treaty were made with, say, Fiji, agreeing on the way in which garbage is to be collected in each country, the federal parliament should not thereby increase its power to make laws about garbage. This is what the founders intended and no doubt this is what the people intend. However, this has been circumvented by the High Court. In the example of Australia and Fiji entering into a treaty about garbage, the parliament would then have the power to legislate on this subject. This is of course a ridiculous example, but it demonstrates how the power has been interpreted by the High Court to give the parliament vast powers, never intended by the founding fathers nor indeed, approved by the people of Australia.

This can be dangerous. It increases the potential for the federal government to act in an authoritarian and undemocratic way.

Take one example. The Roxon Draft Bill released in late 2012, an exposure draft of a proposed anti-discrimination law, has been widely criticised as being likely to result in substantial restrictions on free speech. The legislative power under which it is proposed to justify this is the external affairs power.[14]

In other words, without the benefit of this reinterpretation of the external affairs power by the High Court, it would have been beyond the power of the federal parliament to pass such a law.

That of course should be the situation today. This was the intention of the founders of the Commonwealth, and of the people who approved the Constitution.

It should not come as a surprise to readers that on almost every occasion when the Australian people have been asked by referendum to increase the powers of the federal parliament and government, they have refused.

In fact the people have been asked to vote more than once on transferring some powers to Canberra. Four of these have been each submitted twice – marketing schemes, freedom of religion, price control and local government recognition. At the time of writing the attempt to put the latter to the people for a third time in 2013 failed due to the timing of the election Two powers have been submitted on three occasions – trade and commerce and simultaneous elections. Three powers have been submitted on five occasions – monopolies, corporations and industrial matters.[15]

It is sad to have to tell Australians that none of those referendums proposing an increase in Canberra's powers would be necessary now.

The High Court has sufficiently reinterpreted the Constitution to hand a swag of powers to Canberra, although the original intention of the Constitution was that all of these were reserved to the states. This was done by a later High Court denying that there was any such concept of reserved powers – although everyone knew, including and especially the judges, that this was the very basis of federation.[16]

A recent example of this approach concerned the validity of the Howard government's WorkChoices legislation.[17] The power of the federal parliament to legislate in this area is set out in section 51 (xxxv) of the Constitution. This provides that parliament may make laws for the peace order and good government of the Commonwealth with respect to "conciliation and arbitration for the prevention and settlement of industrial disputes extending beyond the limits of any one State".

The original intention of the Constitution, as approved by the Australian people, and as confirmed in five referendums, is that the federal parliament must not have a general power over industrial relations. Nothing could be clearer.

The legislation was essentially justified by the Howard government as being based on the corporations power. Under Section 51 (xx), the federal parliament may legislate with respect to "foreign corporations, and trading or financial corporations formed within the limits of the Commonwealth".

The argument was that the law related to the employment activities of corporations. The Howard government was relying on a series of cases which gave an extended meaning to the corporations power and thus to the powers of the federal parliament and government in clear contradiction to the original intention of the Constitution and that the wishes of the Australian people on the original approval of the Constitution and on five subsequent occasions. Although Labor opposed WorkChoices, and the Labor states went to the High Court to have the legislation declared invalid, they failed to challenge the extended use of the corporations power. So did the Labor states run dead in the High Court, not arguing that the corporations power did not extend to allowing the federal parliament to pass laws controlling all industrial contracts?[18]

The fact is that Labor, as much as the Coalition, supports the use of the corporations power to centralise government in Australia.

As with the external affairs power, the corporations power can also be used to allow the government to act in an authoritarian and undemocratic way. In March 2013, the government introduced legislation to exercise control over the content of newspapers.[19]

The result of this patchwork of legal development is that, as former Keating government minister Gary Johns puts it, Australians now live under not three but four levels of government, including the UN.[20]

He warns that by entering into so many treaties, not only has power been transferred to the Commonwealth, but it has also enabled some citizens to override the national government. Substantial funds, he says, are leaving Australia to flow into the hands of international agencies.

In the meantime the ability to agitate on behalf of non-citizens has resulted in the federal government losing control over Australia's borders and has shifted substantial costs to the states.

As we have seen, many of these treaties are with the most dictatorial and corrupt powers. Australian politicians and bureaucrats are not so naive as to assume the other powers intend to observe the terms of the many treaties we enter into.

They enter into them at least partially because, thanks to the High Court, this is a convenient cover under which they can circumvent the original intention of the Constitution, and the wishes of the Australian people as expressed in the series of referendums, to apply their agenda.

There is another advantage in entering into international treaties, and that is convenience. International treaties allow some of our politicians to act in a way which the Australian people clearly do not want. Thus some of our politicians hide behind the Refugee Convention, insisting that international law requires that we accept illegal immigrants.

This is untrue. It is not a correct statement of international law. The point is that the interpretation of a treaty is a matter for Australia, and in any event, no treaty is sacrosanct. If on a proper interpretation, a treaty requires a government to act contrary to the national interest, the easiest solution would to ensure the treaty no longer applies, to "denounce" the treaty.

In any event there is a clear wish on the part of many politicians to cede their nation's sovereignty. This is not supported by any mandate from the electors.

The British have seen how their politicians have transferred many of the nation's sovereign powers to the quasi-federal European Union. Unlike the Australian federation, this was conceived as and is intended to be an essentially undemocratic organisation, governed by unelected bureaucrats, judges and select politicians from member countries. There is an enormous democratic deficit. The current crisis in the EuroZone is one result. In fact the British could have had all the advantages – without any of the disadvantages and costs of the common market – by entering into free trade agreement with the EU as Norway and Switzerland have.

We see similar trends in Australia, with, for example, the then Prime Minister Kevin Rudd calling for discussions on an Asian Union along EU lines.

Friedrich Hayek long ago warned of the dangers of political agendas based not on competitive markets and freedom, but of centralisation and planning. He argued that the separation of economic power from political power is an "essential guarantee of individual freedom".[21]

The point surely is that if our independence, our sovereignty, is to be surrendered, this should only be done with the explicit approval of the Australian people.

Endnotes

1 See Chapter 15.

2 Bob Brown, *The 3rd Annual Green Oration*, 23 March 2012. Bob Brown http://greensmps. org.au/content/news-stories/bob-brown-delivers-3rd-annual-green-oration (retrieved 1.01.2013).

3 Dick Morris and Eileen McGann, *Here come the Black Helicopters: UN Global Governance and the loss of Freedom*, Broadside Books, Northampton, 2012, Part 1.

4 Freedom House, *Combined Average Ratings – Independent Countries*, 2011.

5 Adopted at the UN Conference on Environment and Development (UNCED), the Earth Summit, held in Rio de Janeiro in 1992; Amy McGrath, *Wolves in Sheep's Clothing*, Towerhouse Publications, Brighton Le Sands, 2012.

6 Morris and McGann, op. cit., Part 9.

7 *The New American*, 24 September 2012. http://www.thenewamerican.com/reviews/movies/item/12947-powerful-new-video-explores-how-agenda-21-will-affect-you (retrieved 0.02.2013).

8 Morris and McGann, loc. cit.

9 *Constitution*, Article II, section 2, clause 2. The President acting alone or with Congress may enter into executive agreements which are still valid.

10 *Senate Bill* 477 bars the taking of private property in Alabama without due process and says that "Alabama and all political subdivisions may not adopt or implement policy recommendations that deliberately or inadvertently infringe or restrict private property rights without due process, as may be required by policy recommendations originating in or traceable to Agenda 21."

11 See Chapter 5.

12 *Minister for Immigration and Ethnic Affairs* v *Teoh* (1995) 183 CLR 273.

13 51. The Parliament shall, subject to this Constitution, have power to make laws for the peace, order, and good government of the Commonwealth with respect to: (xxix.) External Affairs.

14 *Human Rights and Anti Discrimination Bill, 2012, Exposure Draft Legislation*, Attorney-General's Department. http://www.ag.gov.au/Consultations/Documents/Consoli-dationofCommonwealthanti-discriminationlaws/Human%20Rights%20and%20Anti-Discrimination%20Bill%202012%20-%20Exposure%20Draft%20.pdf (retrieved 6.01.2012).

15 David Flint, *The Cane Toad Republic*, Wakefield Press, Kent Town, 1999, pp 160-161.

16 *Amalgamated Society of Engineers* v *Adelaide Steamship Co Ltd* (1920) 28 CLR 129 (the Engineers' Case)

17 *New South Wales* v *Commonwealth* [2006] HCA 52; 81 ALJR 34; 231 ALR 1 (14 November 2006) http://www.austlii.edu.au/au/cases/cth/high_ct/2006/52.html (retrieved 0.02.2013).

18 Julian Leeser, "WorkChoices: Did The States Run Dead?" Samuel Griffiths Society, Vol 19, Chapter 1, 2007. http://www.samuelgriffith.org.au/papers/html/volume19/v19chap1.html (retrieved 06.05.2013).

19 *News Media (Self-regulation) (Consequential Amendments) Bill* 2013; *News Media (Self-regulation) Bill* 2013; *Public Interest Media Advocate Bill* 2013.

20 Gary Johns, "Health, education and industrial relations must face reform test", *The Australian*, 5 January 2013. http://www.theaustralian.com.au/opinion/columnists/health-education-and-industrial-relations-must-face-reform-test/story-fn-8v83qk-1226547661408 (retrieved 5.01.2013). Hayek, F.A. von, *The Road to Serfdom*, Chicago, University of Chicago Press, 2007, p. 168.

CHAPTER 7

Another witch-hunt: Slandering
our sports men and women

Politician Craig Thomson and former politician and powerbroker Eddie Obeid are entitled to the presumption of innocence. But actual allegations, supported by evidence, have been made against them. Mr. Thomson has been charged.

No evidence whatsoever has been produced by the government against the sports men and sports women of Australia. So why did the Gillard government in February 2013 effectively slander every clean athlete in the country? Why did it launch such a witch-hunt? It should have waited until prosecutions were ready to be made against specific people.

As noted earlier, the Gillard government, against advice, closed down all of the live cattle export trade with Indonesia as a knee jerk reaction to a television program. This included trade involving abattoirs under Australian control as well as Indonesian abattoirs observing high standards. This resulted in enormous and permanent damage to businesses some of which went into liquidation. A significant number of Australians, including indigenous Australians, were thrown out of work. The Indonesians came to the conclusion that Australia was an unreliable source, and when the trade reopened reduced our quota by about one half.

Australians had hoped that the government had learnt its lesson from this sad exercise. It had not.

Instead we had two Gillard government ministers, the Sports Minister Kate Lundy and the Justice Minister Jason Clare, effectively "frothing at the mouth" at their contrived press conference over an Australian Crime Commission enquiry into sport, as the *Daily Telegraph*'s leading NRL sports writer, Andrew Webster, put it in his column on 9 February 2013.[1]

The result was that there were headlines around the world reporting that Australian sports were wallowing in drugs and crime.[2]

The Sydney Institute's Dr. Gerard Henderson made the important point that the Minister for Justice is not expected to be simultaneously "an investigator, prosecutor, judge and jury", nor is the Minister for Sport expected to "hector and threaten" the sporting organisations she is responsible for supporting.[3]

Andrew Webster slammed Ministers Clare and Lundy because they "indirectly but unfairly slandered every clean athlete in the country".

Pointing out that the ACC is supposed to be "shrouded in secrecy", he asked why the enquiry was made so "very, very public".

He pointed to the elementary fact, which the Minister for Justice should have recognised, that "evidence is what is important in this country".

All that the nation was given was "a 47-page glossy brochure bereft of detail and full of unconnected propositions". The result was that the whole of Australian sport was smeared perhaps irrevocably.

John Black chaired the first government-appointed enquiry into drugs in sport under the Hawke Labor government. A former Labor senator, he describes the ACC investigation as an "amateur hour".[4]

The ACC have admitted they possess no evidence, merely intelligence. John Black says if you have intelligence, "almost by definition you sit on it and you use it. You don't tell the world".

Former Detective Sergeant Tim Priest referred to the ACC's brief but chequered history. This included its long and damaging case against actor Paul Hogan. They alleged he was guilty of tax crime and fraud on a massive scale but they were subsequently forced to withdraw this.

Tim Priest says the ACC's finding that the growth of the illegal firearms market was the result of thefts rather than illegal gun importations was seriously flawed. To many this conclusion was incomprehensible and was most convenient for the federal government, which could then point the finger at the state government. Subsequent events have shown the federal government has lost control over the borders in relation not only to illegal immigrants but also in relation to illegal weapons.

Tim Priest asks why, in a country "awash with mind-altering substances, illegal firearms and massive unexplained wealth of a growing number of individuals", the ACC went so public about its investigation into sports. In particular it apparently provided no brief on evidence sufficient for directors of public prosecutions to proceed to a criminal trial.

Andrew Webster gives the government the benefit of the doubt as to whether this move against Australian sport was just a distraction to get embarrassing news off the front page. Possible examples included Eddie Obeid, Craig Thomson, the missing surplus, fraudulent taxpayer-funded pamphlets claiming there was a surplus and the suggested raid on superannuation while ministers who retire earlier than other Australians can can benefit from large, mainly taxpayer-funded, superannuation.

In the meantime a Senate committee is considering proposed changes to the law that would invest the Australian Sports Anti-Doping Authority (ASADA) with extraordinary powers to compel any Australian athlete to attend interviews with an investigator.[5] The burden of proof would be shifted to a defendant if he or she did not co-operate. At a hearing on 1 March 2013, the President of the Australian Olympic Committee (AOC), John Coates, called for those who did not co-operate with ASADA investigations to be liable to imprisonment.

Under the Australian Sports Anti-Doping Authority Amendment Act 2013, ASADA has powers similar to those in the *Australian Security and Investments Commission* (ASIC) *Act* to protect the financial markets. But ASIC investigates possible criminal activity, not the taking of banned substances on lengthy lists, including some medications and supplements. The inclusion of some of these is questionable.

But when asked by Senators to provide specific examples as to why the new laws should be implemented neither the Australian Sports Commission nor ASADA could comply. Liberal Senator Cory Bernardi labelled the powers ASADA were seeking as "almost unparalleled", and Senator George Brandis was scathing in his assessment of the evidence provided by the enquiry witnesses.

"All we've heard is that Australia is the world leader, the world's best practice and we've got to stay ahead of the curve," Senator Brandis said. "That's no argument to up-end fundamental legal rights."

So there is a pincer movement. Defame Australia's athletes, and introduce legislation to remove their civil rights. It is difficult to understand why the government has embarked on this gross injustice to the nation's athletes.

This demonstrates yet again the need for all politicians to be made accountable to the public not only in elections every three or four years – ones where the powerbrokers have chosen many of the candidates – but on every day, in every month and of every year.

Endnotes

1 http://edition.cnn.com/2013/02/07/sport/australia-doping/index.html?iref=allsearch (retrieved 11.02.2013).

2 E.g., *CNN* http://edition.cnn.com/2013/02/07/sport/australia-doping/index.html?iref=allsearch; *BBC* http://www.bbc.co.uk/news/world-asia-21363100; *The Guardian* http://www.guardian.co.uk/sport/2013/feb/07/australian-doping-report-blackest-day?INTCMP=SRCH (retrieved 12.02.2013).

3 http://www.smh.com.au/opinion/politics/ministers-turn-judge-and-jury-in-sport-case-20130211-2e8tw.html#ixzz2Kd206g7n (retrieved 12.02.2012).

4 http://www.theaustralian.com.au/sport/drugs-enquiry-amateur-hour-former-senator-john-black-slams-acc-investigation/story-e6frg7mf-1226578247263 (retrieved 15.02.2013).

5 "Senators scathing of ASADA evidence", *Sydney Morning Herald*, 1 March 2013. http://news.smh.com.au/breaking-news-sport/senators-scathing-of-asada-evidence-20130301-2fanb.html (retrieved 6 March 2013).

CHAPTER 8

Puppets in the parliamentary theatre

8.1 Introduction

Australia, a Federal Commonwealth under the Crown, is a representative democracy. Government is based on the Westminster system. Under this the government is responsible to the lower house which consists of the representatives of the people from the various electorates. In the UK this is the House of Commons – in Australia, at the federal level, the House of Representatives. So a government must resign if it loses the confidence of the House.[1]

As a representative democracy, we elect representatives to act on our behalf. This is to be contrasted with direct democracy especially in ancient Athens where the people – at least the free men who had served in the army – actually took decisions and governed the city.

While such a system may be feasible in a small city or even a province, it is not possible in a country with a large population. This is especially so in a country like Australia with a very large land mass. In some advanced jurisdictions,[2] while government and lawmaking is that of a representative democracy, there is a significant addition of the tools of direct democracy – the right to recall a government, to veto legislation or to introduce legislation.

In Australia, we could readily graft these tools onto our existing representative democracy, significantly enhancing the power of the people, but in no way threatening our constitutional stability.

Let us look at our system of representative democracy.

The great Irish statesman and member of the House of Commons, Edmund Burke, famously made this observation about politicians in a representative democracy: "Your representative owes you, not his industry only, but judgment; and he betrays, instead of serving you, if he sacrifices it to your opinion."[3]

He was more concerned that the representative might abandon the exercise of his personal judgement to carry favour with the electorate. He was not to know that the problem which would develop in Australia would be not so much that MPs would more and more sacrifice their opinion and judgement to the electors, although the parties are obsessed with polling more to manipulate the media and the public. The problem is that our MPs have too often sacrificed their opinion to the factional powerbrokers who control the executive organs of the relevant party structure.

Burke lived at a time when parties were not as powerful as they are today – especially the Australian brands which are some of the least democratic in the English-speaking world. Rather than the politicians in our parliaments exercising their opinion and judgement, their behaviour is too often that of puppets in a theatre. The public sees this at its worst during Question Time which, with all its amateurism and appalling vulgarity, is choreographed down to the most exquisite detail.

Contrast this with the behaviour of British parliamentarians whilst recently debating the contentious gay marriage bill. Although both lively and passionate, members were able to conduct themselves in a more-or-less polite manner.[4]

When Burke lived during the early years of our representative democracy, representative democracy worked in that members were chosen for the value of their judgement and in most parties were free to vote as they wished. But while Australia is one of the six or seven oldest continuing democracies in the world, our Westminster system of representative democracy has been thoroughly compromised through the machinations of the powerbrokers controlling the major political parties.

As a result most MPs no longer vote according to their judgement, but vote as they are told. Even their right to ask questions or to address the House is controlled. Candidates are chosen by the parties more often because they will remain obedient to a faction or even the party, rather than voting on their assessment of the merit of each proposal. Burke would have been saddened, if not outraged, by this decline of representative government in Australia since the late 20th century century. He would have concluded that members of Australian parliaments have today sacrificed their judgement, not to the electors, but to their parties, factions and "faceless" powerbrokers.

This can be even true of some so-called independents. In 2010, even those who had campaigned as independents signed deals making them effectively coalition partners of the minority government, and rarely thereafter exercised any independent judgement.

There are of course exceptions, a good example of which can be seen in New South Wales in the Hon. Rev. Fred Nile MLC, who takes strong independent positions and also has a unique ability to assess on its merits the legislation that comes before the parliament.

The centralisation of control within the political parties has no doubt contributed towards the shrinking of their membership. This is particularly so when preselections are forced on local branches by power cliques at the top, and when members are threatened with sanctions if they exercise their freedom to speak publicly on party matters.

In the meantime, politicians have elevated the major parties to positions of enormous privilege created by the laws they make, policies they administer and substantial sums of money from the taxpayers which they have sequestered.

In return for these considerable advantages, the parties should be required to act openly, transparently and democratically, and not run by small cabals of powerbrokers who too often exercise their power to advance their own interests, including, at times, their financial interests.

The fact is that their electoral expenses are subsidised generously. They enjoy exemptions from privacy law and much of their campaigning costs are paid for by the taxpayer. In government they hit gold, appointing political apparatchiks as advisers whose principal task is to advance their chances of re-election, as well as vast numbers of media advisers to generate spin to go to the media and even using expensive government advertising for party political purposes.

They enjoy privileges in elections with the party's name appearing on ballot papers. In federal elections their deals as to the direction of their Senate preferences are hidden from all except the most persistent. The practice of preselecting candidates by tiny cabals within the already small ruling politburos is completely undemocratic and bordering on corrupt – something the Americans did away with a century ago through the introduction of democratic primary preselections.

Under these, candidates are normally chosen by registered voters, with some primaries being open to all comers.

In summary, the parties and the factions have compromised Australian representative democracy in four main ways.

1. Most politicians are constrained from the free exercise of their opinions and their judgement in parliament in a way which goes much further than party politics could reasonably require.

2. The preselection of party candidates for elections will often not reflect the choice of party members and supporters. Worse, the choice is too often determined not by merit, but by factional loyalty.

3. The electoral process has been reorganised to suit the needs of the parties or a party, and not to ensure the purity and integrity of the process.

4. Other important institutions of the state and of society have been and are being compromised in order that the factional powerbrokers retain their power and influence.

Burke, the man of principle that he was, would surely agree that some countervailing power to the parties and the factions in the Australia of the 21ˢᵗ century is desperately needed. He would be appalled that the neutering of Australian representative democracy has been so inexorable and that the demands of today's major parties and the factions for power, privilege and taxpayer funding have been so insatiable.

We hope that he would have concluded that, since representative government has been so neutered in Australia, the people should now be armed with the tools of direct democracy.

8.2 Controlling parliament's business

In the meantime, we have seen the conduct of parliamentary business placed more and more under the control of the parties. In particular, the practices adopted at Westminster to ensure the full independence of the Speaker have not been followed in Australia, for example, with the Speaker no longer participating in party business and contesting the next election as an independent. More specifically, the British Speaker remains relatively independent in controlling parliamentary debates. Of course the government, through its numbers, can ensure its legislation is considered according to a timetable it desires, but the Speaker is permitted a wide discretion and members themselves are also accorded considerable freedom.

Question Time in Canberra, in all its embarrassing vulgarity, is under the absolute control of the political parties. For too long questions asked by government backbenchers have been so obviously prearranged as to be a public embarrassment. Questions from the opposition give every appearance of being allocated by the party whip, rather than as a result of the Speaker choosing between different contenders. By way of contrast, when the opposition is entitled to a question, different members will stand to attract the Speaker's attention.

The members of parliament at Westminster are accorded greater freedom by the parties in relation to the way they vote. For example in March 2003 the then Prime Minister Tony Blair needed the support of Tory MPs when 121 British Labour MPs voted against the Blair government over the Iraq war, something which, it seems, could never happen in Canberra.[5]

Tony Blair's chief "spin doctor", Alistair Campbell, recalls that questions from MPs on the Labour side of the House of Commons in respect to the second Iraq war were more vicious and critical than anything levelled at the government by the Conservative opposition.[6]

8.3 Controlling MPs

While representative democracy is based on the proposition that the electors choose their representative for the quality of his or her judgement, the fact is that most MPs do not and cannot always speak or vote in accordance with their considered judgement.

This began when the ALP, in its early days, adopted what is called the "caucus pledge" to control how Labor MPs could vote. Never a feature of the British Labour Party, it was justified in the early days as necessary to keep the elected politicians to a party agenda, especially concerned to protect working class interests. It was soon accompanied by a strong commitment to the tools of direct democracy, including Citizen Initiated Referendums.

But as the party became strong enough to win government, it became less interested in direct democracy. The commitment to direct democracy remained in the platform until it was removed in 1963.

In the meantime, the caucus pledge has remained and still requires Labor MPs and even local government councils to vote according to binding decisions of their caucus, which is bound by the party platform.

The platform is determined from time to time by the party conference. This is only partly made up by representatives of the rank-and-file members, but a sizable block comes from the trade unions. In recent years, the trade unions have more and more fallen under the control of professional officials who have not risen from the shop floor, but who are ambitious young members from the elite class, often law graduates. Their interests too often centre around the accumulation of wealth and power. They learn to operate under cover without the standards of accountability and transparency consistent with a democracy, protected from any legislative reform by a parliament in which there is always a considerable block of former union officers. There is of course a serious conflict of interest here. The result is that the proper standards of transparency and financial integrity which the parliament requires of company directors do not apply to union officers. They control the resources of their members based on fees which for low paid workers are considerable and which are large in the aggregate.

At the federal level, the caucus is a meeting of all Labor MPs and senators. Once a vigorous and independent assembly, under the Rudd and Gillard governments it surrendered its crucial power to elect the ministry and, on most important matters, to determine policy.

This did not liberate Labor MPs to vote as their consciences require. Still bound by the caucus pledge, they have become the puppets of the Prime Minister and his or her inner or "kitchen cabinet". Their sole real power is to elect the leader.

The result has been that while Labor MPs once voted in accordance with caucus decisions, they now treat the directions of the leader or the small inner committee surrounding the leader as if they were caucus decisions.

One example related to the announcement, on 11 July 2011, of the details of the carbon tax to the Australian people by the Prime Minister, Julia Gillard. The day before this was announced to the nation (and not incidentally to the Parliament) Prime Minister Gillard gave the details to the caucus in a telephone hook up. She had already given the details to her allies, the Greens and Independents. The result was that the caucus was given a *fait accompli*, with Labor MPs lamely treating this as a caucus decision binding on them.[7]

The once lively and robust Labor caucus had been turned into a rubber stamp. Their predecessors would have been both amazed and appalled. This is the behaviour we would expect in a backward dictatorship, not one of the world's oldest democracies.

It is also clear that even in the caucus some Labor MPs do not necessarily express and act on their opinions. They are subject to significant outside pressures and directions – and not necessarily from their constituents. This power is wielded by the factional powerbrokers.

An example of the power of the factions occurred in July 2012, when Tony Sheldon of the Transport Workers Union threatened the withdrawal of union election funding if the caucus replaced the unpopular Prime Minister Julia Gillard.[8] Then in a meeting of the "faceless men", a group of union leaders pledged their allegiance to Julia Gillard indicating thereby that they could direct a substantial body of caucus votes in her support.[9]

Although the Liberal and National Parties do not have a caucus pledge, there is an expectation that MPs should normally vote in accordance with the party policy which is not necessarily settled in the party room or the joint party room, but determined by the leaders.

The result is that most MPs and senators vote according to their caucus or party room, and in many instances even according to the faction within the caucus or party room. To the credit of the Liberal and National Parties, backbenchers remain free to cross the floor.

But as Professor Peter van Onselen points out, any Coalition politician doing this today faces two "openly articulated consequences".[10] The first threat is that there will be no chance of executive promotion. Second, and worse, he says a member crossing the floor will be warned of an almost certain challenge at the next preselection. This, he says, is the threatened punishment for "disrespecting the powerbrokers and the leader".

The quality of representation has been affected by the preselection of candidates not always on merit, but on loyalty to a factional powerbroker. This phenomenon is also not restricted to the Labor Party.

8.4 Factions across the political spectrum – two case studies

Factions – in the sense of sub-parties whose members are bound to vote in certain ways – seem to have first emerged in the Labor Party.

While seeing nothing wrong with people sharing the same convictions working together to advance those issues, Federal Labor Senator John Faulkner has expressed concern at the power of factions within the ALP.[11]

There is, he says, a great deal wrong with a situation where a "Russian doll of nested caucuses" allows a tiny minority of MPs exercising a controlling interest over the majority.

Senator Faulkner explains his Russian doll analogy by an example. This is of a group with 51% of what may be termed a sub-faction, making up 51% of a faction, and then having 51% of the caucus numbers, being able to force the entire caucus to adopt their position. Thus, a group of only 14 members could control a caucus of 102 members and senators – the size of the caucus in January 2013.

Senator Faulkner comes to the conclusion that the practice of "factions, affiliates or interest groups binding parliamentarians in parliamentary party votes of ballots must be banned".

But he defends the caucus pledge saying that it ensures consistency with the party platform and stability in government. But it depends for its integrity, he warns, on "democratic decision-making within caucus".

Thus while the caucus pledge is acceptable, factional pledges are objectionable. It can be argued that in the early days of the Labor Party, surrounded by its "class enemies", it was imperative to maintain discipline. As Labor has so often been in government, the original justifications for the caucus pledge have surely disappeared. The caucus pledge is now little more than a very effective tool to keep the caucus under the thumb of the powerbrokers.

Labor case study

Senator Faulkner was no doubt embarrassed by, but not in any way personally involved, in a 2012-2013 investigation by the NSW Independent Commission Against Corruption (ICAC). This is into claims the family of former Labor MP and right faction powerbroker Eddie Obeid had planned to enrich itself by up to $100 million through corrupt dealings in coal exploration licences.[12]

The allegation was that Mr. Obeid was privy to inside information on new coal mining licence allocations at Mount Penny, about 125km west of Newcastle. It was claimed that this came about through his relationship with Ian Macdonald, who was the minister responsible for mineral resources between 2005 and 2008.

How did Mr. Obeid become so powerful? Once the owner and publisher of the Sydney Arabic language newspaper, *El Telegraph*, he was to become a protégé of Labor powerbroker Graham Richardson in the 90s.

Senator Richardson decided that Mr. Obeid should replace NSW politician Jack Hallam who had displeased him by speaking out against uranium mining.[13]

Graham Richardson was successful. At a joint meeting of the New South Wales Parliament in 1991, the then Premier Bob Carr moved the nomination of Eddie Obeid as an MLC. He soon established a caucus sub-faction soon known as "the Terrigals", from the name of a central coast resort near Sydney where they met.

The sub-faction was soon in a position to control not only preselections of candidates but also the appointment of ministers. Their overriding concerns, concludes Alex Mitchell political editor of the *Sun-Herald* for many years, were "jobs for the boys, branch-stacking, accumulating a war chest from developers and hoteliers, and extravagant advertising".

In 1999, Eddie Obeid was made a minister, but demoted by Premier Bob Carr after the 2003 election. Through his factional power, he drove three Premiers from office: Bob Carr, Nathan Rees and Morris Iemma. The latter two gave evidence to ICAC about Obeid's power to make and un-make ministers and even premiers.

Former Premier Morris Iemma told of the pressure put on him from Eddie Obeid and Joe Tripodi to replace the former planning minister Frank Sartor with Ian Macdonald, who is under investigation by ICAC.

Alex Mitchell says that under Premier Iemma, the mineral resources portfolio previously held by Eddie Obeid was handed to Ian Macdonald, the leader of the left faction.[14] But when Premier Rees sacked Ian Macdonald in late 2009, he was in turn removed as Premier.

The Terrigals then installed Ms. Kristina Keneally as Premier. Ian Macdonald was then appointed as Minister for Mineral Resources.

Alarmingly, the rise in the influence of Obeid's faction was in direct proportion to the collapse in ALP membership and the folding of branches. At the 2011 election, NSW Labor suffered its biggest defeat in 100 years and its numbers in the lower house were decimated to a rump of 20 MPs.

Liberal case study

A process has also emerged in parts of the Liberal Party where candidates are "cleared" prior to the preselection as to their acceptability, a form of guided democracy with the potential to narrow the choice to the preselection panel. In July 2012, Greg Mayfield, the editor of the *Port Pirie Recorder*, was not allowed to proceed with a nomination to become a Liberal Senate candidate because the party's candidate review committee decided it was not in the party's interests for his nomination to stand.

In the meantime, the NSW Liberal Party has also become dominated by factions, which has led to rank-and-file moves to democratise the party. The noted *Sydney Morning Herald* columnist Paul Sheehan described the NSW Liberal Party in 2012 as one dominated by a small clique of unaccountable powerbrokers.[15]

The NSW executive has gone further by regularly centralising preselections under "emergency powers".

This has been done so frequently that there has been a groundswell of repugnance among the rank-and-file party membership, leading to calls for reform. The principal proposal is that preselection be through what is called a "plebiscite" or primary of party members in the electorate, an example of direct democracy. The inclusion of this on the agenda of the state executive was resisted by party powerbrokers, leading to expensive litigation.

Paul Sheehan reports that a senior member of the NSW Liberal Party telephoned Tony Abbott in August 2012 to make this blunt warning against his supporting moves for reform: "If you insist on supporting these motions there will be World War III. We will blow the division up from underneath you. You will lose the [next] election."

This was a reference to moves inside the NSW Liberal Party to democratise the party, this man feeling so undermined by the reforms "bubbling up from the grassroots" that he threatened the federal leader with the loss of an election.

Paul Sheehan slams the NSW Liberal Party as a party of "black box politics", a party of questionable elections, rampant self-interest, personal fiefdoms and institutional duplicity. Black box politics occurs, he says, when there is an accumulation of power by a small group of powerbrokers who run the party largely unencumbered by the restrictions imposed by governance, accountability or transparency.

While black box politics were once the exclusive province of the unions and the Labor Party, especially in NSW, he revealed that this malaise has now spread to the NSW Liberal Party. "The party has corrupted its own ideals," he says.

During the previous 12 months, the State Executive has invoked "emergency powers" more than 100 times to impose its will on the party. It is, he writes, constantly backdating elections, overriding local votes, striking out memberships, and voiding local branch elections, in the name of stability.

The NSW division of the Liberals thus operates under a state of "perpetual emergency". He sees an analogy with a government which suspends civil liberties during times of war: "Except there is no war, other than warring personalities. There have been no emergencies, let alone a hundred of them."

The obvious solution in the New South Wales Liberal Party is to make the party more democratic. But when a party member and a branch sought to have these matters discussed at a meeting of the Party's ruling State Council, the powerbrokers ensured the motions did not appear on the agenda paper.

The member, Denis Pogson, a rank-and-file party member in the Robertson electorate and a self-funded retiree, took exception to having his vote and his branches vote "treated like garbage".

In declaring himself a "Menzies Liberal", Mr. Pogson was horrified about the extent to which the powerbrokers had taken the Party away from its great founder's ideals.

He began proceedings in the Supreme Court, which were resisted at great expense, no doubt with funds raised by the rank-and-file to fight elections.

New South Wales Supreme Court Justice Nicholas agreed with Mr. Pogson and forced the powerbrokers to put the motions on the agenda for the State Council meeting.

In the meantime, John Ruddick, a young and forward-thinking member of the party has called for the broad democratisation of the Liberal Party and proposed a program of action to achieve this.[16]

The Australian Labor Party has also been affected by demands that it democratise its internal processes.

Senator John Faulkner has called for the preselection of party candidates to be undertaken by primaries consisting of members of the party in the relevant electorate. In relation to the Senate, he proposes this be done by party members across the relevant state or territory.[17]

If the major Australian parties were to agree to democratise the ways in which candidates are selected, they would be following a century-old reform adopted in the United States, a country whose constitution in significant respects inspired the founders of the Commonwealth of Australia. In the United States, the institution of primary elections has led to the widespread involvement of party members and registered voters in the choice of candidates. Australians may be wary of primaries because of the inordinate amount of time presidential elections take in the United States. This has not so much to do with primaries but rather to do with fixed elections for an executive presidency or executive governors.

8.5 Controlling the choice of candidates

As the parties developed, the selection of candidates in an election would be left to party preselections with some involvement of local party members. With declining party memberships, and with party executives being captured by factional powerbrokers and lobbyists, the influence of rank-and-file party members has been diluted if not pushed aside. Pre-selections have become tools through which patronage can be dispensed by those acting with an agenda other than the best interests of firstly the country, and then the party. This means that the electors are often presented with very limited choices.

In 2010, against the wishes of the local ALP branches, the ALP leader Mark Latham parachuted former rock star and former Nuclear Disarmament Party candidate Peter Garrett into the safe Labor seat of Kingsford Smith in a part of Sydney in which he had shown no interest.

During the election, a radio commentator Steve Price revealed that Peter Garrett had admitted that a Labor government would change all its policies once it got into power. Peter Garrett, who was accused of abandoning policies he once stood for, denied this.[18]

The candidates of the major parties are selected not for their independent judgement as a representative democracy requires, but to act according to the instructions of an inner leadership group. While this is ultimately responsible to the party rooms or caucuses, overshadowing this is the authority of factional bosses who can instruct members even on who is to lead the party. The factional system is most developed in the Labor Party, but the Liberal Party has a similar system more in some states than others, especially in New South Wales.[19]

Party preselections have led to a most unrepresentative federal parliament. Thirty-four moved straight to parliament from being political advisers to other MPs, often with little other life experience (19 Labor, 14 Coalition and one Greens). Thirty came from the unions into the Labor Party, most the new class of union executive. Twenty-nine came from the legal profession (14 Labor, 12 Coalition and three Greens).[20]

Further, parliamentarians are much more likely to have a tertiary education than the general public, with 69% having a bachelors degree, compared with 14.2% of the general Australian population aged 28 and older. 18.5% have a Masters degree, compared with 3% in the general population, and 3.5% have a Ph.D. compared with 0.7% in the general population.

But as Dr. Katherine Betts found in her 2004 study, the most marked division within Australian politics is not between different groups of voters, that is working class versus middle class. The most marked division is between a majority of voters, including the traditional working class, and candidates for the Labor, Greens and Democrats parties.[21]

Labor, Greens and Democrat candidates tend to share the views, attitudes and values of what has been described as the elites, a privileged class concentrated mainly in the inner-city electorates in the Sydney-Canberra-Melbourne triangle.[22]

As a former vice-chancellor and foundation Chairman of the Australian Research Council observes, and as attitude surveys suggest, most Australians are, in comparison with the ABC and most academics in the humanities and social sciences, rather "more conservative, less internationalist, less sympathetic to the disadvantaged, less convinced about any human contribution to 'climate change', less worried about endangered species, more critical of handouts to indigenous Australians, less welcoming of boat people, and so on."[23]

Dr. Betts study was itself based on Australian Election Studies of the Australian National University. This research would not have pleased the party powerbrokers. It would not be surprising that if there were a further survey undertaken, the candidates would be advised either not to respond or to provide answers which were less revealing, just as politicians do in parliament or to the media. We leave it to the reader to judge whether we are being harsh on the party powerbrokers.

The attitudes of respondents were measured by their responses to different questions. Let us take three as examples.

One was whether the death penalty should be reintroduced for murder. While only 4.5% of Labor candidates were in support, 27.6% of social professionals, 68.1% of working class voters and 55.19% of all voters wanted the death penalty reintroduced.

Another question was whether higher income tax made people less willing to work. 18.2% of Labor candidates supported this, 55.9% of social professionals, 76.1% of working class voters and 69% of all voters.

Asked whether the government should choose in favour of reducing taxes or spending more on social services, 85.2% of Labor candidates thought the government should spend more on social services, but only 46.5% of social professionals, 25.3% of working class voters and 30.2% of all voters were in favour.

Dr. Betts believes this rift between the voters and the candidates may stem from "an adherence to national loyalties" on the part of most voters and "an enthusiasm for international cosmopolitanism" on the part of new-left candidates.

She points out that Labor's constituency is divided into two groups. One is a smaller group of new-class social professionals tending to work in education, social professions and the arts – referred to in this book as the elites. The other, larger group consists of the old working class.

She says that Labor's problem is not so much just trying to serve two very different kinds of voters. It is that those who gain preselection share the values of the new-class, the elites, and seek to advance these. Dr. Betts writes that they may even see their old style working class supporters not as "old comrades whom they are proud to lead and protect, but as narrow-minded strangers tending towards the racist right".

She points out that on one issue, Coalition candidates are also distant from their constituents. This is high immigration. She thinks candidate support for this results more from pressures from the growth lobby within the business community rather than any feeling for internationalism. She thinks this could be a hazard for the Coalition.

In summary, the control by the factional powerbrokers over preselections, more so in the Labor Party, means that in safe seats the real election is often held among the party elite.

With the increasing power of the factions, party preselections often reflect their battles for control of the party rather than the interests of the electorate which tends to be ignorant of the factors that led to the choice of the candidate, or the merits of different candidates. Where a candidate is chosen for a safe electorate, the preselection obviously determines the final result and will be eagerly contested by the factions. The electorate will have no say whatsoever in choosing between factional candidates and their agendas. The candidate in the election will be foisted on them.

Prime Ministerial preselection

In January 2013, Prime Minister Julia Gillard decided to override the preselection of a Labor candidate for the election of a Northern Territory senator in January 2013.[24]

She had expected applause across the country for her decision to impose an indigenous candidate, the former athlete Nova Peris.

But party members – and not only in the Northern Territory – were upset at the reopening of the preselection, pointing out that Ms. Peris' political policies were unknown and that she was not even a member of the Labor Party when she was nominated. The veteran Senator Crossin, whom Ms. Gillard had effectively sacked, did not go away quietly.

Under the electoral system the politicians chose, most Senate places are effectively reserved for the major parties to fill. This is usually decided by the "faceless men" – the factional powerbrokers who dominate the state executives.

There might as well not be an election. To add insult to injury, the people are forced to go along with this charade by being compelled to go to the polling stations.

Bad enough as normal Senate preselections are, this one made public a number of issues, including factional fights, and the fact that Senator Crossin is a supporter of the former Prime Minister whom Ms. Gillard replaced, Kevin Rudd. Was Senator Crossin being punished, was she being replaced by a supporter of Ms. Gillard?

Ms. Gillard's explanation was that it was time for the Labor Party to have its first indigenous member of the federal parliament. Critics pointed out that she had her chance to achieve this last year. This was when the NSW Senate vacancy created by Senator Arbib's resignation was expected to be filled by the former party president with an indigenous background, Warren Mundine. Instead, Ms. Gillard ensured that her then favourite, former Premier of New South Wales Bob Carr, was parachuted into a Senate position. He would then become Foreign

Minister and thus overshadow the memory of Kevin Rudd in that position.

That didn't work out as well as the Prime Minister intended. Senator Carr broke cabinet solidarity in late 2012 to campaign in the caucus against the Prime Minister's wish to maintain our traditional position in relation to Israel in a recent UN vote. It was alleged that Senator Carr said that he would be unable to explain that when he was speaking from "the steps of the Lakemba mosque".[25]

Whatever the relative merits of Senator Crossin and Ms. Peris, the process has been tainted by the Prime Minister's assumption that membership of parliament is within her gift. This is the mark of an authoritarian political system, a guided democracy and not the system bequeathed to us by our forefathers.

One hundred years ago, the Americans took preselections out of the party backrooms and out of the control of the smoke-filled backrooms where the factional powerbrokers used to operate. The Americans have primaries. In most of these supporters of a particular party decide who should be the party candidate in their electorate or their state.

That is how it should be in a democracy.

That is how it should be in Australia.

Why aren't our taxpayer-funded political parties required to democratise their preselections?

It is time the law was changed and the parties were required to be transparent and behave as if they were democratic parties and not ancient oligarchies.

If they are unwilling they should be required give up the wealth and privilege they have so improperly – and some would say corruptly – granted themselves.

It is time that this nation returned to being the democracy our forefathers bequeathed to us, and which many have fought for and died for.

Endnotes

1 This obligation to resign also extends to a failure to secure supply. This is an authorisation by the Parliament for the government to spend taxes to carry on the government. At the Federal level the Senate must support any such authorisation.

2 See Chapter 17.

3 Speech at his arrival at Bristol, 3 November 1774.

4 http://www.smh.com.au/world/gay-marriage-passes-in-a-very-british-debate-20130206- 2d ynt. html

5 Matthew Tempest, "Labour MPs revolt over Iraq", *The Guardian*, 26 February 2013. http://www.guardian.co.uk/politics/2003/feb/26/foreignpolicy.uk2 (retrieved 30.04.2013).

6 Peter van Onselen, "Parliament plods along party lines", *The Australian*, 19 January 2013. http://www.theaustralian.com.au/opinion/columnists/parliament-plods-along-party-lines/story-fn53lw5p-1226556966209 (retrieved 20.01.2013).

7 http://www.theaustralian.com.au/national-affairs/carbon-tax/pm-respects-labor-mps-still-waiting-for-carbon-tax-briefing/story-fn99tjf2-1226089838755 (retrieved 20.07.2012).

8 http://www.theaustralian.com.au/national-affairs/industrial-relations/union-cash-lost-if-labor-dumps-julia-gillard-threatens-twu/story-fn59noo3-1226430459867 (retrieved 22. 07.2012).

9 http://m.theaustralian.com.au/national-affairs/union-leaders-back-julia-gillards-leadership-dismiss-reports-shes-losing-their-support/story-fn59niix-1226429720980 (retrieved 22.07. 2012).

10 van Onselen, op.cit.

11 John Faulkner, "Political Integrity: The Parliament, the Public Service, and the Parties," speech to the *Integrity in Government Conference*, University of Melbourne Law School, 4 December 2012. http://www.senatorjohnfaulkner.com.au/file.php?file=/news/QCRMVHXKFO/index.html (retrieved 21/12/2012).

12 Imre Salusinsky, "Roll up, roll up as Rum mob puts on one hell of a show", *The Australian*, 22 December 2012. http://www.theaustralian.com.au/opinion/columnists/roll-up-roll-up-as-rum-mob-puts-on-one-hell-of-a-show/story-e6frg76x-1226541984202 (retrieved 22.12.2012).

13 Alex Mitchell, "With friends like these", *Sydney Morning Herald*, 10 February 2010. http://www.smh.com.au/nsw/with-friends-like-these--20130209-2e4z0. html#ixzz2KSl01XDQ

14 Ibid

15 Paul Sheehan, "Lid lifted on NSW black box", *The Sydney Morning Herald*, 24 September 2012. http://www.smh.com.au/opinion/politics/lid-lifted-on-nsw-black-box-20120923 -26ewc.html#ixzz2FiSaDJf1 (retrieved 22.12.2012).

16 See Chapter 21.

17 Faulkner, op. cit.

18 Jewel Topsfield, "Garrett stripped of climate change role", *The Age*, 30 November 2007. http://www.theage.com.au/articles/2007/11/29/1196037074839.html (retrieved 20.01.2013).

19 Andrew Clennell, "Teacher's pet has designs on the principal's office", *Daily Telegraph*, 10 January 2013.

20 Edmund Tadros and Jason Murphy, "The men and women of Federal Parliament", *Australian Financial Review*, 10 January 2013.

21 Katherine Betts, "People and Parliamentarians: The Great Divide", *People and Place*, vol. 12, no. 2, 2004, pp 64-83. http://arrow.monash.edu.au/hdl/1959.1/480481 (retrieved 11.01.2013).

22 David Flint, *The Twilight of the Elites*, Freedom Publishing, North Melbourne, 2003.

23 Don Aitken, "Someone please tell the ABC it's not all doom and gloom out here", *The Australian*, 19-20 January 2013. http://www.theaustralian.com.au/media/opinion/someone-please-tell-the-abc-its-not-all-doom-and-gloom-out-here/story-e6frg99o-1226556989384 (retrieved 19.01.2013).

24 http://www.theaustralian.com.au/national-affairs/julia-gillards-push-for-nova-peris-sets-off-week-of-brawls/story-fn59niix-1226560454673 (retrieved 24.01.2013).

25 See Chapter 2.

CHAPTER 9

Controlling elections

9.1 Voting methods

Australian electoral laws are frequently changed or, as the politicians will so often say, "reformed", allegedly in the public interest. It is to be expected that a ruling party will only make changes which do not disadvantage it. What is objectionable is where a change is made to favour a political party and which opens up the system to abuse. This is often done on the pretext that it will make voting easier. The problem is that it too often does – fraudulent voting.

Compulsory voting for state elections was introduced in Queensland in 1915 and for federal elections in 1924. Victoria introduced compulsory voting in 1926, New South Wales and Tasmania in 1928, Western Australia in 1936 and South Australia in 1942.[1]

The argument that people are not forced to vote, i.e., forced to attend the polling station, is the equivalent of hiding the White Australia Policy behind the dictation test.

The claimed reason for compulsory voting is self-evident, to improve the turnout at elections. Since the introduction of compulsory voting for federal elections, the turnout has never fallen below 90%. While the advantages and disadvantages of compulsory voting are regularly debated across the country, the real reason for this "reform" has been to relieve the major parties of something which is properly considered a normal obligation in most democratic countries, actually motivating the electors to vote. This has reduced the parties' activities on polling day to being present outside the polling stations to harass voters, pollute the streets and emit vast amounts of carbon dioxide in producing flyers and signage to tell voters how they should vote, rather than that they should come out to vote.[2]

Former minister and senator Nick Minchin rightly condemns compulsory voting as a "conspiracy among the political parties to use the force of law to save themselves the trouble of having to persuade people to vote". This, he says, debilitates our democracy and is a denial of a basic right in a liberal society – the right to decide whether or not to vote. One of the "best things" which could be done to restore the health of our democracy would be to remove the compulsory voting provisions of the Commonwealth Electoral Act "so insidiously inserted there by self-serving politicians".[3]

Compulsory voting has allowed the parties to commit a blatant and improper misuse of taxpayers' funds.[4] This was when the politicians decided that the campaigns should be funded by the taxpayers. In proposing this, the politicians have an obviously serious and continuing conflict of interest. By enacting a law providing for public funding, and simultaneously requiring the electors to vote, the politicians have a vested interest in compulsory voting which artificially increases the amount of money the parties receive.

The politicians should have chosen between compulsory voting and compulsory funding by the taxpayers of their election campaigns. To require both is deceitful and dishonest.

Voting methods abuse

In the meantime, the politicians have regularly changed the method of voting in ways that they hope will suit them, for example through the introduction of preferential voting, to ensure that votes in favour of minor parties or independents are not lost by the major parties.

A particular method of voting will advantage some parties and disadvantage others. But this is never permanent. When the Labor

Party split in 1955, the Coalition benefitted from the Democratic Labor preferences for almost two decades. But in recent years Labor has benefitted from Greens preferences.

The preferential system means the results are often delayed, sometimes unduly so. The worst feature is that voters are forced to make preferences when they clearly would prefer not to do so. In some states optional preferential voting has been introduced, where the voter does not have to record more than their first preference. This is fairer and should speed up counting.

In one state, Queensland, this was thought to advantage the ALP against the two Coalition parties. The theory was some Coalition voters would not allocate any preferences. When the Coalition parties amalgamated into one, any advantage to Labor disappeared. Indeed with Labor's current low primary vote, and its need for Green preferences, optional preferential voting may work against Labor.

At least there is some justice for politicians who seek to manipulate the voting system to their advantage.

9.2 Senate vacancies

The filling of most casual vacancies in the Senate has now been effectively captured by the major political parties. As party membership has fallen, and the powerbrokers have taken control of the major parties or significant parts of them, a Senate vacancy has become an attractive prize for the ruling faction. Too often, the Senate vacancy is filled on the basis of the loyalty of the candidate to one particular faction, and not necessarily on merit.

Consider this in terms of Edmund Burke's prescription for representative democracy. This is that we choose our representatives for the quality of their judgement and opinions, and of their strong determination to exercise their judgement when in office. Because of the malevolent activities of the powerbrokers, the system which we have today is the precise opposite of this. Indeed, it is shameful for Australians to admit that they have produced a system which is probably the most corrupted among comparable democracies.

It is as though the filling of a Senate vacancy had been redesigned to allow the ruling powerbrokers to choose candidates who they believe will readily act on the instructions and in the interests of the faction.

This dereliction of democracy has been effected though an elaborate process devised by the major political acting together.

Unlike the House, a Senate vacancy is not filled by the people, or even filling the position by the next ranking candidate at the last election. Instead, the founders left the election to the relevant state parliament. An understandable practice soon developed that it would be fair to choose a politician from the same party as the departing or deceased Senator. But it was only a practice.

A proposal that the constitution require that casual vacancies be filled by the party of the outgoing senator arose out of the tumultuous events which occurred during the term of the second Whitlam government, 1974 to 1975.

Highly critical of the way the country was being governed, and in light of information that the Whitlam government was actually seeking an enormous amount of foreign funds through an obvious carpetbagger and not through normal commercial channels and that this was for questionable purposes, the Coalition parties were searching for ways to force the government to an early election.

However questionable politically, this can be done through the Senate delaying or refusing supply to the government. In doing this, the Coalition parties followed precedents set by the Labor Party in opposition. In fact the Labor Party had made 170 attempts to reject supply during the course of the previous Coalition governments.[5] These usually failed because the Democratic Labor Party refused to vote with the opposition.

The opportunity arose on two occasions in 1975 when NSW Labor Senator Lionel Murphy was appointed to the High Court, and when

Queensland Labor Senator Bertie Milliner died. The New South Wales vacancy was filled by the state parliament appointing an independent or so-called "political neuter", a long-standing Albury Mayor, Cleaver Bunton. In Queensland, the Premier, Sir Joh Bjelke-Petersen, rejected the nomination of one Mal Colston, and following one precedent, invited the Labor Party to submit three names to him for consideration. Labor insisted on the appointment of Mal Colston, and the Queensland Parliament appointed Albert Field, a French polisher who had been a member of the Labor Party for 30 years. He was clearly hostile to the Whitlam government and was then expelled from the Labor Party. (The party's power to expel was to be given constitutional effect in the subsequent "reform" which the politicians colluded together to push through).

Senator Field's appointment was challenged for other reasons in the High Court, and he was never able to vote. Senator Bunton refused to join in motions blocking or delaying supply.

(Incidentally, Mal Colston was elected as Labor Senator in 1975, proving to be a controversial senator).[6]

Because of its failure to guarantee supply, Governor-General Sir John Kerr withdrew Mr. Whitlam's commission as Prime Minister on 11 November, and in the subsequent election on 13 December 1975, the Fraser government was elected to office.

The Fraser government proposed four constitutional amendments in 1977, including one to require the filling of vacancies for the same party as the departing senator. This was put to the people by way of a referendum. The provision – effecting a deal between the major parties – was specifically and unequivocally designed to enlarge the powers of the politburos – the executives – of the major parties. This was to deny state parliaments a role in choosing a senator on merit, even one from the same party as the departing senator. This was done by inserting a provision that if the selected member "before taking his seat ceases to be a member of that party" the selection shall be nullified.

Accordingly, a political party need only make a rule automatically expelling any member who accepts Senate selection by a state parliament without the endorsement of the party executive. This would be sufficient to block an appointment made on merit by a state parliament.

Although emanating from the Coalition government led by Malcolm Fraser, the proposal seemed tailor-made for the Labor Party. And of course, it encouraged the emergence of the factions and powerbrokers within the Liberal Party, who now have a valuable prize to dangle in front of ambitious young men and women – provided that they understand that their first duty is to be loyal to a particular factional boss.

It would not be too long before members of the Liberal Party would face expulsion for doing what was once accepted as a member's right in a democratic party – standing against an endorsed candidate, or even lending support to such a candidate (even an independent candidate).[7]

Just as Gresham's law decrees that bad money drives out good, there is no doubt that in Australian politics, bad practices in one major party drive out good practices in the others.

Not only did the major political parties collude in putting this "reform" to the people, instead of concentrating on this important issue, the people were distracted by having to vote on five different issues, including a non-binding plebiscite to choose a national song, not as it is so often reported, a national anthem.

The other referendums were for simultaneous elections – the only one not carried – to allow territorians to vote in referendums and for a retirement age for judges. (The latter was an ill thought out measure. It incorporated a retirement age in the Constitution rather than leaving it to parliament in relation to future appointees. The result is that we have lost some excellent judges who were still in their prime. Unusually, not one politician opposed this measure, so no opposing case was submitted to the people).

Apart from confirming that the parties should control Senate vacancies, the agenda of the major parties was to have the cleverly named Simultaneous Elections referendum passed. The spin was that this was merely to prevent House and Senate elections being out of synchronisation. It was said that this would avoid the holding of additional unnecessary elections.

If this had been approved by the people, it would have significantly increased the power of a prime minister who on advising and securing an election for the House, would be able to empty half the Senate immediately. This would not have been an inadvertent and unintended result. The proposal was designed to achieve this.

It was designed to subvert the original intention of the Constitution. This is that the Senate is intended not to be affected by the vagaries and excited opinions surrounding the holding of a House election. Senators are intended to have six year terms taking effect on the first day of July every three years, no matter when the House term runs. The Senate, emulating the concept of the House of Lords, is intended to be a check and balance on the house, and through its composition, to see issues from a wider perspective. The only exception would be when there was such a deadlock between the houses that a double dissolution was justified.

Recalling that the Coalition parties had opposed a similar proposal by the Whitlam government in 1974, a small number of Senators fortunately persuaded the people to reject the measure.

Unfortunately, the people were also persuaded by the arguments of politicians of both sides that the filling of a vacancy in the Senate should be from the same party as the departing senator. This in fact was what normally happened in the past. Sir Joh Bjelke-Petersen's requirement that three names be submitted was perfectly reasonable in the circumstances. Labor Party leaders would probably subsequently agree with his objections to Mal Colston.

If the people were to have known in 1977 that the constitutional change was designed to give absolute power to the politburos, the party executives – and thus to the powerbrokers – to appoint their lackeys they would not have agreed.[8] If the people were made aware of this abuse now, they would probably wish to reconsider this. Indeed, if this were Switzerland, it would be possible for citizens to call for a reconsideration of this without the prior approval of the likely losers, the key politicians. Unfortunately this is not possible in Australia.

So we have today the situation where a Senate vacancy can be offered by the powerbrokers as a reward, or a consideration for either doing or refraining from doing something, to a loyal member of the faction without any consideration of the merits of the candidate and the representation of the people of the State.

This result is disgraceful and embarrassing for our ancient democracy.

9.3 Senate preferential voting

It is extremely difficult for voters in an election to vote for candidates whose opinion and judgement they trust. In other words, the key criteria of representative democracy as explained by Edmund Burke is extremely difficult to apply.

Voting "above the line" induces a vote for a party, not for individual senators. This was introduced because of the number of candidates in an election resulting in a very large ballot paper. But voting above the line was not the only way in which the task of the voter could be simplified.

A more simple solution would have been to introduce optional voting, that is voting for as many candidates as the elector chooses, from one to the number of candidates. This is not in the interest of the parties, as it would reduce the number of preferences and give the voter absolute control over his or her preferences.

Under the present system voting below the line is not only time-demanding, it is easy to make mistakes and can result in votes being too easily declared informal and lost.[9]

Instead the politicians introduced voting above the line under, by which voters may cast one vote for a group of candidates usually, but not always, under a party label. Each of these groups appears at the top of the ballot paper, and most will bear the name of a party, for example, "Labor", "Liberal", "National", "Greens", etc. It is a requirement that the voter insert the numeral "1" in only one box.

This was an ingenious move by the politicians. Most people are going to vote above the line; voting below the line being too likely to lead to an invalid vote.

Voting above the line forces the voter to choose a party. It stops the voter from thinking about the relative merits of different candidates on a party list, or voting for some candidates from one party and candidates from another. It also stops a voter from voting for some but not all party candidates and some independents.

But there is another consideration which greatly advantages the political parties. The scheme could have allowed voters above the line to express their own preferences. For example a voter voting for a small party, say the Greens, might not wish his or her preferences to go to Labor. That voter might have preferred his or her preferences to go to a group of independents.

The politicians have ensured that voters cannot do this.

This involves a primary vote for a party, without any ability to allocate preferences between the parties. The allocation of preferences is determined by the party executive – after all deals have been done with other parties.

The powerbrokers deals about preference are secret and only become public if someone talks. There is of course absolutely no question of these being available under a Freedom of Information application.

The preferences are set out in a Group Voting Ticket filed with the Australian Electoral Commission. They are accessible on the AEC website, but only a very persistent voter with the computer skills, time, interest and patience can find them. And even if they can, they can't change them.

It is said the preferences are available at polling stations. Neither author can recall seeing them. They are certainly not displayed prominently enough to have noticed, even when looking. We suggest readers ask for these at the next election. If the powerbrokers read this book they may well ensure that these are available, so we will have achieved one thing. We will not however have achieved the democratic right of Australian voters to express their preferences above the line.

The point is that while a party may recommend how preferences should be awarded, surely it is wrong in principle that a party should effectively determine voter's preferences.

Or have the Australian people delegated their voting preferences to the powerbrokers as if we were living in some tin pot dictatorship?

The fact is that the powerbrokers in the major parties have blatantly arranged matters against the public interest to suit them, and in doing so vastly enhanced their influence.

9.4 Making it "easier to vote"

Significant changes to federal electoral law were made in the 1980s to make it "easier to vote", although there was no evidence that there were any serious obstacles to voting, or a public demand to make voting easier.[10]

In 1996, an electoral reform movement, the H.S. Chapman Society was formed by people who are described on the movement's website as victims of, or witnesses of, electoral fraud concerned by the 1983-4 changes to the *Commonwealth Electoral Act*. They quote former Senator Graham Richardson's words in his memoirs that the amendments would "ensure Labor would stay in power as long as possible and make it as difficult as possible to change it".[11]

Notwithstanding the regular assertions that there is little electoral fraud, there remain obvious incentives for fraud that neither the post office nor any credit card provider would tolerate. It would be incredibly naive to believe that powerbrokers in the major parties do not take advantage of these possibilities, especially those with a background in organisations versed in electoral matters, electoral slush funds and the like.

Official inquiries apart, the media have shown very limited interest in investigating this. A major investigation by Sydney's Channel 9 was an exception.[12] Radio station 2GB has also pursued the matter, the latest being by Michael McLaren.[13]

In the meantime, the parliament continues a campaign to increase enrolments and make it easier to vote. In 2012, it authorised the Australian Electoral Commission to directly enrol potential voters via "automatic enrolment", a term which the AEC discourages.[14] This was widely criticised at the time. If that criticism is incorrect, and this is an honest attempt to increase enrolments, the question remains: why are such obvious incentives for fraud accepted? Why are those incentives not removed?

The obvious answer is that the existence of those incentives is in the interests of the powerbrokers. There can be no other possible answer.

Those incentives for fraud relate to identification – or the lack thereof – on voting in person, on enrolling to vote and in the process of declaration voting.

Some have also suggested that we make it "easier to vote" through the introduction of online voting – a proposal completely unrelated to the implementation of an electronic roll (which we explore below).

If implemented, such a proposal is fraught with dangers. Without a paper trail, there is massive potential for fraud. There is also the potential to compromise voter anonymity. And even if it were possible to implement technology which achieves the required level on anonymity, it would be next to impossible to reassure voters of its merits.

9.5 Identification on voting

When the name of the voter is crossed off the roll in one polling station, or when casting an absentee vote, that name should ideally be crossed off on every copy of the roll, in every polling station in Australia, and overseas.

After the 2010 elections 29,920 letters were sent to people who appeared to have voted more than once, an increase of 45% over the previous election. The actual ballot papers cannot be identified. In the Senate election that year there were 85,726 more votes than for the House of Representatives, an increase of 50% over the previous election.[15]

The solution appears simple. In one stroke, the possibility of voting more than once could be eliminated, provided of course the first vote was by the actual voter and not someone else. That could be avoided by requiring the voter to provide identification.

The technology to link the rolls in order to rule off a name of a voter has long been available, and is used constantly in relation to credit cards. Providing such a link would involve some cost, but nothing compared with the waste which is so typical of government. At the beginning of the year 2013, it was estimated that the interest on government debt amounted to about $20 million a day. The waste on the Building the Education Revolution project was officially found to be over $1 billion, but estimates following investigative reporting by *The Australian* and by Ray Hadley on the Macquarie Broadcasting Network indicate that it would be more in the vicinity of $5 or $6 billion.

That such a computer link is not in place in polling stations is because it is not in the interests of the powerbrokers to install this. We cannot believe that the ministers are so naive that they actually believe people do not vote more than once, or that it is possible this is not always brought to the AEC's attention. If they are so naive they should surely not be entrusted with any official position.

Is it not then reasonable to conclude that not linking the polling stations must be the preferred policy of this and previous governments?

The future direction of the country can depend on one election. This can mean the difference between good government; and incompetence, massive waste and duplicity on a grand scale.

Why should it be possible that an election be decided fraudulently?

9.6 Identification on enrolment

Then there is the problem created when the High Court upheld a challenge by GetUp!, the left wing activist organisation, just before the 2010 election, to the closing of the rolls at 8pm on the day the election writs are issued.[16] This was introduced by the Howard government to prevent the potential for substantial fraud concealed in the last minute flood of registrations which can be effected by minimal formalities – a driving licence number and the signature of another voter.

The fact that the applicants to the High Court were in breach of the law and had plenty of time to register did not stop the court from granting an expedited hearing, as if some grave injustice had occurred.

Then the Court announced its decision on 6 August 2010 without indicating that it was a narrow decision. It was not until 15 December, over four months later and just before Christmas, that the Court released the judges' reasons, with the majority relying on an activist interpretation of the Constitution.

GetUp! has not been backward in claiming that they won a great victory in this case. They say it had 100,000 disenfranchised voters on the roll. And it just so happened that in 11 electorates, those voters determined the result.

On past experience a number of these would be fraudulent enrolments.

The point is the Constitution clearly intends that the detail about running an election – including the time for the closing of the rolls – is for parliament, and not the High Court. The Constitution had even left the determination of the franchise to parliament. Accordingly, female suffrage was granted by parliament soon after federation and not under the Constitution itself.

Nowhere in the Constitution does it say that the rolls must stay open after the election is called. Without any authority, on the nominal application of two persons both in breach of the law, and organised by a left wing activist group, four judges have amended the Constitution.

The judges are not above the Constitution. It surely does not mean what they want it to mean.

As with the politicians, the judges need to be reminded that they are the servants and not the masters. Their role is to apply the Constitution, not to rewrite it.

It is therefore completely understandable that one of our great constitutional lawyers, Emeritus Professor Geoffrey de Q. Walker, has proposed that High Court judges too should be subject to recall by the people.[17]

9.7 Declaration voting

In 2002, Dr. Amy McGrath warned that the number of voters applying for pre-poll and postal votes was then so great that it could change the fate of many a candidate in an election, and even elections themselves.[18]

When over 84% of votes were being cast in the polling stations, Dr. McGrath warned that the dramatic increase indicated that voters were using the declaration voting arrangements as a form of convenience voting, rather than for their original intention. She warned that the increase in declaration votes meant that elections could be delayed, the cost of administering them increased and with the increased usage of postal voting there might be negative implications on the secrecy of the ballot.[19]

Her conclusion was that these are issued, and cast, with scant regard to the original requirements of declaration voting. The first requirement has since been withdrawn. This was that the voter be well-known to the witness, who had to be drawn from a limited list of authorised witnesses. In actual practice the second requirement is not observed. This is that it would be difficult to attend a polling place on polling day.

The point surely is that an election should reflect the choice of the nation on election day, after we have all been exposed to the same debates.

Since Dr. McGrath made these comments, the number of declaration votes has increased even more. In the 2010 election, only 74% of the votes were cast at polling stations. Declaration votes were almost 26% of the total vote.

A British expert in these matters, Richard Mawrey QC, visited Australia in 2010 and gave his opinion on convenience or easy voting. Sitting as a British High Court judge, he had found six Labour councillors guilty of electoral fraud in the 2004 Birmingham Council election. This made news not only in the UK, but around the world. And in a splendidly bipartisan approach, he subsequently found that Conservative councillors had engaged in fraud in the Slough Council election.

He discussed these findings in the two interviews given in Australia. In these, he referred to "[e]lectoral fraud which would disgrace a banana republic," and observed that "[e]asy voting is fraudulent voting". He warned that the longer the period between the calling of an election and the closing of the rolls, the greater the likelihood of undetectable fraudulent registrations.[20]

Clearly, declaration voting should only be allowed when it is established that a person cannot reasonably be expected to go to a polling place on election day. And it should be cast in such a way to ensure that it is a secret ballot.

The politicians have ensured that these basic requirements are not being observed – indeed they are encouraging the use of declaration voting and the submission of requests for a declaration vote through their offices. This leads to the obvious temptation to filter these, whether or not this is exercised. The temptation would be not to activate those requests where the party database may indicate a hostile vote was likely. Such a temptation should not exist in a democratic society.

According to one report, voters known to be hostile to a political party have had their applications for postal votes delayed – and in some cases destroyed – by party campaign workers.[21]

Declaration voting is a tool in the arsenal of the major parties to increase their votes, making it more difficult for candidates from smaller parties and independents to succeed, and allowing the most skilled at abusing the requirements to obtain more votes, not the party with the more appealing policies.

Such advantages should not be allowed in a democratic society.

9.8 Taxpayers' funding of elections

The political parties' election campaigns are now, to a very significant degree, funded by the taxpayers.

When the politicians proposed the funding by taxpayers of their political parties, they had a serious conflict of interest. This was because there is an obvious incentive to continue to force taxpayers to vote. Without compulsory voting the amount taken from the taxpayers would fall. A declaration of interest should at least have been made, as should politicians who today benefit from this scheme.

The amount of funding is calculated by multiplying the number of formal first preference votes received by the election funding rate. This is indexed and from 1 January 2013 to 30 June 2013 is 248.800 cents per eligible vote.

This favours the established parties and allows them to increase their grip on parliamentary representation. The argument usually advanced is that this reduces the chances of large benefactors gaining advantages from government.

But Australian politicians from the major political parties have it both ways. To a considerable degree their election is funded by the taxpayer. When they leave office they frequently gain a considerable commercial advantage from the connections they made while serving the people.

The mere knowledge of this while in office is an incentive to act corruptly. There is no need to agree in advance on such a connection even with a wink and a nod.

That there is not a ban on entering into any such arrangement for a reasonable period of time is in itself a scandal. After that period a former politician should still be accountable for such lobbying.

The politicians have never attended to providing, if not a barrier to this, some significant disadvantage to this nefarious practice. Instead they have voted themselves increased remuneration from the taxpayers – or the "independent" machinery to ensure this – arguing in part that this will prevent corrupt influence over their actions.

In the 2010 election the ALP received $21,225,869.96, the Liberal Party $21,097,860.24, the Greens $7,212,923.38, the National Party, $2,485,700.16, Family First $407,268.37 and Country Liberals (Northern Territory) $179,411.15.

Independents also received funding, including Tony Windsor (New England, NSW) who received $130,426.40, Robert Oakeshott (Lyne, NSW) who received $92,617.43, Bob Katter (Kennedy, Qld) who received $88,245.60 and Andrew Willkie (Denison, Tas) who received $31,876.62.[22]

9.9 Conclusion

It is clear that over the years, Australian politicians have manipulated the electoral system to suit their narrow purposes, or indeed, the narrow purposes of the factional powerbrokers. No significant reform has been introduced with the public interest in mind. Everything has been done to secure the narrow interests of the major parties and especially the powerbrokers. Ten simple reforms would overcome this.[23]

This is an area of the law which should be especially subject to the correcting influence of the Australian people through the tools of direct democracy.

Endnotes

1 *Electoral Reform*, a Discussion Paper, Department of Justice and Attorney-General, January 2013, p. 35. http://www.justice.qld.gov.au/__data/assets/pdf_file/0007/171529/disc-ppr-electroal-reform.pdf (retrieved 5.01.2013).

2 Loc. cit.

3 http://www.theaustralian.com.au/opinion/cut-paste/once-upon-a-summetime-when-the-long-bows-are-drawn-and-the-chatter-is-high/story-fn72xczz-1226547816239 (retrieved 5.01.2012).

4 See below, 9.8 Taxpayers funding of elections.

5 Sir David Smith, *Head of State*, McLeay Press, Paddington, 2005, pp. 264-266.

6 Senator Colston became an independent in 1996 and sitting as a Queensland First Senator thereafter. In 1997 he was charged with defrauding the Commonwealth but the prosecution withdrew the charges on medical evidence that he would not live long enough for a trial to be completed. He retired on 30 June 1999 and died in 2003.

7 Constitution of The Liberal Party of Australia NSW Division as amended 12 September 2009 (3.12.1 State Executive May Expel Member). In 2004, after an acrimonious preselection for the seat of Wentworth involving accusations of branch stacking , the Liberal MP Peter King stood as an independent against the newly endorsed Liberal candidate, Malcolm Turnbull. Peter King was expelled, as were several members of the party who lent him support.

8 It was first implemented in relation to SA Senator Steele Hall, who was elected as a Liberal Movement Senator, but later changed to the Liberal Party of Australia. As the Liberal Movement had merged with the Australian Democrats, a nominee of the Democrats was chosen, Janine Haines.

9 Some errors are tolerated, see http://www.aec.gov.au/Voting/How_to_Vote/Voting_Senate.htm (retrieved 5.01.2013).

10 *Commonwealth Electoral Act*, 1918; on electoral fraud see the website of the HS Chapman Society: http://www.hschapman.org/(retrieved 31.07.2012).

11 http://www.hschapman.org/ The movement's Dr. Amy McGrath OAM has written *The Forging of Votes 1995* about union fraud in the Federated Ironworkers' Union, and *The Frauding of Votes 1996* about parliamentary fraud.

12 http://www.youtube.com/watch?v=Y6NaKnoq9k0&feature=related http://www.youtube.com/watch?v=nv1nkrOacQ4&feature=related   http://www.youtube.com/v/IzXUCQ0CIIE&hl=en&fs=1 (retrieved 07.05.2013).

13 Interview with Bruce Kirkpatrick http://www.2gb.com/article/vote-fraud-part-1.ed. (retrieved 07.05.2013).

14 *Commonwealth Electoral Act*, 1918 (Cth) s.103A.

15 R.A. Beatty "Vote Early & Vote Often" Analysis – Federal Elections 2007 and 2010. http://www.bosmin.com/ICS/FederalElections07-10.pdf (retrieved 07.05.2013).

16 *Rowe* v *Electoral Commissioner* [2010] HCA 46.

17 Geoffrey de Q. Walker, *Initiative and Referendum:The People's Law*, Sydney, Centre of Independent Studies, Sydney, 1987, pp. 157-162.

18 http://www.hschapman.org/pdfs/Styles%20of%20Voting/Pre-Poll%20and%20Postal%20Votes.pdf (retrieved 31.07.2012).

19 Gerry Newman, *Research Report 3, Analysis of Declaration Voting*, Australian Electoral Commission, 2004, updated 2011. http://www.aec.gov.au/About_AEC/Publications/Strategy_Research_Analysis/paper3/(retrieved 29.12.2012).

20 Interview by Professor David Flint with Richard Mawrey QC, 25 February 2010. http://www.norepublic.com.au/index.php?option=com_content&task=view&id=2 310&Itemid=4

21 Peter van Onselen, "Political parties' postal vote abuse in firing line", *The Australian*, 29 July 2011. http://www.theaustralian.com.au/national-affairs/political-parties-postal-vote-abuse-in-firing-line/story-fn59niix-1226103797474 (retrieved 4.01.2013).

22 http://www.aec.gov.au/about_aec/media_releases/e2010/13-10.htm (retrieved 31.07.2012).

23 Ten reforms:

1. Enrolment is as important as opening a bank account and should be similar.
2. The obligation should be on people to register, not bureaucrats to do it for them.
3. Everybody should be able to see the rolls to see if people are illegally registered in our house, in neighbouring houses, in house numbers that don't exist, in parks, cemeteries or rivers.
4. The rolls should close the same day that the G-G calls the election.
5. With only special exceptions, everyone should vote on the same day.
6. We should all vote in our subdivision – not in any one of, say, twenty places in a large electorate.
7. When we go to vote, we should identify ourselves with a card from the electoral commission printed with a barcode – just like the ones on goods at the supermarket.
8. When our card is read, our name would be simultaneously ruled off everywhere.
9. Not everybody has a spare $100,000 to go to the High Court. A respected Electoral Ombudsman should be appointed to check on any problems to resolve disputes.
10. Any enquiries should be referred to a respected standing Special Commissioner

CHAPTER 10

Manipulating the system

10.1 The law does not apply to politicians

Voters would be surprised to know how federal politicians, using the powers of the parliament to make laws for the "peace, order and good government" of the nation have established a scheme which gives massive advantages to the major political parties which as we have seen are too often the personal fiefdoms of the factional powerbrokers.

We can see here an elaborate pincer operation designed to favour the major political parties. A law on privacy was enacted by parliament for Australians to obey; but with the first side of the pincer operation, a special exemption for the political parties.[1] Accordingly the politicians can keep information about Australians which would be illegal for most organisations.

The other side of the pincer operation is in the provisions of the *Commonwealth Electoral Act*, 1918, under which they are entitled to privileged access to the electoral rolls. Not only are members of parliament, senators and registered political parties supplied with print and electronic copies of the rolls, they also get access to confidential electoral roll information.[2]

This has allowed the parties to develop databases containing information which would not be available to other organisations. In addition, it allows them to enter information on the databases obtained by politicians from electors in the course of representing them.

This includes information gleaned from electors who approach their local members for advice and assistance. The electors would be entitled to think this is confidential unless, of course, they have specifically agreed to its release.

It is not.

This information is effectively stolen from the electors who have revealed it to a member of parliament or a senator – or more likely a member of their staff – in the course of their public duties. This can include information about their weaknesses, health, religion, financial status, family relationships, taxation issues – anything which is extremely private and personal information.

This can be improperly converted to advantage one of the major political parties. If just about any other person or entity retained such information there would be outrage, no doubt including outrage from the political class.

This information and the confidential details from the Australian Electoral Commission provide valuable profiles on electors. They are consolidated into growing databases which can be accessed for electoral purposes by staff whose salaries, computers and offices are funded by taxpayers.

Electors do not of course have access to these databases to see what is stored about them and to correct errors.

A serious abuse of these privileges can involve the sending out of invitations to electors to apply for a postal vote before an election. When these are returned to the politician's office the databases can be checked. According to one report by a respected commentator, voters known to be hostile to a political party have had their applications for postal votes delayed – and in some cases even destroyed – by campaign workers.[3]

And who created this very cosy arrangement – one which other organisations cannot duplicate? The answer is of course our elected representatives – the politicians. Did they vote for this in the public interest? Or was it in their interest – and not yours?

10.2 Building up support

The emergence of an essentially Labor Party and Greens loyal power base made up of healthy people capable of working but dependent on government is not unique to Australia. This is a modern version of the "bread and circuses" which the Roman emperors used to keep the populace docile.

Marx referred to their 19th century predecessors of the welfare dependent as the lumpenproletariat. They were then a marginal group of no electoral importance, eking out an existence so precarious that in some countries starvation was not an unknown prospect. Today those capable of working but welfare dependent are generously subsidised through the taxes of mainly ordinary Australians struggling to keep up with the cost of maintaining a family. They are neither aged, nor injured through accident, nor ill through natural causes, nor indeed otherwise deserving.

In Australia in 2009-10, 60% of households received more in direct social benefits than they paid in taxes and 26.4% of individual taxpayers paid no net income tax. Twenty years ago, this proportion was only 14.3%.[4] The Australian welfare dependent class has become so large that we have one of the lowest workforce participation rates in the developed world.[5] The Centre for Independent Studies has found that almost one in six working age Australians relies on welfare for all or part of their income.[6]

Robert Carling concludes rightly that the welfare state has gone far beyond a "safety net" concept. There is a large constituency whose direct financial interests are best served by the preservation or enhancement of social benefits. And the top 40% of households are bearing the burden, paying 72% of the taxes and receiving 22% of the benefits.

Rarely disturbed by Coalition governments, this class nevertheless fears them and thus tends to direct their votes to those whom they expect to protect their interests. They are "rolled gold" in any election especially in a country with compulsory and preferential voting.

The United Kingdom government recently attempted to review aspects of the welfare safety net. The question was whether there were significant numbers of welfare recipients who were improperly taking advantage of the system. This is of course what any prudent government should do. Indeed we would suggest that every government has a duty to do this.

So in late 2010 to early 2012, 431,100 claimants for the UK Incapacity Benefit were re-assessed; 145,000 were found to be fit for work. Almost 40,000 of these claimants had been claiming the Incapacity Benefit for more than 10 years.[7] Then in May 2011, unemployed claimants were deemed lacking the personal skills necessary to find and keep a job (i.e., those thought to be "work-shy") were required to undertake a one-month work placement. If they refused, or failed to complete the placement, they could lose their benefit for three months; repeated failures triggered longer sanctions.

In the first 15 months of the scheme, 90,000 claimants were referred to a work placement with 33,000 attending. The rest either found themselves jobs, or simply stopped claiming. As Professor Saunders says "some undoubtedly already had jobs in the 'black economy'."

National Disability Scheme

It is appropriate to recall this in the light of the fact that both parties support the introduction in Australia of a National Disability Scheme, a desirable reform for the disabled. Andrew Baker of the Centre for Independent Studies predicts that by 2023-24, "the NDIS eligible population will likely grow to about 500,000, and cost nearly $30 billion a year. The NDIS will need more than 8,000 public servants to administer the scheme."[8]

This is a desirable and important reform. But on past experience, the scheme is likely to be mismanaged and a number of claimants will successfully receive benefits under the scheme without any justification. Will there be safeguards in place to avoid this and ensure the scheme only benefits the deserving? From previous experience we can have no confidence that the politicians and bureaucrats will ensure this.

The experience of a widely respected general practitioner is apposite. He told one of the authors how a 40-year-old patient came to see him seeking the doctor's certification that he should receive a disability pension. The doctor undertook the necessary examination and found that the man was in good health. When he advised his patient, the patient responded: "Don't worry; I'll find a doctor who will help me."

The GP saw his former patient some months later. He boasted that he was now in receipt of a disability pension. The doctor said: "I won't report this to Centrelink. When I've done it in the past they have done nothing and admitted that they would be doing nothing. Worse, the unworthy pensioner was told of what I had done. We honest doctors know that is not worth our while to tell Centrelink."

In early 2013, people were surprised to see a photograph in the Sydney *Daily Telegraph* of a rioter, Omar Halaby, smashing a milk crate into a police car in a riot in Sydney in September 2012.[9] It was about an American video on YouTube. His Legal Aid lawyer, Sophie Eden, told the court that he suffered from "certain disabilities" which led him to claim the pension for the past three years. "He has some physical problems in relation to football accidents ... he has literacy issues, a short attention span, things to that effect."

Because of this he receives a $200-a-fortnight disability support pension, but works as well.

The controversial Sydney magistrate Pat O'Shane put him on a 12 month good behaviour bond. Muslim community leader Keyser Trad said it was often difficult for Muslims to find employment. Mr. Trad seems to assume the disability pension is for the unemployed. This is a view held by some politicians because it reduces the unemployment figures.

At June 2012, 827,460 people were receiving the disability pension, costing taxpayers about $15 billion a year. This is expected to rise to close to $17 billion in 2015-16. This contrasts with 588,807 receiving the unemployed benefit.

There is a clear incentive to move from the unemployment benefit, which is $257.70 a week, to the disability support benefit which at $404.20 a week is not only significantly higher, but offers the added attractions of easier income tests, significant fringe benefits and fewer work tests.[10]

The numbers receiving the disability support benefit are obviously bloated by shifting the unemployed, especially the older unemployed, onto this, as well as able-bodied people who have elected not to work.

Mission Australia chief Toby Hall recently warned, "The evidence absolutely shows, with the right support, about 350,000 to 400,000 people could go back into the work force, which is why we think it is such an important issue."

"Those people, through no fault of their own, are left without a proper level of support. They don't have access to employment like everyone else. That is wrong."[11]

The responsibility for this is lies with the politicians. They have failed in their duty to ensure that the disability pension operates only as a safety net for deserving cases. They have let it grow to an impossible level through a mixture of deceit, negligence and plain vote buying.

This is yet another reason to make the politicians truly accountable to the people.

The politicians introducing and administering the National Disability Scheme have a duty to see that it acts as a safety net for some very deserving people and only them, and not also as a scheme to defraud taxpayers.

Abuse of the immigration power

It seems that the practice of improperly funding or otherwise favouring voters for electoral purposes may extend to the use – or rather the abuse – of the federal government's immigration power.

According to *The Sydney Morning Herald*'s Paul Sheehan, the former federal minister and at that time President of the Australian Labor Party, Barry Jones, addressing the annual conference of Australians for an Ecologically Sustainable Population, conceded that this had occurred under Labor.[12]

Paul Sheehan quotes Barry Jones as saying:

> The handling of immigration by the previous [Labor] government was, I'd have to say, less than distinguished. Partly because, I think, immigration was seen as very important – tremendously important element – in building up a long-term political constituency.
>
> There was a sense that you might get the Greek vote locked up or, from the other party-political points of view, you might get the Chinese vote locked up ... As a result, the idea of bringing groups of people to fulfil family reunion requirements, and so on, was seen at the time as being a real advantage to the party in power at the time.

The truth, Paul Sheehan said, was even more brutal. The immigration program proved tremendously important during the 13 years of Labor federal government to 1996, as it has in recent years.

"The family reunion program was, as Jones said, crucial to this strategy. Labor used immigration to restock its urban seats with people who would be dependent on government largesse – seen as Labor's largesse."

According to Paul Sheehan, neutral grassroots activists such as Sheila Christophedes – she worked for the No Aircraft Noise Party in Sydney during the 1996 Federal election – found that Labor's strategy had captured the bulk of these new voters.

"When I was door-knocking I could tell that Labor propaganda was really working with migrants who had little English skills," she says. "A lot of them told me, `We only vote Labor'. They believed that if John Howard were elected, Medicare would be in jeopardy, immigration would be in jeopardy, (and) that Howard would actively discriminate against ethnic minorities."

Paul Sheehan concludes that this strategy worked.

He says that the only section of the electorate to "hold firm" for Labor in the 1996 Federal election were the urban electorates with heavy non-English-speaking background (NESB) immigrant populations.

He says that Labor's policy of "skewing immigration" towards family reunion increased the number of unskilled migrants. This he says resulted in some migrant streams that have been economic disasters. They formed "pockets of unemployment and welfare dependence at levels not seen since the Depression".

Eventually the mainstream electorate realised this, turning against Labor "with a fury". The Labor primary vote fell to 38.8%. This he says was a massive rebuke for a government at a time of economic growth and relatively sound economic management.

"The depth of this anger was in part fuelled by an electorate tired of being ignored and patronised and silenced on the issues of social cohesion and special-interest rorting."

Since the Rudd government dismantled the Howard government's successful "Pacific Solution", we have seen the development of people smuggling businesses which have delivered to the date of writing around 40,000 "clients" to Australia, magnified by a factor of perhaps three with the reapplication of the family reunion program to those with the now permanent residency visa which replaced the now abolished temporary protection visas.

Most of the people smugglers' clients have not come from a place of alleged persecution but from a safe third country, usually Indonesia. Most have hidden or destroyed their passports. Once released into the community most go on to welfare, some even working as people smugglers.

Paul Sheehan says the police have not seen as large a gap in quality control in the flow of unskilled and welfare-dependent arrivals since the refugee flow from Lebanon in the 1970s.[13]

After four years, only about 25% are in full-time work.[14] Vast numbers of asylum seekers are being released from the overcrowded detention centres with bridging visas which allow detainees to enter the community, work, and most importantly to receive something regular immigrants cannot receive for two years, welfare benefits.

Among the benefits available in addition to welfare is a one-off household formation package for those in community detention of up to $9,850, with education assistance of up to $9,220.[15] They receive Medicare assistance for medical, hospital, dental, medicine and optical costs. Some are given mobile phones. In addition they receive free legal aid. While even Australians on welfare must pay the recent very large increases in court fees, illegal immigrants are exempt.[16] So not only are illegal immigrants welcomed to Australia, they receive what no one else does, a standing invitation to sue the government completely at the taxpayers' expense.

Paul Sheehan points out that this has reduced the average time spent in detention from nine months to three months, but "the quicker turnover has compressed the scrutiny process".

He refers to the scandal revealed by the ABC of "Captain Emad", Abu Khalid, a people smuggler, who came claiming to be an asylum seeker. "He brought his wife, three children and a grandchild. All received refugee status, settled in Canberra and were provided with public housing despite using different identities to those they used to enter Indonesia from Iraq. Yet even after Khalid's activities were exposed by the ABC's *Four Corners* program, he was allowed to leave."

One of the most disturbing features of this wave of illegal immigration was the revelation by *The Australian*'s Paul Maley that full ASIO security checks were suspended on 13 August 2012 when the processing of asylum-seekers was suspended. Because the detention centres are full, many are being released into the community with the full security check being delayed until they are assessed as refugees.[17] Most will have no identification, although those from Indonesia must have arrived with passports. This is an extraordinary breach of security.

The government has lost control of the borders. Is it just that the government is incompetent? Or is it, as some believe, part of an agenda to change Australia, an agenda of boats for votes?

10.3 Using taxpayer funds to influence voters

In recent years Australian governments have been spending between $100 and $200 million dollars a year in government advertising.[18] Much of this is political advertising. The major political parties have all abused government advertising. The systems put in place to restrain such misuse by various governments have proved ineffective, no doubt deliberately so.

In 2011-12, the government spent $139.7 million on campaign advertising media placement, 20% more than in the previous year. But in the year from 1 January 2007, the Howard's government spent $254 million, 60% of which was spent during its final five months in office.[19]

Taxpayer funded political advertising is an abuse which calls out for a cure. It is unlikely that those who benefit from this are prepared to put in place sufficient controls to ensure this never happens and that there are no exceptions.

In addition to such political advertising, the taxpayers are funding opinion polling, focus groups and customer surveys which are undertaken by federal government departments and agencies in order to finesse the government's political and policy messages. In an analysis of the available data, *The Australian* found the Rudd and Gillard governments spent $126 million over the four years 2008-2012 for this purpose.[20]

The Australian's Tom Dusevic writes that:

The ability to commission and draw on the information

collected from these forays into community attitudes is one of the key advantages of incumbency. It allows a government to fashion ministerial talking points, to identify problems in service delivery and to assess the popularity of policies – before and after they are implemented.[21]

In the meantime the government has significantly increased the number of spin doctors working on the government's message. Their 1,600 or so spin doctors cost taxpayers about $150 million dollars a year.[22]

In addition, there are also more spin doctors in the parallel public service that governments now surround themselves with, the so-called ministerial advisors.

Among the Prime Minister's, there is her chief spin doctor, John McTernan, imported under the government's maligned 457 visa from the UK. He had gained, shall we say, certain notoriety when he spun for the Blair government.

He became well known here when he phoned 2GB's financial commentator, Ross Greenwood, who described the call as an "absolute tirade" laced with incessant use of the "F" word.

Recognition ceremonies

In a bizarre program which is redolent more of an authoritarian country or even a dictatorship, schools with recently finished Building the Education Revolution buildings will be required to hold "recognition ceremonies" during this election year. They are to praise the government and invite federal Employment Minister Bill Shorten to speak, according to a report by Gemma Jones in the Sydney *Daily Telegraph* on 24 January 2013.[23]

This $16.2 billion program, administered by the then Minister of Education Julia Gillard, led to a scandalous waste of money particularly in a number of public schools. An enquiry was established without the power to compel witnesses to appear, to protect them or for the production of documents. That found that the waste involved extended to well over $1 billion. The *Australian* and radio station 2GB's Ray Hadley concluded that the waste point to several billion dollars. This included the provision of buildings not asked for and the tearing down of buildings and their replacement by buildings of lesser use. In at least one case, a building was completed in a school which was soon to be closed.

Gemma Jones reported that an online kit sent to schools advises teachers they are to make "provision in the official proceedings for the Minister Bill Shorten or his representative to speak" at ceremonies which are not to be planned for parliamentary sitting days.[24]

Students can only be asked to speak "where possible and where time permits". Schools are directed to "acknowledge the government's assistance in all speeches and publicity issued by the school such as newsletters, websites or local media articles".

Staff are also instructed to "record the day through photographs or video footage" and publish the material on the school website and to provide parking for guests, with a government plaque to be fixed to the building.

Ceremonies have taken place for several years based on the same guidelines. The government has been criticised for continuing them in an election year.

The ceremonies could take place at more than 1,000 schools, with about 13 per cent still to host the recognition events the Department of Education says are "required".

10.4 Potentially improper influence

The practice has developed in recent years of politicians taking lucrative positions usually as lobbyists soon after leaving parliament, notwithstanding generous superannuation (often announced to be for the purpose of spending more time with their families). This will often involve lobbying governments to obtain decisions favourable to their clients, and even assuring opposition support.

There is of course the distinct possibility that such positions may be granted as a reward for past favours. The incentive for corrupt behaviour is obvious.

In any event, in the new role the ex-politician will invariable rely on time spent and contacts made while in office.

All of this is unacceptable. The politicians are generously cared for under their superannuation and other arrangements.

These practices are unacceptable in a representative democracy but are tolerated by a consensus among the principal parties who have compromised the system.

It should obviously be illegal for MPs to accept positions in any business which is related to matters on which they may have been involved as a politician, whether in voting, speaking or other legislative or executive roles. This should last for a reasonable period. After that period a former politician should still be accountable for such lobbying.

10.5 A parallel public service

From the time of the Whitlam government, a parallel public service of ministerial advisers has been set up in ministers' offices, with smaller staff establishments made available to the opposition parties. Where once a prime minister, even in wartime, functioned with less than half a dozen assistants, a prime minister today now seems to see the need to have around sixty advisers.

Their principal task is to advance the political interests of the minister.

A large number seem too inexperienced to be advisers. Rather many seem to be ambitious young embryonic politicians, who spend a vast amount of time in Machiavellian plotting.

A highlight was the Australia Day riot in 2012 when an adviser was involved in the misrepresentation of an observation by Opposition Leader Tony Abbott about the future of the so-called "Aboriginal Embassy", semi-permanent structures which disfigure the foreground of old Parliament House, but which the politicians have been unable to remove.

Tony Abbott did not say that the "embassy" should be pulled down but that message was conveyed indirectly to the aboriginal meeting. The result was a riot outside of a Canberra restaurant where awards for bravery were being presented by Prime Minister Gillard in the presence of Tony Abbott as Opposition Leader. Instead of "reading the Riot Act", the police decided that the Prime Minister and the Leader of the Opposition should flee from the restaurant to their car. The Prime Minister was carried bodily part of the way with her face almost in the ground, video reports of this went around the world and made the nation a laughing stock. In accordance with police practice these days, no arrests were made then or indeed subsequently. Although the adviser said he did not misrepresent Mr. Abbott's words, he resigned.[25]

The danger of maintaining a large highly politicised parallel public service of advisers was clearly demonstrated on this occasion.

Not content with that the politicians – of all parties – have moved to politicise what was once a splendid ornament of Australian democracy, a truly independent public service, which is the subject of the following section. The existence of a parallel public service has exacerbated this.

In 2012, the head of the Business Council of Australia, Jennifer Westacott, warned public servants: "Your authority has been undermined by political gatekeepers, often with little expertise and no accountability ... Australia now has more personal staff per minister than many other comparable countries."[26]

University of Queensland Professor of Public Administration Ken Wiltshire supported these views and told *The Australian* that bad decisions were costing billions of dollars.[27]

"Ministerial advisers are a worry – they're part of the politicisation of the public service and having heads of departments on contracts is part of that politicisation as well," he said.

"The public service should provide frank and fearless advice to the minister. If the minister wants political advice, they should go to the advisers but we shouldn't mix the stew."

Professor Wiltshire worked with the Institute of Public Administration Australia earlier this year to test 22 major federal programs including Building the Education Revolution, the National Broadband Network and the home insulation scheme. Three-quarters of those programs failed a test devised by Professor Wiltshire to judge them by their ability to demonstrate a policy need and other factors. Based on federal government outlays in the period 2007 to 2012, he estimated that the poor decision process had probably cost taxpayers $15-$20 billion. The National Broadband Network was, he said, probably the greatest example of poor policy in the history of the nation.[28]

10.6 Politicising the public service

The emergence of a non-partisan public or civil service under the Westminster system coincided with the withdrawal of the Crown from political activity and the emergence of the constitutional monarchy as we know it. It is said the great Walter Bagehot advised the Canadians in 1867 that to ensure popular rule, there were only two constitutional models available for them: the British or the American ones.

Not only did a non-partisan public service not exist in the US, he believed it was impossible to have one. Under the Westminster system, the loyalty of the public servant is to the non political Crown and not to the politicians. This enforces the obligation of the public servant to act within and according to law, and to provide advice not influenced by and indifferent to political considerations.

Unlike an American president, our prime minister is untenured and at all times dependent on the confidence of the lower house. This allows for one of the jewels of our system, a peaceful and efficient transfer of political power. A leading example of this difference between the American and Westminster systems came after the failed Bay of Pigs invasion of Cuba in 1961.

President Kennedy, who agreed he was responsible for the failed intervention, told the CIA deputy head, Alan Dulles: "Under a parliamentary system of government it is I who would be leaving. But under our system it is you who must go."[29]

The contrast between the public services of the countries of the Commonwealth and the states of the US remains, even if in Australia in recent years there has been some regrettable weakening of this principle in regard to the higher echelons of the public service.

If the 2009 Australian OzCar (or "Ute-gate") affair demonstrated anything, it was that the ideal should remain that of an independent public service.[30] A constitutional monarchy is a fertile field for this because it is designed to allow an easy transfer of political power, the prime minister being untenured and at all times dependent on the confidence of the lower house.

Our great wartime Labor Prime Minister John Curtin accepted this. When, as Leader of the Opposition, he was offered confidential material by a delinquent public servant, he said: "No matter has given me so much concern, as it affects the public administration and the loyalty of persons in the service of the Crown, and I had to choose what my highest duty to my country was." According to his biographer Lloyd Ross, he showed the documents to the then Prime Minister Robert G. Menzies and Treasurer Arthur Fadden at the earliest opportunity.[31]

In the Westminster realms, the Crown remains the central institution providing leadership beyond the political arena. As Viscount James Bryce is reputed to have said, it is not so much the power the Crown wields, but the power it denies to anyone else, which is important. This means that the politicians are required to justify proposals and, in the area of the reserve powers, must accept decisions made by the viceroy in his or her discretion.

In addition, the other institutions outside of the political arena, the judiciary, armed forces, police and public service, do not in the

Westminster system owe their allegiance to the politicians, even if chosen through the political process. They owe their allegiance to the Crown which is a trustee for the people. They, as well as the politicians, owe allegiance to the Crown. This is reinforced by their swearing an oath of allegiance.

We have over the years seen a serious diminution of the independence of the higher echelons of the public service. Some say this began when Mr. Whitlam introduced the office of the ministerial "staffer", a party political advisor who is paid by the taxpayer. The number of these has increased substantially. They do not give disinterested advice in the public interest, as public servants do: they act in the narrow party political interest of their minister or opposition shadow minister.

The turning point was when the Hawke government removed the tenure of the heads, and took control of appointments. Once this powerbrokers' delight was put in place, his successor would follow, whether reluctantly or joyfully. As soon as John Howard came to office, he appointed new heads of several departments. Mr. Rudd waited until August 2009 to do the same.

John Curtin would have been horrified. He would not have accepted the gift of a utility, nor would businessmen pay a small fortune to meet his ministers, nor did he expect a lucrative lobbyist role after early retirement on a generous superannuation.

John Curtin died in office, having led the country through war. He gave his life for the nation.

There is a fundamental difference between today's politicians and statesmen of the calibre of John Curtin. This was that he honoured and respected our institutions and our heritage. He had a deep understanding of them.

He understood that the independence of the public service can only be achieved if they owe their allegiance not to the politicians, but to the Crown and therefore all of the people.

At the time when the noble, humble and incorruptible John Curtin was in Parliament, the leaders of all the parties and the great majority of members and senators understood and supported the respect and acceptance of our institutions.

It is sad that only a minority of politicians do so today. The consequences are apparent.

10.7 Broken promises

There is often a debate about whether a government has a mandate to adopt a particular policy. For example the release in late 2012 of an exposure draft of a human rights and anti-discrimination bill would have effected significant changes. Critics feared it would lead to the gagging of the press and the encouragement of litigation based on conduct some people found offensive. It was a proposal about which there was absolutely no notice in the election manifesto of the governing parties in 2010. In a similar way when the Coalition introduced the work choices legislation after the 2004 election, it was also argued that the Coalition parties had given no notice that such legislation would be introduced. That said, the direction of the legislation, namely the deregulation of much of the labour market, was clearly consistent with broad Coalition policy.

When however a government breaks a promise clearly made during an election campaign, the electorate will necessarily feel aggrieved and ask why the politicians did not wait to seek a new mandate at the next election, as John Howard did over the GST. Where a government does not seek a new mandate, Australians should be able to vote again on the issue, either by recalling the government, or at least vetoing the legislation.

For example, prior to the 1993 election, ALP leader Paul Keating promised two rounds of income tax cuts, legislating them to prove they would become "L-A-W law". The law was later repealed so the money could be put into superannuation.

John Howard promised before the 1996 election never to introduce a Goods and Services Tax, a GST. But then he changed his mind, going to the 1998 election clearly promising to introduce a GST to replace the Commonwealth Sales Tax and various state taxes. Although people frequently refer to John Howard's 1996 promise, he did go to the next election clearly indicating what he would do if he were re-elected.

In the 2010 election, the leader of the Labor Party, Julia Gillard, promised that under no government which she led, would there be a carbon [dioxide] tax. However, as a result of negotiations with the Greens, she became committed to the introduction of such a tax.

10.8 The solution

The people are aware that the political system is not working well. The politicians will from time to time propose solutions, which are either cosmetic or pointless distractions, or which actually increase their hold on office.

Rather than reducing the opportunities of the people to judge the quality of the government, there should be more opportunities for the people to give effect to their assessments.

Australia's founding fathers recognised the limits to representative government in deciding that matters of the greatest importance, such as the amendment of the Constitution, should be referred to the people, to be determined by them both nationally and federally.

Because of the compromise of our constitutional institutions by the factional powerbrokers – the "faceless men" and the elites – it is time that the Australian people took charge. It is time that those who govern us should be made accountable, not every three or four years in somewhat confected elections, but every day, of every week, and of every month. We shall return to this in Part 3.

Endnotes

1 *Privacy Act,* 1988 (Cth) s 6C(1).

2 *Commonwealth Electoral Act,*1918 (Cth) s 90B.

3 Peter van Onselen, "Political parties' postal vote abuse in firing line", *The Australian,* 29 July 2011. http://www.theaustralian.com.au/national-affairs/political-parties-postal-vote-abuse-in-firing-line/story-fn59niix-1226103797474 (retrieved 4.01.2013) .

4 Robert Carling, "Self-sustaining leviathan", *Centre for Independent Studies,* 19 October 2012. http://www.cis.org.au/publications/ideasthecentre/article/4585-self-sustaining-leviathan (retrieved 19.01.2013).

5 David Burchell, "Haunted by hasty populism", *Weekend Australian,* 7-8 June 2008.

6 http://www.cis.org.au/research/social-policy/welfare-state (retrieved 16.01.2013).

7 Peter Saunders, *Centre for Independent Studies,* 23 November 2012. http://www.cis.org.au/publications/ideasthecentre/article/4617-mead-dutiful-but-defeated (retrieved 16.01.2013).

8 http://www.cis.org.au/publications/ideasthecentre/article/4611-ndis-the-new-leviathan (retrieved 16.01.2013).

9 http://www.dailytelegraph.com.au/news/life-on-the-pension-is-a-riot-for-omar/story-e6freuy9-1226558635258 (retrieved 07.05.2013).

10 Tim Colebatch,"Disabled make up bulk of those out of work", *The Age,* 9 March 2013. http://www.smh.com.au/national/disabled-make-up-bulk-of-those-out-of-work-20130308-2fr3b.html#ixzz2N5q8UrIV (retrieved 09.03.2013).

11 Gemma Jones, "The welfare system in Australia is broken", *Daily Telegraph,* 8 April 2013. http://www.dailytelegraph.com.au/news/the-disability-welfare-system-in-australia-is-broken/story-e6freuy9-1226614493682 (retrieved 08.04.2013).

12 Paul Sheehan, "The politics of embarrassment", *The Sydney Morning Herald,* 23 May 1998.

13 "The truth on refugees is worse than fiction", *The Sydney Morning Herald,* 30 July 2012. http://www.smh.com.au/opinion/politics/the-truth-on-refugees-is-worse-than-fiction-20120729-2369z.html#ixzz223LwOWkl (retrieved 2.08.2012).

14 *Settlement Outcomes for New Arrivals,* Department of Immigration and Citizenship, 2010. http://www.immi.gov.au/media/publications/research/_pdf/settlement-outcomes-new-arrivals.pdf (retrieved 2.08. 2012.)

15 Gemma Jones, "Asylum seekers made to feel at home, thanks to a $10,000 welcome pack", *Herald Sun.* http://www.heraldsun.com.au/news/victoria/asylum-seekers-made-to-feel-at-home-thanks-to-a-10000-welcome-pack/story-fn7x-8me2-1226273251317 (retrieved 04.05.2013).

16 Chris Merritt, "Poor slugged for court fees as boatpeople get free ride", *The Australian*, 3 May 2013. http://www.theaustralian.com.au/national-affairs/immigration/poor-slugged-for-court-fees-as-boatpeople-get-free-ride/story-fn9hm1gu-1226634256413 (retrieved 04.05.2013).

17 *The Australian*, 5 April 2013. http://www.theaustralian.com.au/national-affairs/asio-sets-asylum-checks-to-light/story-fn59niix-1226612879117 (retrieved 10.04.2013).

18 http://www.aph.gov.au/About_Parliament/Parliamentary_Departments/Parliamentary_Library/pubs/BN/2011-2012/GovernmentAdvertising (retrieved 05.08.2012).

19 Tom Dusevic, "Labor spins research to record high", *The Australian*, 7 January, 2013. http://www.theaustralian.com.au/national-affairs/labor-spins-research-to-record-high/story-fn59niix-1226548577112 (retrieved 8.01.2013)

20 Ibid.

21 Ibid.

22 Nicola Berkovic, "PM's $150m spin doctor brigade", *The Australian*, 13 August 2012. http://www.theaustralian.com.au/media/pms-150m-spin-doctor-brigade/story-e6frg996-1226448739077 (retrieved 4.01/2013).

23 http://www.dailytelegraph.com.au/news/schools-used-as-election-pr-fodder/story-e6freuy9-1226560422676 (retrieved 25.01.2013).

24 http://deewr.gov.au/ber-recognition-ceremony-kitBER Recognition Ceremony Kit (retrieved 25.01.2013).

25 Matthew Franklin and Joe Kelly, "Tony Abbott to seek Australian Federal Police report into Australia Day riot", *The Australian*, 30 January 2012. http://www.theaustralian.com.au/national-affairs/abbott-to-seek-afp-report-into-riot/story-fn59niix-1226256747994; http://www.youtube.com/watch?feature=player_embedded&v=MCVf5mzudd8 (retrieved 07.05.213).

26 Jennifer Westacott, "Restoring a High-Performing Public Service", *Institute of Public Administration Australia*, edited extract http://www.bca.com.au/Content/102032.aspx (retrieved 6.01.2012).

27 David Crowe and Annabel Hepworth, "Business declares war over ministerial staffers 'costing us billions'," *The Australian,* 21 September 2012. http://www.theaustralian.com.au/national-affairs/business-declares-war-over-ministerial-staffers-costing-us-billions/story-fn59niix-1226478444994 (retrieved 6.01.2012).

28 Ibid.

29 "Untold Story of the Bay of Pigs", *Newsweek*, 14 August 2011. http://www.thedailybeast.com/newsweek/2011/08/14/bay-of-pigs-newly-revealed-cia-documents-expose-blunders.html (retrieved 07.05.2013).

30 "OzCar scandal: controversy explained", Emma Rodgers, *ABC Online*, 23 June 2009. (retrieved 6.01.2012).

31 Laurie Oakes, "Time to quit shonky politics, Mal," *Daily Telegraph*, 8 August 2009. http://www.dailytelegraph.com.au/news/opinion/time-to-quit-shonky-politics-mal/story-e6frezz0-1225759113617 (retrieved 07.05.2013).

CHAPTER 11

Gagging the media

Freedom of speech and freedom of the press are essential to democracy. Democracy requires that both good and erroneous ideas be allowed, and indeed, encouraged in the marketplace of ideas. As John Milton declared: "Let truth and falsehood grapple; who ever saw truth put to worse in free and open encounter?"[1]

Thomas Carlyle expressed the role of the press in informing the nation eloquently when he said: "Burke said there were three estates in Parliament; but in the Reporters' Gallery yonder, there sat a fourth estate more important far than them all."[2]

The American Supreme Court Justice Hugo Black in 1971 accurately described the ideal role of the press in the Pentagon Papers Case, *New York Times Co. v. United States*,[3] although his historical reference is somewhat romantic – it was not the founding fathers but the Supreme Court which gave the current meaning to the First Amendment.

In the First Amendment, the Founding Fathers gave the free press the protection it must have to fulfil its essential role in our democracy. The press was to serve the governed, not the governors. The government's power to censor the press was abolished so that the press would remain forever free to censure the Government. The press was protected so that it could bare the secrets of government and inform the people. Only a free and unrestrained press can effectively expose deception in government. And paramount among the responsibilities of a free press is the duty to prevent any part of the government from deceiving the people and sending them off to distant lands to die of foreign fevers and foreign shot and shell.

It should not be forgotten that, outside of wartime, Australia's federal parliament and government have no authority over the print media. The High Court has not unreasonably interpreted the posts and telegraph power to extend to the granting of licences for radio and television transmission.[4]

The High Court has also found implied in the Constitution a freedom of political communication which clearly limits the use of this licensing power to impose restraints on freedom of the media.[5]

This implied freedom is fortunately and sensibly restricted to political communication. In the United States in recent years, the Supreme Court has ignored what was clearly in the minds of the founding fathers of the United States – that political speech is different. This is not so surprising in a court which was to view human life so cheaply as to invent a constitutional right to abortion.

Guided by their belief that Americans had brought with them the fundamental rights of Englishmen, they revered freedom of speech – that is freedom of political speech. They would have been horrified and outraged that this guarantee has today been used by the Supreme Court to declare invalid, for example, a law to protect children from indecent materials on the internet, or to make laws regulating obscenity unenforceable.[6]

In any event it is absolutely essential for the media to play its role in informing the public on all matters, especially political matters, that it be free from government control.

As Lord Jacobson once informed the House of Lords, "My Lords, relations between government and the press have deteriorated, they are deteriorating, and they may deteriorate even more. And on no account, on no account, must they be allowed to improve."[7]

Clearly freedom of speech and the press cannot be absolute. As the Americans say, no one should be allowed to shout "Fire" in a crowded theatre without justification.[8]

11.1 Defamation and freedom of political communication

Until the 1980s, some politicians became very well-known for using our highly technical defamation laws to control the media. One celebrated device was the "stop writ" which involved the taking out of a writ for defamation to create the justifiable fear that any further publication would significantly increase the amount of damages likely to be awarded.

The use of the "stop writ" was restricted to a number of politicians, some of whom famously celebrated the damages received often in a an out-of-court settlement by referring to their "Packer" swimming pool or their "Fairfax" holiday cottage.

After the High Court found that a freedom of political communication was implied in the Constitution, the number of defamation cases brought by politicians declined significantly.[9] The Constitution does not expressly guarantee freedom of speech, but the democratic form of government which it established assumes that people will be free to inform and be informed on political matters.

As a result the use of the "stop writ" to block the legitimate investigation and public disclosure of matters of public interest disappeared, even before the emergence of a uniform defamation law agreed by the Commonwealth and the states.

However, the unfair situation has not arisen in Australia as in the United States where public figures can be defamed with impunity because of careless and excessive interpretation of the United States Constitution.[10]

11.2 Journalists and proprietors

There is a celebrated declaration by an editor of *The Manchester Guardian*, C.P. Scott that "comment is free, but facts are sacred".

This division between news and comment was once rigorously observed. Editors in most newspapers insisted on the news being objective. Comment was reserved to the editorial pages. This was enforced by strong editors supported by strong proprietors. This has changed. Now news and comment are quite often intermingled.

In the meantime, proprietors or media moguls are few on the ground, and of these Rupert Murdoch is no longer a resident.

The media is now less hierarchical. The authors of reports are usually identified and many journalists are now multi-media celebrities, directly controlling more content than ever before.

Research indicates that the typical journalist's position on a range of issues tends to be well to the left of the general population.[11] This in itself should not be a cause of concern if news is presented objectively and comment is clearly distinguishable.

There is a particular problem with comment on the public broadcasters, the Australian Broadcasting Corporation (ABC) and the Special Broadcasting Service (SBS). Unlike the press, neither may have an editorial agenda and comment should be balanced. Moreover both have charters setting out their responsibilities and both are funded by the taxpayer. However, there can be little doubt that comment on the ABC more often than not leans to the left, and that this affects the determination of whether an item is newsworthy. For example, the ABC shows a distinct reluctance to report news which contradicts the theory that man-made carbon dioxide emissions are the principal cause of global warming – if indeed the planet is still warming.

Of the principal media, the Rudd and Gillard governments seem particularly happy with Fairfax, the ABC, and FM radio.

They are less happy with some commercial radio talkback but here there are many more outlets available. They are especially displeased with News Ltd. newspapers, particularly *The Australian*, forgetting that News Ltd. and *The Australian* subjected the Howard government to probably greater critical scrutiny, *The Australian* editorialising in favour of a Rudd victory in 2007. Commercial radio talkback, which is by definition opinionated, was often critical of the Howard government and in any event has an obligation to seek balanced opinion. Commercial radio news is on the whole balanced; commercial television news is understandably driven by video availability and an understanding that their audiences are not interested in the minutiae of politics.

The Coalition opposition would be happier with commercial radio talkback both because of the access it gives, and the fact that commentators tend to be conservative – no doubt responding to the audiences these stations attract. The Coalition would also be happier to an extent with News Ltd., but these are certainly not blind supporters of conservative positions.

And with the rise of the internet, which is challenging the viability of the traditional media, the filtering monopoly they once enjoyed has been weakened.

11.3 Drip and spin

Until recently, no Australian government has attempted to exercise undue control over the media. As governments always do, most have attempted to present news in ways that put the government in the best possible light. Nor do they willingly release information which will embarrass them. All of this is part of the natural adversarial relationship which really should exist between the government and the media. Indeed, we should become concerned when government puts journalists on a drip as it were, leaking stories in return for an understanding that the relevant journalist will not come down too harshly on the government.

In addition, we should be concerned that the number of journalists and public relations officials working for government is out of all proportion. For a number of years now governments have exceeded what could be considered to be reasonable.

An investigation by *The Australian* in 2012 revealed there are about 1,600 media and public relations staff employed by federal government departments and agencies with a further 60 media advisers directly working for ministers. The cost is about $150 million a year.[12]

With newspapers and television stations having to reduce their staff, the likelihood of the media circulating the government line increases. The purpose of much of what is released is to present the government in a favourable light. In other words, a good part of the $150 million is really private expenditure which should be undertaken by the governing party, and not the taxpayer.

Why should taxpayers be subsidising the Labor Party – or the Coalition – to this extent?

11.4 Media silenced

We do not know the full story yet, but we do know that in 2011 the leading executives of Fairfax and News Ltd. decided to call off investigations into the role of the Prime Minister Julia Gillard in the setting up of the "AWU Workplace Reform Association" for her then boyfriend as an "electoral slush fund". Police suspected that over $400,000 was defrauded through the fund from major construction companies.

A senior Fairfax executive required that an interview by Michael Smith be pulled from radio station 2UE although it had been approved by an expert defamation lawyer and by the station's internal editorial process. It had also been extensively promoted. This action was taken notwithstanding the Fairfax charter of editorial independence which the Fairfax board was emphasising in its negotiations with Gina Reinhart who was asking for a seat on the board.

The Prime Minister telephoned John Hartigan, the CEO of News Ltd., to complain about a column on the same subject by Glenn Milne in *The Australian*. *The Australian* published a very general apology and withdrew the column from the web.

2UE broadcaster Michael Smith was suspended and his employment with Fairfax came to an end, as did Glenn Milne's with *The Australian* and the ABC. Andrew Bolt was warned and considered leaving News Ltd.[13]

The ABC did not report on the AWU slush fund in any meaningful way, if at all. Worse, it failed to report – again in any meaningful way, if at all – the fact that the government had been so successful in silencing the two major press chains.

Never before in the history of the Commonwealth has a government been so successful in silencing the media. Australians must be concerned at this naked abuse of power. In particular, Australians are entitled to know what threats and promises were made to stop a legitimate investigation into a matter of public interest.

11.5 Government regulation of the media

The Prime Minister personally insisted that News Ltd. in Australia had "questions to answer" in the wake of the UK phone hacking scandal concerning initially the Murdoch Sunday newspaper *The News of The World* even though she was not able to specify what these might be. There were no suggestions that News Ltd. outlets had engaged in any similar activities in Australia.

As the Prime Minister was putting out the message that News Ltd. had questions to answer, the then Greens leader Senator Bob Brown launched an attack on the Murdoch press (News Ltd.) labelling it the "hate media".

Then, on 14 September 2011, the Minister for Broadband, Communications and the Digital Economy, Senator Stephen Conroy, announced an "Independent Inquiry into the Australian Media" although under the terms of reference it was to concentrate on the newspapers and the Press Council.[14]

This was notwithstanding the fact that there was no recent evidence that there was anything seriously wrong with the way in which the press were reporting matters.

The enquiry was led by former Justice of the Federal Court of Australia, Mr. Ray Finkelstein QC. The enquiry reported to government on 28 February 2012.

The report claimed that News Ltd. had walked out of the Press Council in 1998-2002, which was completely untrue. This was crucial as the report made much of the fact that newspapers could leave the council.

The Finkelstein enquiry concluded that a powerful News Media Council should set journalistic standards, enforce news standards and have the power to require a news media outlet to publish an apology, correction, or retraction. Yet the Constitution gives no power to the federal parliament to pass legislation to give effect to such recommendations although the High Court has given an extraordinarily extensive meaning to the power of the parliament to legislate with respect to corporations.

From these decisions of the High Court it would seem that any section in any piece of legislation which begins with the words, "Any corporation", is valid. Of course this was never the intention of the founding fathers or of the people of Australia when they approved the Constitution. Further it was not their intention when they approved or more importantly rejected proposed changes to the Constitution.

The recommendations look very much like an attempt by the government to warn off News Ltd. from pursuing anti-government stories.

As opposition leader Tony Abbott observed, the most "shameless example" of this was Senator Doug Cameron accusing the "Murdoch press" of actually "fabricating stories", stories about the "prospect of a Rudd challenge – for which he was, himself, one of the numbers men!"[15]

Recalling that the government had just replied to seven media CEOs saying that it might not proceed with a new regulator if the media were to establish more effective forms of self-regulation, he said this was in effect saying "censor yourselves or we will do it for you".

"Any government that demands changed behaviour from the media under circumstances like these is not trying to raise journalistic standards but to lower them to the long-term detriment of our country."

In March 2013, the Minister for Communications, Senator Conroy, brought a package, the so-called Media Reform Package Bills, to the cabinet and caucus with no notice but with the support of the Prime Minister, Julia Gillard. They were approved for introduction, apparently with some reluctance.

He announced that they would be introduced into parliament with a requirement that they be passed by the end of the following week after which parliament would rise for seven weeks.

The package contained carrots and sticks.[16] The carrots were essentially for the television broadcasters, involving the halving of their substantial licence fees. Central to the package were the bills on the self-regulation of the print media and the creation of an official, the Public Interest Media Advocate (PIMA).

Briefly, the PIMA would determine standards for the print media, and approve self-regulatory bodies such as the Press Council. If the PIMA did not approve a self-regulatory body, or approval was withdrawn, then newspapers and journalists associated with the self-regulatory body would lose their Privacy Act exemption.[17]

This would make investigative reporting impossible. The consent of any target of an investigation would need to be obtained. Moreover, the powers of the PIMA were to be beyond review and beyond appeal. The reaction was hostile, including from those who were supposed to be attracted by the carrots. The government did not seem to recognise that this would be the first licensing of the press in peace time, and that this was beyond the original intention of and probably against the freedom of political communication found in the Constitution.[18] The government obtained insufficient support from the crossbenchers.

The introduction of the bill was probably the catalyst for a demand within the Labor Party for a vote on the leadership, and the bills were withdrawn. In addition, it was indicated that an amendment to the *Racial Discrimination Act* to make offending unlawful would not proceed.

The result was that the government has been tainted by these measures as being authoritarian in the extreme. Further, it is likely that the government's policy on freedom of speech and of the press will be an issue in the coming election.

11.6 Alan Jones breaks the media silence on AWU

Alan Jones is the doyen of radio broadcasters, commanding huge audiences in the crucial breakfast time slot from Sydney radio station 2GB and across the Macquarie Broadcasting Network.

He is extraordinarily well prepared for his program. Assumed to be locked into the Coalition, his cross examination of Barry O'Farrell on CSG mining demonstrated his attachment to principle. Opposed to free trade and capital punishment he can never be typecast. He covers a wide range of issues not just each week but each program, often those which the mainstream media will not touch but which are matters which concern rank-and-file Australians.

He conducts interviews with an intensity which has to be heard. He can be aggressive where the person interviewed is refusing to answer properly and to inform the people. Politicians who have something to hide are terrified of appearing on his program; nevertheless he is compulsory listening for the elites and for ordinary people across the length and breadth of the land.

There have been numerous attempts to silence him, sometimes even with the involvement of taxpayer-funded entities. The ABC even funded a book, *Jonestown: The Power and Myth of Alan Jones*, until the impropriety of the national public broadcaster doing this became the story.[19]

On 23 July 2012, he startled the nation by reopening something which the Prime Minister had gone to extraordinary lengths to close and lock up, just as parliament so improperly locked up the papers relating to the late Justice Lionel Murphy's legitimate public investigation.[20]

On that day he interviewed Michael Smith and by this act reopened the issue not only of the Prime Minister's involvement in the AWU slush fund, but of fraud and misappropriation in the union movement. Above all, he asked the question why the rules of transparency and disclosure which applied to company directors do not apply to trade union officials given that they are handling vast amounts of other people's money.

The AWU slush fund was to become the subject of further investigation by *The Australian*, Alan Jones and 2GB and the subject of numerous questions addressed to the Prime Minister in the federal parliament. Soon the Fairfax press and the ABC were reporting the affair, including the police investigations. On 23 April 2013, 2GB's Ben Fordham reported that the Victorian police were still investigating the matter, and this extended to his earlier interview with the Prime Minister.[21]

11.7 Stifling free speech through "anti-discrimination law"

One of the most effective means by which free speech can be silenced is under the cover of laws about racial discrimination.

A leading example is section 18C of the Federal *Racial Discrimination Act*, which prohibits statements that "offend, insult, humiliate or intimidate" another person or a group of people on grounds of race or ethnicity.

When Andrew Bolt wrote a piece about some very prominent "fair skinned" Aborigines who, he said, had chosen an Aboriginal identity in order to further their careers, they did not sue him for defamation, but relied instead on section 18 C.[22]

One of the complainants, Professor Larissa Behrendt, subsequently became famous for a tweet concerning the chair of the Northern Territory's Indigenous Affairs Advisory Council, Bess Nungarrayi Price, who was appearing on the ABC's *Q&A* television program, and who spoke favourably about the Howard government's 2007 intervention into Territory communities. "I've seen progress. I've seen women who now have voices," Bess Price said. "Children are being fed, and young people more or less know how to manage their lives."

In response, Professor Behrendt sent a Twitter message to an ABC radio presenter, saying: "I watched a show where a guy had sex with a horse and I'm sure it was less offensive than Bess Price."

No action was taken by the Human Rights Commission about the denigration of Bess Price, presumably because no complaint was made. Just as one of the authors of this book has not complained concerning posts on a republican website describing him as "perma-tanned" and as an "Indonesian born blow-in". (He gives notice that if anyone complains on his behalf, he will not co-operate with the investigation as a matter of principle).

This "hurt feelings" test too easily restricts freedom of speech. It is too far below the defamation threshold which applies when a person has been brought into "hatred, ridicule or contempt".

But in late 2012, the Attorney-General Nicola Roxon effectively indicated that the "hurt feelings test", as used against Andrew Bolt, was not enough.

The Attorney released an Exposure Draft which many feared would gag free speech in Australia.[23]

"I am not aware of any international human rights instrument or national anti-discrimination statute in another liberal democracy that extends to conduct which is merely offensive," declared the former Chief Justice of New South Wales, and one time chief of staff to Labor leader Gough Whitlam, Mr. Jim Spigelman.[24] He added:

We would be pretty much on our own in declaring conduct
which does no more than offend to be unlawful. The
freedom to offend is an integral component of freedom of
speech. There is no right not to be offended.

The legislation would also make it easier to complain. Most
extraordinarily, it would also reverse the onus of proof.

A Senate Committee has given a mixed reception to the Bill.[25] The
Coalition indicated the fundamental opposition to the bill for four
reasons:[26]

a) The provisions of the bill violate fundamental human
   rights.
b) The scope of the bill is impossibly wide and dangerously
   vague.
c) The bill is internally inconsistent and liable to produce
   unintended consequences.
d) The bill would damage Australia's social fabric by encouraging a "culture of complaint".

On 19 March 2013, the government indicated the Bill would not
proceed at least in its present form.[27]

NSW government moves against critics

In January 2013, it was announced that the NSW Premier Barry O'Farrell
was concerned there have been no successful criminal prosecutions in
the history of the NSW anti-discrimination laws and that they have fallen
out of step with community expectations.[28]

Section 20D of the Anti-Discrimination Act, 1977, creates the
offence of serious racial vilification.

This requires that a person – by a public act – had incited hatred
towards, serious contempt for, or severe ridicule of, a person or group
of persons on the ground of their race by:

a) threatening physical harm towards, or towards any property of, the person or group of persons, or

b) inciting others to threaten physical harm towards, or towards any property of, the person or group of persons.

New South Wales voters might be more concerned about the collapse of law and order in parts of Sydney and other towns.

It was ominously reported that leading media commentators Alan Jones and Andrew Bolt were to be called before the enquiry. Alan Jones has been a trenchant critic of CSG mining on prime agricultural and urban land and under water catchments.

11.8 Gagging leading Dutch politician

In 2013, the Q Society organised a speaking tour of Australia by probably one of the best known Dutch politicians, Geert Wilders. He is the founder and leader of the Party for Freedom (Partij voor de Vrijheid – PVV), the fourth-largest political party in the Netherlands.

His political agenda is not extreme, and includes a commitment to direct democracy. It includes a restoration of respect for teachers, police, nurses and others and a more accessible and humane health care system. He is best known for his opposition to what he calls the Islamisation of the Netherlands. He does not dislike Muslims, but what he sees as a totalitarian political system ruling through terror. From 2009 to 2011, he fought a prosecution for hate speech, eventually being acquitted.[29]

When he was first invited to Australia, consideration of his visa was delayed for four months which made it impossible for him to come. On this occasion, the visa was delayed but eventually granted.

Pointing to the double standard about Geert Wilders, Senator Cory Bernardi recalled that in 2012 the government had no issue granting a visa to Taji Mustafa, the British leader of Muslim extremist group Hizb ut-Tahrir.[30]

When here, he argued for Australia to be put under sharia law, and approved a demonstration in Sydney about a video released in America. The demonstration turned into a riot.

Nor was there any difficulty in granting a visa to one Sheikh Abdul Rahman Al-Sudais who has called Jewish people the "rats of the world". He says Christians are "influenced by the rottenness of their ideas and the poison of their cultures".

Geert Wilders came to Australia to warn that Islamism is a totalitarian political ideology enforced by violence and rigid adherence to it.

Australians may not agree with him, but surely he is entitled to argue this and people are entitled hear him. So why were thugs allowed to attempt to stop people from hearing him in Melbourne. One person was thrown to the ground. Why did the Victorian police allow them to break the law with impunity?

Instead the authorities – including the Liberal Premier of Western Australia, Mr. Colin Barnett – wanted him silenced. Mr. Barnett made his views very clear: "As far as I am concerned ... he is not welcome", even claiming he "had a hand" in the Perth venue cancelling the function at the last minute.[31] Do Australians find it acceptable that a Premier would, like some tin-pot dictator, seek to decide who will and will not speak in his state?

Westpac refused to be involved in a payment system for his bookings. At least 30 venues refused to host his function. The booked Perth venue was cancelled when it was too late to arrange an alternative. A large number of politicians were invited to hear him – not to agree with him. Some declined, many ignored him and four accepted, including the courageous Christian Democrat New South Wales politician, the Rev. Fred Nile. A radio interview was called off because of threats to arrest him. Speaking on behalf of the Australian Human Rights Commission, its President Professor Gillian Triggs, told ABC radio that "we'd have to say that there's a risk he's sailing close to the wind".[32]

Whether or not you agree with his solutions, there can be little doubt that the situation on the ground in the Netherlands indicates a serious decline from the once tranquil and very liberal society that one of the authors of this book remembers.

This very truthful, honest letter from Ulrike Lackner appeared in *The Australian* on 22 February 2013. It would be difficult for anyone to challenge the facts.[33]

> I lived in The Netherlands in the 1970s and 80s and loved its tolerant and peaceful society where citizens and foreigners were treated as equals no matter what colour or opinion we had. It was safe and friendly.
>
> I was not in the least worried about my then 15-year-old daughter walking home through Amsterdam's central park with her girlfriend in the early hours of the morning. There was no crime to speak of and rapes were as good as unknown.
>
> How different it was when I visited in 2007. The streets were unsafe and immigrants threatened patrons in pubs. My daughter had bought a pub there. What was once a place of entertainment to locals had become the domain of Islamic troublemakers.
>
> Gone were the musicians. The tolerance of the Dutch had become a doormat. My daughter's beautiful pub was repeatedly trashed by people who would not listen to her pleas to stop.
>
> I agree with Geert Wilders. If one of the most tolerant, welcoming and least violent countries in Europe has closed its heart and compassion, there must be a very good reason. I have seen the reason with my own eyes.
>
> It is time to stop blaming the victim and start debating this issue of Islamification and try to prevent another Amsterdam happening here. It is also time to stop calling anyone with a different opinion a racist.

There are a number of questions about the visit. Why was there such an attempt to silence him? Why did the commercial interests go to water? Were they threatened? Why were our politicians unwilling to even hear his very important message?

There is a warning here. It is clear that the powerbrokers and the elites who govern this country are quite prepared to limit and restrict freedom of speech and of the media if it serves their narrow interests. And those interests are the retention and accumulation of power and the financial advantage which it brings.

In April 2013, it was revealed that the Boston bombers, the Tsarnaev brothers, were fans of a Sydney Islamic radical cleric Sheik Feiz Mohammed who had called for the decapitation of Geert Wilders. Mr. Wilders said he was not surprised, but did not share the "great faith" of Australia's Attorney-General Mark Dreyfus in the "conversion of the hate-preacher".[34]

Australians must be constantly on their guard and insist upon being empowered sufficiently to control those who rule us.

Endnotes

1 *Areopagitica: A speech of Mr. John Milton for the Liberty of Unlicensed Printing to the Parliament of England*, 1644.

2 Thomas Carlyle, 19 May 1840. "Lecture V: The Hero as Man of Letters. Johnson, Rousseau, Burns". *On Heroes, Hero-Worship, & the Heroic in History. Six Lectures. Reported with emendations and additions* (Dent, 1908 ed.). London: James Fraser. p. 392. http://www.gutenberg.org/files/20585/20585-h/20585-h.htm (retrieved 12.02.2013).

3 *New York Times Co. v. United States*, 403 U.S. 713 [1971].

4 R v *Brislan* (1935) 54 CLR 262.

5 *Australian Capital Television Pty Ltd v Commonwealth* (1992) 177 CLR 106.

6 David Flint, *Malice in the Media Land*, 2005, Freedom Publishing, North Melbourne, pp. 56-60.

7 http://www.quadrant.org.au/magazine/issue/2010/7-8/media-bias-and-the-federal-election/page:printable (retrieved 10.08.2012).

8 *Schenck* v. *United States* 249 U.S. 47 (1919), per J. Holmes at p. 52.

9 *Australian Capital Television Pty Ltd v Commonwealth* (1992) 177 CLR 106.

10 Flint, op. cit., pp. 68-69.

11 Ibid., pp 27-31.

12 Nicola Berkovic, "PM's $150m spin doctor brigade", *The Australian*, 13 August 2012. http://www.theaustralian.com.au/media/pms-150m-spin-doctor-brigade/story-e6frg996-1226448739077 (retrieved 23.02.2013).

13 See interviews with Michael Smith, www.cando.org.au, http://www.youtube.com/playlist?list=PL8E5A18C590E33B9A&feature-view_all (retrieved 5.01.20130 see http://www.michaelsmithnews.com/ (retrieved 05.05.2013).

14 http://www.dbcde.gov.au/newsroom/department_media_releases/call_for_submissions (retrieved 22.02.2013).

15 https://www.youtube.com/watch?v=IA77oVdr_ZA (retrieved 22.02.2013).

16 *Media Reform Bills Package: Broadcasting Legislation Amendment (Convergence Review and Other Measures) Bill* 2013, *Broadcasting Legislation Amendment (News Media Diversity) Bill* 2013, *News Media (Self-regulation) (Consequential Amendments) Bill* 2013, *News Media (Self-regulation) Bill* 2013, *Public Interest Media Advocate Bill* 2013, *Television Licence Fees Amendment Bill* 2013.

17 *Privacy Act*,1988,s.7B(4.)

18 David Flint, "Press gagging is the last resort", *The Australian*, 25 March 2013. http://www.theaustralian.com.au/media/opinion/press-gagging-is-the-last-resort/story-e6frg99o-1226604498497 (retrieved 07.05.2013).

19 David Flint, "Psychosexual treatment of Alan Jones relies on rumour: His hatchet job on a renaissance man does Chris Masters no credit", *The Australian,* 30 October 2006. http://www.theaustralian.com.au/opinion/david-flint-psychosexual-treatment-of-alan-jones-relies-on-rumo/story-e6frg6zo-1111112436223 (retrieved 23.02.2013).

20 http://www.quadrant.org.au/blogs/qed/2012/07/alan-jones-interviews-michael-smith (retrieved 23.02.2013).

21 http://www.2gb.com/audioplayer/8620 (retrieved 05.05.2013)

22 *Eatock v Bolt* [2011] FCA 1103, 28 September 2011, Bromberg J.

23 *Human Rights and Anti Discrimination Bill, 2012, Exposure Draft Legislation,* Attorney-General's Department. http://www.ag.gov.au/Consultations/Documents/Consolidationof-Commonwealthanti-discriminationlaws/Human%20Rights%20and%20Anti-Discrimination%20Bill%202012%20-%20Exposure%20Draft%20.pdf (retrieved 6.01.2012).

24 James Spigelman, "Free speech tripped up by offensive line", *The Australian,* 11 December 2012. http://www.theaustralian.com.au/national-affairs/opinion/free-speech-tripped-up-by-offensive-line/story-e6frgd0x-1226534034425 (retrieved 07.05.2013).

25 http://www.aph.gov.au/Parliamentary_Business/Committees/Senate_Committees? url=legcon_ctte/anti_discrimination_2012/report/index.htm (retrieved 07.05.2013).

26 http://www.aph.gov.au/Parliamentary_Business/Committees/Senate_Committees?url=legcon_ctte/anti_discrimination_2012/report/d01.htm (retrieved 07.05.2013).

27 http://www.theaustralian.com.au/national-affairs/discrimination-reforms-dumped/story-fn59niix-1226601065130 (retrieved 01.05.2013).

28 *Anti-Discrimination Act,* 1977, s.20D.

29 http://www.foxnews.com/world/2011/06/23/dutch-court-acquits-anti-islam-lawmaker/ (retrieved 23.02.2013).

30 http://www.corybernardi.com/2013/02/free-speech-double-standard.html/ (retrieved 23.02.2013).

31 http://www.news.com.au/national-news/western-australia/dutch-mp-geert-wilders-perth-gig-cancelled/story-fndo4e3y-1226581432645

32 http://www.abc.net.au/worldtoday/content/2013/s3696020.htm (retrieved 07.05.2013).

33 http://www.theaustralian.com.au/opinion/letters/protests-against-wilders-show-disdain-for-democracy/story-fn558imw-1226583000065 (retrieved 07.05.2013).

34 Geert Wilders, "No surprise the Boston bombers were fans of the sheik", *The Australian,* 27 April 2013. http://www.theaustralian.com.au/national-affairs/opinion/no-surprise-the-boston-bombers-were-fans-of-the-sheik/story-e6frgd0x-1226629578097 (retrieved 01.05.2013).

CHAPTER 12

False solutions

12.1 Introduction

There is clearly something seriously wrong in the way in which we are governed in Australia. Federation started out so well; we were one of the most advanced countries in the world, with the secret ballot, the Westminster system, responsible government, votes for women, the requirement that the people approve of any constitutional change, and the remarkable achievement of federation itself.

As our venerable founding fathers Sir John Quick and Sir Robert Garran wrote:

> Never before have a group of self-governing, practically independent communities, without external pressure or foreign complications of any kind, deliberately chosen of their own free will to put aside their provincial jealousies and come together as one people, from a simple intellectual and sentimental conviction of the folly of disunion and the advantages of nationhood.
>
> The States of America, of Switzerland, of Germany, were drawn together under the shadows of war. Even the Canadian provinces were forced to unite by the neighbourhood of a great foreign power. But the Australian Commonwealth, the fifth great Federation of the world, came into voluntary being through a deep conviction of national unity.
>
> We may well be proud of the statesmen who constructed

a constitution which, whatever may be its faults and its shortcomings, has proved acceptable to a large majority of the people of five great communities scattered over a continent; and proud of a people who, without the compulsion of war or the fear of conquest, have succeeded in agreeing upon the terms of a binding and indissoluble Social Compact.

The Australian experiment was an exciting venture. We were a world leader in democratic and constitutional innovation. Governments, state and federal, attended to their core responsibilities with diligence. We toyed with strengthening our democracy by empowering the people with the tools of direct democracy. The 1891 draft of our Constitution actually provided for this, and although this was removed, direct democracy became part of the Labor Party platform from 1897 until it was removed in 1963 on the motion of Don Dunstan, later Premier of South Australia.[1]

There were great achievements in education, in building our infrastructure, in the pioneering of great agricultural ventures and in the valour of our defence forces. The period following the Second World War was one of promise, with new immigrants coming, assimilating fully to our fundamental values and contributing enormously the development of the country.

Since then we have seen a dramatic decline in government performance, in law and order, maintaining and supporting our soldiers, sailors and airmen, in the standard and content of education, in transport, in harvesting water, in the nefarious campaign to destroy our farmers, in an immigration policy which led to the formation of criminal gangs and of a significant level of dependency, the loss of control of our borders, and the outsourcing of a significant part of our immigration policy to foreign criminals. We are seeing dramatic incursions into the right to private property and even our traditional freedom to say what we are thinking.

All of this has coincided with the takeover of our institutions by what we call the AAA, the axis between those who seem to hate traditional Australia, the factional powerbrokers and the elites.

Were our founding fathers and the men and women who served to defend this country – so many of them giving their lives – to return today, they would be horrified when they see the shallow uninspiring corrupt rule by this Anti-Australian Axis.

Our system of government was never perfect – no system ever is. So there have long been proposals to change it. In recent years the very forces who have overseen the decline in standards of governance have rushed to join in and offer their own solutions. Readers will not be surprised that not one of these halted, or will halt, the decline and some will only speed it up to some awful conclusion.

The dominant solution to each and every problem has been to centralise even more power in Canberra, neutering if not dissolving the states, increasing the power of the federal government to control the people, and spending even more of the taxpayers' funds, even borrowing against the future. Other solutions have often related to this craze for the centralisation – removing or weakening the Senate, prescribing simultaneous elections (an apparently innocuous proposal until one digs deeper), making double dissolutions easier, appointing ministers from outside parliament, increasing the remuneration of the politicians, lengthening and fixing parliamentary terms, removing the Australian Crown from the constitutional system, shredding the Flag, establishing a common currency or union with New Zealand, entering an Asian Union along the lines of the EU and, as we have seen, even world government.

There have been other solutions which have not been brought before the people. A principal one was when certain High Court judges have changed the Constitution from the original intention – that of the founders and the people – through "interpreting" the document in such an artificial and devious way, which would shock and outrage the founders. In this they have assumed a law-making role far beyond that normally understood to be the function of a judge. And they have done this not only in relation to the common law – they have usurped the role of parliament and the Australian people in illicitly amending the Constitution.

Of course none of this has in any way enhanced the role of the people or made the politicians more accountable.

The theme of this book is that the answer to these problems is to place our faith and trust where it belongs in a democracy – in the common sense, good judgement and decency of the Australian people. Empower them to make governments accountable, and the quality of government must improve and return to what it once was.

Australia would remain in essence a representative democracy but the people would have at their disposal the tools of direct democracy as, for example, the people of Switzerland have. They could recall their politicians and even a government. They could veto unacceptable laws. They could, if they wished, enact those laws they believe the nation needs.

The result would be that a government would be improved by the qualities of the Australian people, either by their acting to use the tools of direct democracy, but more often than not, by the politicians then being aware that some proposals or courses of action would never be countenanced by the Australian people.

This would make the political arms of our democracy accountable not just every three or four years in often confected elections, but all of the time – that is 24/7.

Let us address these false friends, the so-called solutions which the political establishment has offered us.

12.2 Centralising power in Canberra

Most centralists today realise that it would be next to impossible to abolish the states. But the next best thing is being achieved. Through a judicious mix of judges with a centralist agenda, power hungry federal politicians, and feeble state politicians prepared to accept a quiet life, preferring to take the federal money and run, Australia has turned itself into the most fiscally centralised federation in the world.

It is now almost standard practice that whenever a problem arises, for example, in education, the dominant well-funded argument will be that the matter must be handled on a national basis and that the solution must be uniform from Perth to Sydney and from Darwin to Hobart. Those states which do not wish to go along with some proposal, invariably described as a "reform", will be subject to a series of attacks in the media. This is notwithstanding the fact that quite often the solutions proposed will mean that the states must hand over their powers and also be required to include some of their budgets. If they resist, it will be said they are holding up progress by blocking the imposition of some so-called national solution which will of course solve the problem.

Usually, nothing could be further from the truth. The Canberra-based solution will often provide an insidious control over behaviour and thinking, it will be wasteful, vast sums will be incurred in establishing a duplicate bureaucracy in Canberra, and much of the so-called solution will be a bureaucratic form-filling template which everyone across the country must observe but which results in no solution at all. Take for example the National Curriculum. In the area of history, this will involve denying our history and our past and imposing on our children propaganda which favours the fashionable themes adopted by the elites. In the principal subjects, for example the teaching of fundamental skills such as spelling, the national curriculum is likely to compound the errors already made by endorsing some fashionable theory emanating from another country by the time it had been abandoned overseas.

Already a large proportion of government in Australia is centralised in Canberra, quite often through a parallel political class and a parallel bureaucracy purporting to perform functions which the states can do so much better. The power to centralise has been attained by the federal government cornering an inequitable and unacceptably high proportion of taxation revenues. The states now account for around 40% of the public sector expenditure, but raise only just under half of this. This offends a fundamental principle of federalism. As Alexander Hamilton observed:

> In a federation, the individual states should possess an independent and uncontrollable authority to raise their own revenues for the supply of their own wants.[2]

Australian states have lost this. To a great extent, they have become mendicants or beggars on the largesse offered by a powerful political class in Canberra. So instead of state governments answering to the people for the money they have raised, the electorate has become confused as to which government is responsible for which function. Accordingly the power exercised by the people at the ballot box has been diluted by the voters being uncertain as to governmental responsibility. There is a significant collateral disadvantage to the Federal authorities trying to duplicate state functions. By concentrating on seizing more and more powers, they have neither the time nor the skills to attend to the core functions of the Commonwealth which are in a serious state of maladministration. Take for example the way in which the federal government has left the country defenceless, and the borders open to illegal immigrants and illegal arms. The Commonwealth needs to surrender sources of income to the states, and not to intrude into state areas such as state minerals and petroleum resources.

It is not only that there has been a concentration of taxation in the federal government. Under the Rudd and Gillard governments this was taken to a new level.

First, the federal government established a taxation review not, as was the previous practice, under an independent highly respected and independent person, for example a retired judge. The taxation review was to be under the very person who would be expected to give them advice on the report from the review, Dr. Michael Henry, the then head of the Treasury.

He came to the not unsurprising conclusion that the state taxation of minerals should be handed over the Commonwealth in return from the Commonwealth doing the same thing that it has long done about everything else. The Commonwealth would take away incentive and competition between the states making them even greater beggars on the Commonwealth. And certainly the states would no longer be competing against one another and therefore offering choice to the taxpayer, as both American states and Canadian provinces do so well.

The last thing the centralists want is a repeat of the superbly valuable lesson offered to the country by the Queensland Premier Sir Johannes Bjelke-Petersen in 1976.[3]

Always a competitive Premier and one prepared to live within his budget, Sir Joh decided something that few politicians would ever concede. This was his brave conclusion that death duties were an evil tax paid only by the middle-class and often coming at the very worst time in the life of a family. This was particularly so for farmers and those in small businesses who would find that a very heavy taxation burden would be imposed at the same time as one of the principals had left this world. The very rich could to a good extent arrange their affairs to reduce the impact of death duties, and of course the poor would not be liable.

Sir Joh abolished death duties, one of the most momentous and beneficial decisions taken by a state premier over the last few decades. To the extent that they could, the elderly voted with their feet. The other states and eventually the federal government realised the game was up. Death and estate duties were soon abolished across the nation, which of course did not stop the federal authorities from bringing them back partially through the capital gains tax. Nor did it stop at least the Greens calling for its return, until they too finally realised that whatever was their socialist agenda, the Australian people would never again accept such an insidious tax being imposed on them.

We have seen a similar story more recently in relation to a federal mining tax proposed in 2009. Under the Henry review this was that state royalties be abolished and there would be one single federal mining tax, a portion of which would be handed back to the states. It would of course only be a matter of time before the states received very clear instructions on how to spend such federal money. The precedents under the Rudd and Gillard governments concerning such exercises are not encouraging. In particular, the Commonwealth's control of the Building the Education Revolution program led to losses ranging between well over $1 billion according to the federal government's own soft enquiry and up to several billion dollars according to radio station 2GB's Ray Hadley and investigative reporters on *The Australian.*[4]

To justify a Federal mining tax in the minds of the electorate, the politicians told what is known in the vernacular as a "porky", that is an untruth or in plain English a lie. There should be a federal mining tax, they said, because the Australian people owned the minerals, and they should be should be getting a decent return from the minerals. Nobody would disagree with there being a decent return but why did the Commonwealth find it necessary to tell untruths? First the mining companies had long been paying the very significant taxes which the Commonwealth had imposed on them. It was not as if they had escaped liability for taxation. And secondly – and more importantly – the politicians were not being truthful about the question of the ownership of these minerals.

Onshore petroleum and minerals are more often than not reserved in the original Crown grant to the Crown. The Crown grant gave the land to the original owner. But not all of the property went with the land as would normally be the case if no restriction were expressed. So minerals and later on petroleum would often be reserved and not included in the grant. This is, as the lawyers say, the Crown in the right of the state of Western Australia or whatever other state is concerned. They were not reserved for the Crown in the right of the Commonwealth, the Federal Crown. As most of the Crown grants were made in the 19th century, they were made by colonial governors in what were to become the states of the Commonwealth. The minerals were not reserved to the Crown in the right of the Commonwealth. The Crown in the right of the

Commonwealth did not exist at that time. Accordingly we may conclude without a shadow of a doubt that land tenure in general is a matter for the states and any price that is levied for the removal of the minerals, that is a royalty, is a matter for the relevant state government.

The Crown in the right of the state is a trustee acting on the advice of the state government and its proprietary rights are determined by state law. In other words minerals found in Western Australia or Queensland effectively belong to the people of Western Australia or Queensland.

Sometimes the minerals were "not reserved" to the Crown. The minerals therefore belong to the landholder. When the NSW government saw that private landholders were receiving royalties from coal mining companies, they decided to seize the coal. Because state constitutions do not require state governments to pay fair compensation on expropriation, the Wran government got away with paying a trivial amount for taking people's property. The compensation was increased by the next Coalition government, but when Bob Carr came to office, he reduced it again.

The case is made by some that there is an advantage in having mineral taxes fixed at the national level. This ignores the great advantage from competition between governments, which the founding fathers of the United States recognised. It also ignores the fact that when the Commonwealth imposes a tax its administrative costs are exorbitant and it kills any spirit in any state government to do better than other governments. This is a typically socialist solution, killing initiative and competition.

12.3 Controlling the people

Over the last few decades, federal governments of both persuasions have demonstrated a tendency to seek to control the people of Australia to a degree not previously thought appropriate in peace time. A record amount of legislation is passed to regulate matters well beyond what was ever thought within the responsibilities of the federal parliament and government. The Gillard government, in particular, has been given to praising itself frequently on the amount of legislation the parliament has passed.

In 2013 the government attempted unsuccessfully through legislation to restrict freedom speech by making it illegal to offend people, and through other legislation to restrict the freedom of the press. It was successful in discouraging the use of electricity by imposing a tax on carbon dioxide, and forcing the subsidising of electricity from renewable sources.

Whenever a problem is identified, one of three solutions, sometimes all, is proposed. First, throw more money at the problem. But as it has been famously said, governments have no money; it all comes from the taxpayers. We should remember this whenever the government's solution is to spend more money. The second proposed solution will be to pass a new federal law, and name, if not a new minister, at least a new ministerial portfolio, probably with a parliamentary secretary. The third solution is to create and house a new federal bureaucracy. These solutions will then give the politicians more opportunities to engage supporters as consultants and office bearers and to dispense financial and other favourites to supporters.

So whenever some new issue hits the news, the politicians will rush in to claim ownership of the solution to it. Even obesity is apparently a matter for concern for the federal government.

The same approach has been adopted in relation to the regulation of business in Australia, thus increasing costs making entrepreneurs wonder whether it is worthwhile opening a business here or even continuing in this country.

12.4 Removing or weakening the Senate

For a very long period of time, one of the proposed solutions to our political problems has been the abolition, or at least the neutralisation of the Senate and other upper houses.

The Labor Party was once affirmatively opposed to the Senate, believing that it and other upper houses were an obstacle to its program. On other occasions the removal of the Senate has sometimes been justified on the grounds of cost, forgetting that the question of cost could be answered by reducing the overall size of parliament, not to mention the insulation from waste it may offer through its longer-term outlook.

The point is that our system necessarily requires an upper house with some considerable power. This is because the executive and the legislature are extremely close under the Westminster system. A government is formed which has the confidence of the House of Representatives. If it has the confidence of the House of Representatives, the government members are bound to support the government on significant matters otherwise the government may be brought down. So to an extent the House of Representatives, in a normal parliament, will become the creature of the government. Even when there was a so-called hung parliament following the elections in 2010, such was the relationship between the government, the Greens members and the independents supporting the government that the House usually voted according to the wishes of the government.

The situation is even worse than our founding fathers expected. This is because of the growth in the rigidity of the two party system and in particular the caucus pledge within the Labor Party which, to an extent, has been mirrored in recent times in the Liberal Party.

The purpose of a liberal constitution is to provide a stable government in which there are checks and balances against the abuse of power. While the Crown remains more important for the power it denies others than the power it wields, there needs to be another check and balance in the political institutions to minimise and counter abuses and rushed decisions. In Australia that power is exercised by the Senate where the states have equal representation, a requirement made by the original states.

Ideally the upper house will have a longer term view than that of the lower house. This flows from the ultimate example, the House of

Lords, where most members were once hereditary peers who had a particularly long-term view indeed. (We are not of course suggesting an Australian House of Lords, just pointing out the original template for parliamentary government). The American founding fathers attempted to create an American version of the House of Lords in their Senate. This was followed in Australia through six year terms and, absent a double dissolution, with half the Senate elected to a fixed term every three years, not two years as in the US. Senatorial terms do not coincide with the terms of members of the House of Representatives, senators taking office on 1 July immediately following their election.

The point is that if there were no powerful upper house, an enormous amount of power would be vested in the party controlling the government and the House of Representatives.

If there is any failure in the present Senate, blame it not on the constitutional system, but in the way the powerbrokers have captured the selection of senatorial candidates who bear the endorsement of the major parties with an inevitable decline in the quality of the candidates.

To reiterate, the problem is not with our Senate as such, but the unscrupulous way in which its election has been captured.

12.5 Simultaneous elections and making double dissolutions easier

Under the Constitution in its original form, senators were to be elected for six years with terms which would begin on 1 January immediately following the election. Assuming that elections would normally be held around the month of March, an amendment was put to the people and approved under which the date for the beginning of the term of members of the Senate was moved to 1 July so that elections to the federal House of Representatives and the Senate could occur simultaneously.[5]

But in recent years, House elections have tended to be in the second half of the year. This has meant that when a Senate election was held at the same time as the House election, which is considered desirable, new senators do not take office for many months. This annoys the major political parties because a hostile Senate may continue during the earlier part of their term.

Three attempts have been made to persuade the people that, subject to rotation of one half of the Senate, the terms should be simultaneous with House terms.[6]

The people have not been prepared to support these attempts to manipulate the Constitution.

The way in which the situation where a government confronts a Senate which rejects legislation which the government deems to be crucial is already addressed – we would say well addressed – by the founders in our present Constitution.[7]

Briefly where the House passes such a bill, and the Senate rejects this bill, the Constitution requires that there be a period of three months before the House re-introduces the bill. If the Senate again rejects the bill – or fails to pass it – the procedure is simple.

The Prime Minister may advise the Governor-General to dissolve both houses. If the Governor-General accepts the advice – as all have – both houses will be dissolved and an election held.

What could be a simpler? What could be more democratic? If a government believes its legislation to be crucial, the final judge of this is to be the Australian people. That is the solution in a democracy just as in 1975, the Governor-General, Sir John Kerr referred the political crisis to the Australian people for their decision.

The Constitution also provides for a further solution in the event that the double dissolution election results in a continuing disagreement between the House and Senate. If after the election the two houses still disagree, the matter can be decided at a joint sitting.

In 2003 the Howard Coalition government, frustrated by a hostile Senate, produced a discussion paper on section 57.[8]

The paper argued that changes to the composition of the Senate over the years had reduced the ability of the government to deliver on its mandate and that section 57 "in its current form is not a workable means of resolving deadlocks".

The paper proposed two options – the paper referred to these as "reforms". Both were to make a double dissolution easier. This would be by obtaining the consequences of a double dissolution without actually having one. One option would be to enable the Governor-General to convene a joint sitting of parliament to consider disputed legislation following the second rejection by the Senate of a bill originating in the House (with a three month interval between each consideration in the Senate). This would avoid the need for a double dissolution election in the event of conflict.

The second option would be to enable the Governor-General to convene a joint sitting of parliament, following an election for the House of Representatives or a House of Representatives and half-Senate election, to consider legislation that had previously been rejected by the Senate twice.

The paper declared that the option of a joint sitting would become a "standard feature" following ordinary elections.

The government appointed a Consultative Group on Constitutional Change to consult and report on the issues raised in the discussion paper. At this point realism prevailed and the Consultative Group wisely concluded that neither option would be likely to succeed if put to a referendum.[9] The Group found that the first option had attracted almost no support, while the second option for a joint sitting after a general election had attracted only limited support. Somewhat optimistically, they concluded that this second option for a joint sitting could have the "greater potential for success in the longer term".

As with any proposal which the Australian people seem to indicate that they do not like, the Group concluded that if the "reform" were to be pursued, a comprehensive program of public consultation and "education" would be required. Readers may interpret this as a heavy program of propaganda.

Fortunately, provided that a good and strong opposition is mounted, the Australian people rarely demonstrate gullibility in the face of such onslaughts.

It is of course a standard and typically devious approach in contemporary Australian political discourse to describe any proposal for change as a "reform" and persuading the public to do something they are unwilling to do is described as "education".

12.6 Appointing ministers from outside parliament

It is frequently argued that the quality of our Australian cabinets would be improved if ministers could be appointed from outside of the parliament as in the United States and in the United Kingdom through the House of Lords.

It is however unlikely that any government dominated by the powerbrokers and guided by the elites would do this.

Where this has occurred on rare occasions at the state level there appears to be little change in the quality of government. And it is unlikely that the politicians elected to parliament would long tolerate their promotion being blocked by ministers who are not members. In addition to this there is the problem that under the Westminster system, ministers are responsible to parliament and are expected to answer questions there.

The American situation is significantly different in that the executive power is vested in the President who is in no way responsible to the Congress, although the appointment of his principal ministers still need to be approved by the Senate. That said, it should be noted that an American minister or secretary does not enjoy the status of an Australian minister. Ministerial decisions in Australia are taken by the cabinet which is a committee of equals. American executive decisions are taken by the President and his cabinet is no more than advisory. Unlike the situation in Australia, no American cabinet can outvote the President of the United States.

12.7 Increased remuneration for MPs, senators and ministers

One frequent argument is that if only we increased the remuneration of members of parliament the quality of politicians would thereby magically improve. However over recent years remuneration has significantly improved, particularly the hidden remuneration they receive. For example, it was calculated in 2013 that if the Prime Minister and Treasurer were to resign, the superannuation payments they would receive would have required an ordinary Australian to have set aside a superannuation fund in the vicinity of $6 million.

When after 15 years service in the parliament, the former Attorney-General Nicola Roxon indicated she would stand down from her ministerial position and not contest the next election, it was revealed that her pension entitlement would be in the vicinity of $120,000 per annum for the remainder of her life, and that to achieve this an ordinary Australian would need to set aside about $2 million. But in addition, Ms. Roxon would receive the pension immediately upon leaving parliament, although she is only in her mid-40s, something which would not be available to the ordinary citizen.

It is not necessarily inappropriate for politicians to be well remunerated. But in a similar fashion to executives who drive corporations into receivership – or close to that – and walk away with millions, so too politicians can be incompetent, wasteful and deceitful without any deleterious impact on their income, their superannuation or their ability to take lucrative positions after politics.

Money alone will not improve the quality of our politicians.

What is clear is that Australia in the distant past had governments and politicians whose overall quality was significantly superior to, and whose remuneration was significantly lower than, those chosen by the powerbrokers today.

12.8 Longer terms and fixed terms

Until some decades ago Australian parliaments ran for three years and terms were not fixed. While this remains the case for the Australian and Queensland parliaments, most of the states have moved to four year terms. Tasmanian apart, all of these involve fixed terms with a known election date.

To achieve this the public was assailed with arguments about the advantages of fewer elections, and elections on known dates. The strongest argument was that this would allow governments the time to govern and not to be thinking of the next election. This would therefore improve the quality of government in Australia.

The results have not been as predicted. There has been no distinct improvement in the standard of government and in the case of New South Wales there has been a very significant decline. Indeed, under the previous government in New South Wales, there were constant calls for an early election. The Governor was frequently the recipient of requests that she act to dismiss the government.

Extending the term of the federal parliament would create an additional problem. It would be necessary to extend the terms of senators to eight years without any guarantee that this would improve the performance.

12.9 Community cabinets

Community cabinets emerged as a result of the need of the Beattie government after the 1998 Queensland state election to stay in power as a minority government supported by an independent MP, Peter Wellington. Premier Peter Beattie rejected Mr. Wellington's proposal for a Bill to introduce Citizens' Initiated Referenda in Queensland, but agreed to a community cabinet process which will involve the cabinet visiting a number of locations throughout the state, with meetings between the ministers and local people.

Mr. Peter Beattie told parliament on 11 November 1998 that the community cabinet process was actually adopted in direct response to pressure for CIR.[10]

This was adopted nationally by the Rudd and Gillard governments. Access to the public meetings with the cabinet is restricted.

Whatever consultation the community cabinet process provides, it cannot be said to empower the people in any way or to make governments truly accountable. Indeed, the process seems to be more cosmetic and for the purpose of photo opportunities for ministers and local members of parliament who belong to the ruling party.

Community cabinets are a spin doctor's delight.

12.10 Removing the Crown

Australian politics and Australian politicians were distracted enormously via the 1990s proposals to convert Australia into a republic, or as constitutional monarchists would prefer it, a politicians' republic. What was precisely proposed was that a core institution be removed from our constitutional system. This is the Crown, which came with the settlement and which had developed over many decades into an institution separate from that in Britain, Canada, New Zealand and other realms – the Australian Crown.

The common point between these separate institutions is that this had become a personal union, something well known in international law, where one person wears the Crown of two or more countries. Our predecessors knew this well. For example in the early years of the settlement, the same person wore the crowns of the United Kingdom and the Kingdom of Hanover. This ended with the succession of Victoria as Queen of the United Kingdom. As a woman she was unable to succeed under German Salic law to the Hanoverian throne. Her uncle, a son of King George III, became King Ernest Augustus I.

The proposal to remove the Crown was stimulated by the Governor-General's dismissal of the Whitlam government in 1975. The Governor-

General did this because the Prime Minister was unable to provide supply, the money needed to administer the government, pay the armed forces, the judges, the public service, pensions and amounts due under a vast number of binding commitments. This was because the opposition had used its power in the Senate to delay the consideration of the supply bills until the government advised an election. As indicated earlier, this was a tactic used on 170 occasions by the Labor Party when in opposition, with the very clear intention that were they able to persuade the Senate to follow their proposal, the government would be brought down and an early election would follow.

Above all of this was a political crisis; it was never a constitutional crisis as the constitutional system provided the answer to the problem – an early election.

The quite deceitful reaction to the 1975 dismissal was for the politicians not to blame themselves, but to blame the Governor-General, the Crown and the Constitution. By 1999, the perpetrators of the tactic to force an early election, Malcolm Fraser and Doug Anthony, were blaming the Crown. Although appointed to the caretaker government in 1975 as Prime Minister and Deputy Prime Minister, and although they were successful in the following election, both actively campaigned for a Yes vote in the referendum. Malcolm Fraser even appeared with Gough Whitlam in a Yes case television advertisement; Australians for Constitutional Monarchy calculated that this helped to increase the No vote.

Since 1975 what was previously no more than a matter for discussions at dinner parties in elite salons in the inner cities became a major political issue. Prime Minister Paul Keating, who had never before shown any great interest in removing the Crown, established a Republic Advisory Committee in 1993 to advise on the ways in which Australia could become a republic. Only those committed to republican change were appointed and the committee was chaired by the chairman of the Australian Republican Movement, Malcolm Turnbull.

The proposal had very strong support among the intellectual elites. This was reflected in the mainstream media which campaigned shamelessly for republican change not only in commentaries but in news reports. The leading authority and former editor and minister, Lord Deedes, observed in 1999:[11]

> I have rarely attended elections in any country, certainly not a democratic one, in which the newspapers have displayed more shameless bias. One and all, they determined that Australians should have a republic and they used every device towards that end.

The pressure of the elites and their refrain that republican change was inevitable fractured the Liberal Party. Hitherto a mainstay of constitutional stability and founded by the strongly royalist statesman, Sir Robert Menzies, the more opportunist and the weaker willed Liberal politicians – but not the party faithful – jumped onto the republican bandwagon.

Successive Liberal Party leaders, Alexander Downer and John Howard, neutralised the issue by promising that it would be referred to a constitutional convention which would propose a republican model for a future referendum. John Howard was good to his promise. Following his election win in 1996, a convention was elected and held in 1998.

Notwithstanding republican propaganda circulated after the referendum to explain the landslide loss, and adopted in the media, John Howard did not rig the Convention. Of the 36 delegates nominated by the Howard government, only 10 were constitutional monarchists. In other words, the majority of delegates nominated by the Prime Minister John Howard were republicans.

The republican delegates at the Convention overwhelmingly recommended a parliamentary model which was submitted to the people on 6 to November 1999. A minority of republican delegates joined with the constitutional monarchists to campaign for the No case. The No case committee, chosen on the basis of votes at the convention elections, consisted of two independent republicans and eight delegates from Australians for Constitutional Monarchy, ACM.[12]

Until the vote, the republican question frequently distracted the politicians from their core responsibilities, dividing the government and the cabinet. Although prominent republicans made many unsubstantiated claims about the advantages of their republic, such as reducing unemployment, improving trade and the economy, liberating artists, clarifying confusion among foreign governments, providing a windfall marketing opportunity for exporters, providing an opportunity for the nation to rebadge and rebrand itself, boosting jobs and invigorating spirits, allowing the then editor of *The Sydney Morning Herald* to honour the nation by deigning to become an Australian, etc, no one seriously claimed that this change would improve the governance of Australia.[13]

ACM and the other four smaller monarchist groups argued that the model proposed would result in an excessive concentration of power in the hands of the politicians. ACM argued that this would be the only republic in the world in which it would be easier for a prime minister to dismiss the president than his cook. As one of the authors observed, the president could be dismissed without notice, without reasons and without any effective appeal. This would have concentrated unacceptably enormous power in the hands of a prime minister and the government. The check and balance that the Crown provides in the Westminster system would disappear.

In any event, and notwithstanding a well resourced campaign – principally funded by Malcolm Turnbull – the strong support of the mainline media, and the support of two-thirds of the politicians, the No case prevailed in a landslide nationally, in all states and in 72% of electorates. The Yes case carried only 28% of mainly inner city electorates.

Then having promised not to raise the republic issue (that is a politicians' republic) in their first term, this emerged as the principal item on the agenda of the 2020 Summit held in April 2008 by the Rudd government.

Attendance at the Summit was rigged as if we were living in some tin pot dictatorship. Such was the extent of the gerrymander that the governance panel of 100 supported moves to a republic, with only one negative vote and one abstention.

No supporters of the present Constitution were knowingly appointed to that panel or, as far as can be seen, to the Summit. The one person who voted for the retention of the constitutional monarchy, Senator George Brandis, had been widely but wrongly assumed to be a republican.

According to one leading republican delegate, it was so mismanaged it had become a Mad Hatter's Tea Party.[14] Then the resolutions passed by the governance panel and approved at the plenary session called for the termination of constitutional links with the UK, links which were ended in 1986.

The record was subsequently changed without explanation to amend the resolutions adopted.

The Summit was an expensive public embarrassment.

To date, there have been 12 major votes and inquiries into how to turn Australia into a politicians' republic. Eleven have been paid fully for by the taxpayer, one partially so. These were:

1. Republic Advisory Committee, 1993.
2. Plebiscite for an Australian Republic Bill, 1997.
3. Convention Election, 1997.
4. Constitutional Convention, 1998.
5. Referendum, 1999.
6. Corowa Conference, 2001.
7. Republic (Consultation of the People) Bill, 2001.
8. Senate Inquiry: Road to a Republic Report, 2004.

9. Plebiscite for an Australian Republic Bill, 2008.

10. 2020 Summit, 2009.

11. Senate Finance and Public Administration Report, 2009.

12. Plebiscite for an Australian Republic Bill, 2010.

The republican politicians clearly believe Australians have to keep on voting until they get it right. In the meantime, they are determined to spend vast and never ending amounts of the taxpayers' hard earned funds.

But since 2010 there has been a lull in politicians pushing a republic. This coincided with the realisation that support for a vague undefined politicians' republic has been declining since the referendum, and not only because of the royal wedding or the Diamond Jubilee. This has been confirmed in polling over time.[15]

This has no doubt been confirmed in the considerable amount of private polling and focus groups which the politicians constantly undertake. That the politicians realise there is little point in pushing the issue at the moment was confirmed by certain events which followed the 2010 election. Parliament's then most passionate republican, Greens leader Senator Bob Brown, entered into negotiations with the Prime Minister, Julia Gillard, with a view to forming a government. As part of those negotiations he was able to persuade the Prime Minister to break her promise concerning the imposition of a carbon dioxide tax. He could of course have had anything he wanted in relation to a republic, a plebiscite or even a referendum. He asked for neither. The reason was not only did he realise it would be doomed to defeat, but that any party proposing this would be punished by the electorate for being sidetracked from the major issues that government should address.

The key point Australians ought bear in mind is that this complicated, expensive, and major proposed change to our constitutional system was never embarked upon to improve our system of government, to overcome the increasing problems flowing from the compromise of our political institutions by the powerbrokers and the elites, or in any way to empower the people. It should come as no surprise to Australians that the model which was put to the people in 1999 would have significantly increased the power of the prime minister and the government. Well before the referendum, some of the leading supporters of the Yes case admitted this before the campaign. Some conceded it subsequently. Australians can draw their own conclusions from this.

The alternative is to have the people elect the president and presumably the deputy president, the governors, lieutenant governors and so on. This would produce up to 27 additional elections every ten years and up to 18 more politicians. We would have two potentially competing politicians at the head of the federation, each state and territory – an expensive recipe for chaos.

The authors, who are interested and involved in the issue, counsel all Australians to be very wary of any proposal to remove the Crown. It will be put up to distract attention from government failings, wedge any party which is foolish enough to be divided on the issue, and be so designed as to increase and concentrate the power of the political class. So beware of the powerbrokers and the elites when they come with some republican proposal in the future – it will not be to improve the quality of government.

12.11 A common currency or union with New Zealand

It is a regular feature of Australian political life that from time to time a proposal will be made that the situation in Australia and New Zealand and the way they are governed will be vastly improved by adopting a common currency or even by entering into a political union so that we would become one country.

A typical example was the proposal made by John Hewson, a former leader of the Liberal Party, who served as Australia's opposition leader in the early 1990s. He claimed it was time to consider incorporating New Zealand into a new independent republic of Australia.[16] But New

Zealand Prime Minister Helen Clark said Mr. Hewson could "dream on".

In the *Australian Financial Review*, Mr. Hewson noted that the two countries had made good progress with bringing their economies together, and that interest in a common currency and full financial harmonisation had grown. "Admittedly, there will be a host of symbolic difficulties, like knighthoods and perhaps the need for a new Australian flag," he said of merging the two countries.

"But none of these issues is insurmountable. Most importantly, New Zealand would be able to maintain its individualistic and competitive character," Mr. Hewson wrote.

These proposals are completely unrealistic. An essential requirement would be that Australia must first clean up the mess which is our federation.

It was always possible for New Zealand and possibly Fiji to enter the Commonwealth of Australia. But since the convention of 1891, New Zealand took no further part in the development of the federal Constitution. New Zealand is mentioned in covering clause 6 as a possible "state" but never took steps to adopt the Constitution.

New Zealand is 1,200 miles away from the mainland of Australia. And even in relation to a currency union, it is clear that from previous experience the two countries are not always in the same part of the economic cycle. One could be going into a recession, the other booming. So the monetary policy appropriate for Australia could well be different from the one most appropriate for New Zealand. For example, a lower rate of interest might be more desirable for New Zealand, but such a rate of interest would be disastrous for Australia. In such a situation it is likely that the combined Reserve Bank of Australia and New Zealand would take a decision most appropriate to Australia, which of course would not be in the interests of New Zealand. In a full political union, the disadvantage of monetary policy which impacts unevenly across the national territory is usually compensated through fiscal policy. But if this happens in a currency union, it is likely to break up.

On the other hand it is unrealistic to propose a political union between the two countries. It is difficult, indeed completely unrealistic, to assume that New Zealand would accept the lowly subordinate status that is the lot now of a state in the Commonwealth of Australia. It is also unlikely that New Zealand would accept the centralist agenda which has been pursued for the better part of the 20th century by the High Court of Australia and by our politicians. While the entry of New Zealand into the Commonwealth of Australia might be a very good thing for the Australian states, it is hard to see how the Australian situation could be quickly rectified so that the status of an Australian State would be something which a proud nation like New Zealand would even consider. The alternative would be to have a two stage federation, with our federation forming a higher federation with New Zealand. Would New Zealand then expect 50% of the seats in the new Senate?

Clearly, we would have to clear up our own mess first before any self-respecting New Zealand government would even consider entering our federation.

12.12 Surrendering our sovereignty in an Asian Union

There are at least two problems with calls for Australia to join an Asian Union similar to the European Union. The first is that such a call is so extraordinarily premature that one must question the reasons why the call is even being made. Is it clearly to gain notoriety; is it merely some form of international grandstanding? An Asian Union along the lines of the European Union would require a commonality of economic development and democratic governance. Australia, despite all the faults since the compromise of our institutions, still remains probably the most democratic country in the region.

The second problem is that such a call is usually made quite deceitfully. It is generally argued that the union – or the common market – is to be essentially an economic arrangement and that there is to be no political coming together and no supranational power and authority over the members.

It is highly likely, however, that those who call for such an arrangement will probably have an agenda similar to those who in the United Kingdom steered that country into her present unhappy and unpopular relationship with the European Union.

The fact is, as Simon Heffer so persuasively argues, that ever since Britain first entertained the idea of entering what was then innocuously called the Common Market, governments of both main United Kingdom parties have consistently lied about the far-reaching implications for this country's future.[17]

He adds that whenever the British public has got wind of plots to remove large areas of Britain's sovereignty, the "usual tactic" has been for ministers to pretend that the consequences of signing any treaty or giving more powers to Brussels will be of very little import. Expect exactly the same manoeuvres by Australia's politicians.

Calls have been made and will continue to be made for Australia to enter such a union with Asian states. In 2008, the then Prime Minister Kevin Rudd proposed an initiative to create an "Asia-Pacific community" by 2020, bringing together countries as disparate both economically, politically and democratically as the United States, China, Japan, India, Indonesia and Australia.[18]

He even appointed a retired 80-year-old diplomat Richard Woolcott to persuade other countries to agree to such an institution. Mr. Woolcott had been closely involved in the formation of APEC in 1989, and came to some prominence as a leading campaigner for the removal of the Crown from the Australian Constitution. Mr. Woolcott was fortunately not able to announce any success in his endeavours. The general view beyond Australia was fortunately that the proposal was premature.

It is to be hoped that if ever such a proposal comes close to conclusion, it will be further submitted to the Australian people for approval in a referendum.

12.13 World government

In Chapter 6 we examined the ways in which government has already subjected this country to foreign rule, particularly in the so-called sustainability policies which are having such a damaging impact on the rights to private property and our living standards.

The point is of course that the Australian people have never been asked to approve this; indeed they have been deliberately kept in the dark as to this development. Once again there is a crying need for the Australian people to be able to decide the extent of our involvement in overseas affiliations which so impact internally.

12.14 Conclusion

Not one of the proposals from the powerbrokers, the politicians and the elites concerning the future governance of Australia addresses what is clearly the principal problem about our quality of government. This is that our institutions have been compromised by the AAA, the axis between the powerbrokers who control the major parties and the elites who have marched through our institutions. The only answer is to rely on the common sense, good judgement and decency of the Australian people.

This should not be left to voting every three or four years, quite often choosing between candidates selected for their factional loyalty or their intellectual attachment to the latest fashionable theories endorsed by the nation's elites. The solution is to give constitutional effect to empowering the people so that the politicians are truly accountable in every week, of every month and of every year.

Endnotes

1 Joseph Poprzeczny, "Australia – A democracy or just another ballotocracy", *National Observer*, No. 76, Autumn 2008, pages 7-32 http://www.nationalobserver.net/pdf/2008_australia_-_a_democracy_or_just_anoher_ballotocracy.pdf (retrieved 05.05.2013).

2 *The Federalist Papers* No.XXXII, http://www.gutenberg.org/ebooks/1404 (retrieved 15.02.2013).

3 *Succession and Gift Duties Abolition Act* 1976, no. 93 (Qld).

4 http://www.theaustralian.com.au/national-affairs/ber-waste-exposed-by-taskforce/story-fn59niix-1225902317500 (retrieved 18.02.2013).

5 *Constitution Alteration (Senate Elections) Act*, 1906 (Cth).

6 *Constitution Alteration (Simultaneous Elections) Bill*, 1974 (Cth), *Constitution Alteration (Simultaneous Elections) Bill*, 1977, (Cth), *Constitution Alteration (Terms of Senators) Bill)*, 1984 (Cth).

7 *Constitution* s. 57.

8 Mark Rodrigues, et al, "Double dissolutions: triggers, elections and proposals for reform, updated 13 May 2010", *Politics and Public Administration Section, Australian Parliament*. http://www.aph.gov.au/About_Parliament/Parliamentary_Departments/Parliamentary_Library/pubs/BN/0910/DoubleDissolutions#_Toc261525882 (retrieved 14.02.2013).

9 Consultative Group on Constitutional Change, *Resolving deadlocks: the public response*, Commonwealth of Australia, Canberra, 2004, p. 9, viewed 22 October 2009. http://pandora.nla.gov.au/pan/79623/20080117-2207/dpmc.gov.au/conschange/report/docs/report.pdf (retrieved 16.02.2013).; Bennett, S, *The Politics of Constitutional Amendment*, Research paper, no. 11, 2002–03, Department of the Parliamentary Library, June 2003, http://www.aph.gov.au/About_Parliament/Parliamentary_Departments/Parliamentary_Library/pubs/rp/rp0203/03rp11(retrieved 06.05.2013).

10 George Williams and Geraldine Chin, "The Failure of Citizens' Initiated Referenda Proposals in Australia", *Australian Journal of Political Science*, Vol. 35, No. 1, p. 42.

11 *Daily Telegraph* (London), 8 November 1999.

12 The authors are respectively National Convenor and Executive Director of ACM.

13 David Flint, *The Cane Toad Republic*, Wakefield Press, Kent Town, 1999, pp. 25-32; David Smith, *Head of State*, Paddington, 2005, Macleay Press, Paddington, pp. 189-192.

14 http://www.norepublic.com.au/index.php?option=com_content&task=blogcategory&id=65&Itemid=71 (retrieved 20.02.2013).

15　http://www.norepublic.com.au/index.php?option=com_content&task=blogcategor
y&id=51&Itemid=56 (retrieved 20.02.2013).

16　http://news.bbc.co.uk/2/hi/asia-pacific/714471.stm (retrieved 17.02.2013).

17　http://www.dailymail.co.uk/debate/columnists/article-228953/HOW-FOR-40-YEARS-
THE-BRITISH-PUBLIC-HAS-BEEN-LIED-TO-.html#ixzz2LJLXAQGQ　(retrieved
19.02.2013).

18 Tim Colebatch, "Rudd's grand vision for Asia-Pacific", *The Age*, 5 June 2008. http://
www.theage.com.au/national/rudds-grand-vision-for-asiapacific-20080604-2lw1.
html#ixzz1y9K8QmIG (retrieved 15.02.2013).

CHAPTER 13

Where it all began

This Chapter is based on essay first published, as "Three and Twenty Years of Freedom," with footnotes deleted, in Quadrant, *November 2008, pp. 40-47. We acknowledge the editor's kind permission to republish the essay.*

The Glorious Revolution has for some decades been airbrushed from the curriculum – or at best treated superficially – in schools and even universities across the nation. But it is as relevant today in Australia, and in the wider world, as it was in England in 1688.

Indeed, the Australian system of government can only be understood through knowledge of the Glorious Revolution. That is because the Australian constitutional system is not wholly based on the federal Constitution of 1900, which was a compact between the people of the several states about the role and function of our federal institutions. Our constitutional system is a golden thread which goes through the federal and state constitutions, back through the Glorious Revolution and to the Magna Carta.

The Glorious Revolution is arguably the most significant single advance in the provision of good government that the world has ever seen. This has been overshadowed by concentrating on its quite peripheral impact on the divisions among Christians. But the Calvinist Prince of Orange who became William III was driven by his fear of absolutist French hegemony over Europe, not by worries about Catholicism whose leader, the Pope, was his temporal ally.

The point is that the freedoms and benefits gained from the Glorious Revolution far exceeded anything gained from any other single event, including the mistakenly more celebrated French Revolution.

The Reign of Terror in the French Revolution was bad enough; but the loss of life from the resulting years of war which ended only in 1815 compares with the First World War – and that with a smaller population.[1] The other great so-called revolution, the Russian one, was more a *coup d'état* by the Bolsheviks, with equally disastrous imitations in Europe and Asia which led to the deaths of around 100 million.[2]

The American Revolution was derivative and confirmatory of the Glorious Revolution. It was the American continuation of the Glorious Revolution.

The Glorious Revolution was in many ways England's great gift to the world. It established those fundamental principles of good governance which best allow people to achieve and to exercise their fundamental rights.

It was of particular significance not only in the constitutional development of Britain and the Commonwealth, but also the United States.

This was recognised eloquently by the founding fathers of the United States when, believing that their rights as Englishmen were being denied, they declared: "We hold these truths to be self-evident: that all men are created equal, that they are endowed by their Creator with certain unalienable Rights, that among these are Life, Liberty and the pursuit of Happiness."[3]

Indeed the American authority on global affairs, Walter Russell Mead, writes that "the Americans justified their overthrow of George III with the same arguments the English used to justify *their* overthrow of James II".[4]

The influence of the Glorious Revolution is not limited to the particular US model of government. Every year for the past two decades the United Nations has, in its Human Development Index, measured nations according to the life expectancy, wealth and education of their people.[5] The form of government of all of the leading ten and the leading twenty nations in every year, with the exception of Switzerland, derives from those principles established long ago in the Glorious Revolution. In most cases the form of government is based on the subsequent evolution of that model in Britain which came after the American Revolution.

As Mead observes, since the Glorious Revolution, the Anglo-Americans have been on the winning side in every major international conflict.[6]

This indicates some advantage in the Anglo-Saxon system of governance. There is no evidence that this has anything to with race but rather, it is to do with the endorsement of what we may call political culture. Mead makes the point that not only is the United States a nation of immigrants, but so was England even at the time of the Glorious Revolution.[7] This augurs well for the current massive immigration into the Anglo-Saxon countries. Good sense will make most realise that the system they have come to works and works well – the great majority will have little inclination to change it.

It is important to stress that the great advantages of the Glorious Revolution were not the result of some philosopher sitting down and designing them. That was what directed the French and Bolshevik Revolutions, near crazed men designing schemes to save the world that came close to ruining it. The style of the Anglo-Saxon is pragmatic; the style of the major continental powers has hitherto been more theoretical.

The wisdom of the Anglo-Saxons has been in allowing institutions to evolve gradually over time and through trial and error. By way of contrast to continental thought, we would refer to the story of the French énarque[8] who when the benefits of something with which we are familiar were shown to him said, "Yes, it may well work in practice, but does it work in theory?"

The Glorious Revolution began with an invitation to invade England made to Prince William of Orange by certain leading Englishmen who were outraged by what they saw as the unconstitutional acts of James II. William was not a stranger to England; he was married to James' daughter, Mary. When William did invade, support for James dissipated and he fled to France.

The Glorious Revolution involved William calling together a Convention Parliament which eventually invited him and Mary to take the throne, but on certain conditions which would limit his powers. This was the beginning of the English and then the British constitutional monarchy, which had the result that the British were to live in a country which was among the freest in the world.

This is in no way an argument that the English, the British or the English-speaking people were or are endowed with any superior intellect. It was that a Dutch Prince was prepared to accept the conditions under which he and his wife might have the throne of England and that thereafter, those in power were prepared to allow the constitutional system to develop by trial and error.

This was to have momentous consequences. David Landes says that the preeminence that Britain enjoyed in the industrial revolution resulted from the fact that the British people had "elbow room".[9]

Far from perfect, by comparison with most communities across the Channel, the British were free and fortunate.

Britain, writes Landes, was soon a precociously modern industrial nation. He believes that the salient feature of a successful society is the ability to adapt to new things and ways. And the key areas of change were the increasing freedom and security of the people. Yet, he says, the British still call themselves subjects of the Crown, while they have longer than anyone else been citizens.

This was due, as Thomas Babbington Macaulay was to put it, to an "auspicious union of freedom and power".[10]

That freedom was taken to the colonies. Before the War of Independence, the American colonies were the freest the world had yet seen.

What was achieved, a great governmental, military, financial and diplomatic revolution, was in many respects unintended and the benefits took some time to become apparent.[11]

King William III was not, as is frequently assumed today, principally driven by a concern for Protestantism. He was instead driven by the need to oppose what he saw as the hegemonic tyrant French King Louis XIV, and the need to ensure England never allied herself with France.

His was a correct assessment of the ambitions of Louis XIV, who showed himself as ambitious for European domination as Napoleon would, and as Kaiser Wilhelm, Adolf Hitler and Joseph Stalin subsequently demonstrated.

William did not come to England as a despot. He was long accustomed to the complex negotiations necessary as *Stadholder* of the United Provinces where high taxation and a huge military establishment were seen as necessary to protect their liberties and were approved by vote in representative assemblies.[12]

It would be wrong to assume that the Glorious Revolution introduced democracy to Britain, at least as we know it. Nor for that matter did the American Revolution. The suffrage in England and Scotland was limited, with the aristocracy and the Sovereign enjoying special rights. But even as Sovereign, William never enjoyed the rights over other Britons which many of the American founding fathers had over those of their fellows whom they owned as their slaves.

The essential point is that the Glorious Revolution introduced conditions essential for good, limited government, something which the American Revolution affirmed.

This was a liberal constitution which came to provide both stable and limited government with adequate checks and balances against the abuse of power. Those checks and balances comply with Lord Acton's subsequent warning, "Power tends to corrupt, and absolute power corrupts absolutely."[13]

That a liberal constitution requires government to be limited is something which socialists have never appreciated. Because much of Western political philosophy in the 19th and 20th century was dominated by socialist thought, (and still is under the guise of, for example, militant environmentalism), this means that little attention has been given to a feature absolutely essential to any society which is governed under a liberal constitution.

This is that the right to private property be protected under the law.

Indeed, Hernando De Soto has demonstrated that the protection of property rights in a formal property system, and one with adequate records, is crucial to economic development, and that its absence in many Third World countries explains many of their barriers to development.[14]

In the context of the debate over the Bush administration's policy to impose democracy across the world, Fareed Zakaria has most notably advanced the argument that democracy works best in societies when it is preceded by "constitutional liberalism".[15]

This is of course the essence of the British and American experience.

Constitutional liberalism, with the people enjoying basic freedoms, including the protection of their property, stable limited government with adequate checks and balances, came before democracy.

This point was not fully appreciated in the occupation of Iraq. We do not speak here of the invasion, which was arguably a continuation of the war with Saddam Hussein that began with his invasion of Kuwait.

It was in the attempt to introduce democracy to Iraq that the lessons of history were not fully appreciated. This, we suspect, was the point made by Prince Andrew, the Duke of York, when he said there were "occasions when people in the UK would wish that those in responsible positions in the US might listen and learn from our experiences".[16]

Prince Andrew was undoubtedly referring to Britain's long experience in government at home and in the empire. This teaches that good limited government requires not only the rule of law but also a panoply of checks and balances, sufficient to prevent abuse, but not so great as to cause instability or paralysis in government. As Zakaria argues, democracy can really only come when a liberal constitution is well and truly in place.

If we return to the British experience, not only did they transmit the benefits of the Glorious Revolution to their first empire in the Americas. They repeated this with their subsequent empire, and first to the settled colonies. To these they transmitted their evolved constitutional monarchy now under the Westminster system. (It can be argued, and we shall advance this below, that this model is on balance superior to that which the Americans adopted).

The Australian, Canadian and New Zealand colonies were soon given the same free institutions, allowed to run themselves, federate if they wished, and in the case of Australia even given the golden key to their constitution, the right to amend this.

No other colonies in any other empire ever had these, quite often because the imperial power did not enjoy them at home. The English-speaking world enjoyed a benefit in advance of others.

According to Andrew Roberts, this is the reason why the English-speaking countries today account for more than one-third of global GDP, despite their combined population being only 7.5% of the world's population.[17]

Living under a liberal constitutional system is reflected in the political judgement of the English-speaking world. Once again, it is not that these people are more intelligent. It is that, accustomed to a liberal constitutional system, the electorate becomes capable of sophisticated judgement and is suspicious of those who challenge the constitution. These electorates typically reject extremes at either end of the political spectrum. The electors can of course be misled, but they are less inclined than others to render heroic status to their leaders or to be swayed by adventurism.

Accordingly it is no coincidence that the communist and fascist parties never attracted any significant support in English-speaking countries, in contrast to many of the apparently sophisticated European continental countries. By maintaining a liberal constitution, the result is that the electorate becomes a guardian of that system.

13.1 The Principles of the Glorious Revolution

William Blackstone, in his *Fundamental Laws of England*,[18] published in 1760, enumerated a stream of signal documents which declare what he saw as the "absolute rights of Englishmen".

It was these rights which the American colonists believed they had taken with them to the new land, and it was these rights which they claimed King George III was infringing.

They saw these documents, all of a constitutional nature, as the spring from which parliament and the common law came. They began with Magna Carta, its various confirmations, the Petition of Right and the Habeas Corpus Acts under Charles I and culminated in the Bill of Rights of 1689 and the Act of Settlement of 1701.

Let us go to the Bill of Rights of 1689, "An Act Declaring the Rights and Liberties of the Subject and Settling the Succession of the Crown."[19]

In summary, this established the fundamental principles of government in what is the first version in England of a modern constitutional monarchy, which we shall call the Constitutional Monarchy Mark I. In this model the King agrees that only the King-in-Parliament can legislate, the King thus having a power of veto. Unlike the present Westminster system, the King also retained control of the executive government. This is the model on which the American republic is based, an irony to which we shall return.

The Bill of Rights was a revolutionary document in that following the landing of Prince William of Orange, the *stadholder* of the Netherlands United Provinces, the legitimate King James II fled to France. It was William who called what became known as the Convention Parliament, and it was that Parliament which offered the throne to William and his wife Mary, James' daughter.

Constitutionally this was irregular, to say the least. If James did in fact abdicate, the Crown would have gone to the young Prince James, the Prince of Wales who was with him in France, and not to his daughter, the Princess Mary, William's wife. Hence it is properly called a revolution, but in comparison to most, a mild one.

The Bill of Rights begins with a recital referring to the Declaration of Right which was read to the Sovereigns before the Crown was formally offered to them. Then follows a general accusation against James II, that "by the assistance of divers evil counsellors, judges and ministers employed by him, did endeavour to subvert and extirpate the Protestant religion and the laws and liberties of this kingdom". This was no doubt recorded to justify the constitutional irregularity in the offer of the Crown to William and Mary. This device was followed by the American revolutionaries in the accusations made against King George III in the Declaration of Independence.[20]

Then follow thirteen specific allegations, principally that James II claimed the power to dispense with the laws of England. Among the accusations is one which will interest Australians, that of "levying money for and to the use of the Crown by pretence of prerogative for other time and in other manner than the same was granted by Parliament". In other words, James is accused of raising taxes without parliamentary approval and ruling without supply.

This is forbidden both under the Westminster system and in the United States, but with different consequences. In the Westminster system, a government which cannot obtain supply must advise a general election or resign.

Thus on 11 November 1975 the Australian Governor-General, Sir John Kerr, withdrew the commission of the then Prime Minister E.G. Whitlam for trying to do this, to govern without a grant of supply.

In his reasons Sir John said:

> Because of the principles of responsible government a Prime
> Minister who cannot obtain supply, including money for
> carrying on the ordinary services of government, must either
> advise a general election or resign. If he refuses to do this I
> have the authority and indeed the duty under the Constitution
> to withdraw his Commission as Prime Minister.[21]

In summary, and in case anyone doubted the illegality of King James'
actions, the Bill of Rights declares that all of these "are utterly and
directly contrary to the known laws and statutes and freedom of this
realm".

Then follows the justification for the invitation to William and Mary
to take the throne, and the calling of the Convention Parliament.

This was that after William landed, and so many went over to William,
that James burned most of the writs prepared for the new parliament,
cast the Great Seal into the Thames and then fled to France.[22]

Parliament debated as to whether he had thus abdicated or,
alternatively, was incapable of acting. There was talk of regency, but
this was rejected when it was realised that under a regency, James could
always return to the throne. He was now even less acceptable, living with
the young Prince of Wales in France under the protection of Louis XIV,
who had revoked the Edit of Nantes which had allowed the Protestant
Huguenots some liberties.

Accordingly, the Bill of Rights declared that the "late King James the
Second" – almost as if he were dead – "having abdicated the government
and the throne being thereby vacant, his Highness the Prince of Orange
(whom it hath pleased Almighty God to make the glorious instrument
of delivering this kingdom from popery and arbitrary power)" had called
an election for the House of Commons which met and formulated the
conditions under which they would offer the throne to William and Mary.

The Bill of Rights then records that "their said Majesties did accept the crown and royal dignity of the kingdoms," and that certain principles were accepted. It was noted in particular that the King and Queen could not, under the prerogative, dispense with the application of the laws, that a standing army would not be maintained in England without parliamentary consent, that the Monarch would not interfere in elections, nor rule without supply, that subjects were free to petition the King, and were to be protected from cruel and unusual punishments, and fines and forfeitures without trial. Parliamentary privilege was established and Protestants were entitled to bear arms for their defence.

Parliament had clearly tired of the Stuart Kings. They looked across the Channel and they did not care for what they saw, the absolutist France of Louis XIV. In particular they did not like the revocation of the Edict of Nantes, which led to the persecution and flight of the Huguenots. They linked their problems with the Stuarts to Roman Catholicism, and so Roman Catholics were to be barred from the throne, parliament claiming that experience had demonstrated "that it is inconsistent with the safety and welfare of this protestant kingdom to be governed by a papist prince."

13.2 Battle of the Boyne

In the year following the passing of the Bill of Rights, William defeated King James in Ireland at the famous Battle of the Boyne. This ended any real hope of a Stuart restoration, at least during James' life.

While this battle is best remembered today in Ireland for its religious connotations, it is important to understand that it was far more about the throne than religion.

Catholics and Protestants were to be found on both sides, with William's elite Blue Guards fighting under the papal banner. William was allied with both Catholic and Protestant powers in the League of Augsburg, which had papal support and was directed against Louis XIV.

In fact, the news of James' defeat was celebrated in the Vatican.[23]

The battle was regarded as more significant on the continent, than in Britain. Two days later an Anglo-Dutch fleet was defeated by the French at the Battle of Beachy Head, and that was of greater concern to the English.[24]

13.3 The Act of Settlement

After the death of Queen Mary, and then the deaths of her sister Anne's son Prince William of Gloucester, William and the parliament felt the need to restate the succession. This was to ensure that the Crown did not return to James' line.

Accordingly the Act of Settlement of 1701[25] vested the succession in the Electress (or Queen) Sophia of Hanover, a granddaughter of James I, and her protestant heirs. The Act still determines the succession to the throne of the United Kingdom and of all the Commonwealth realms, whether by reference to the Act as a British statute, or as a patriated part of the particular realm's constitution.

Any change to the succession today needs the approval of all parliaments of the realms, those Commonwealth countries of which the Queen is the Sovereign.[26]

The Act of Settlement is frequently the subject of debate, principally because of the protestant succession. But there is something far more important in this legislation, something which would have a profound effect on governance in Britain, the US, the Commonwealth and indeed the world.

This is in the provision, that the "judges' commissions be made *quamdiu se bene gesserint*". This means that judges were no longer to hold office "at pleasure," that is, be dismissible by the government whenever it so wishes. And of course a government may well wish to dismiss a judge who rules against it.

From the Act of Settlement, judges hold office now "during good behaviour". That means they can be removed only by an address of both houses of parliament.

This was of single importance. It is the source of the doctrine of the separation of powers in England, the subject of detailed study by Montsquieu.[27] He saw the separation of the three powers, the executive, the legislature and the judiciary as ensuring political liberty. The separation of the judiciary had, he thought, to be real, and this was certainly the case in England.

Subsequently the English model evolved into the Westminster system as we know it today, where the ministry must enjoy the confidence of the lower house, the House of Commons. In the meantime the separation of powers had been carried to the United States, where the judiciary was to become a significant force, and criticised for moving into the area of the legislature.

13.4 The constitutional monarchy Mark II – responsible government

There would be one further development in the constitutional monarchy which followed American independence. Until then, the King or Queen played an active role in the executive. The ministers were not responsible to parliament; they were responsible to the King. So the model the Americans took was one where the head of state was also still head of government.

Paradoxically, it was the American War of Independence which led to the beginnings of what we recognise as the Westminster system, where the government is responsible to the House of Commons.

It was in March 1782 when, following the defeat of the army at Yorktown, the House of Commons voted that they "can no longer repose confidence in the present ministers".

Lord North, who was Prime Minister, resigned.

This was the beginning of the constitutional convention which became firmly established in the middle of the 19th century, that a government must retain the confidence of the House of Commons. This is responsible government. This means that a government is responsible to the lower house of parliament, in Britain, the House of Commons. Unfortunately, it does not mean a government must not be irresponsible.

This was the system which the British gave to their settled colonies in the mid-19th century.

13.5 William as King

But noting that William was not a constitutional monarch as we would know it today is not to say he was not meticulous in observing the obligations he entered into under the Declaration and then the Bill of Rights.

In 1698 a very foolish House of Commons wanted to cut down the size of the army to a mere 7,000 in England. They also decided to send home William's beloved Blue Dutch Foot guards, Catholic and Protestant, the first to enter London and the first to plunge into the waters of the Boyne in 1690.[28]

William did not react as a Stuart king might have. He did not suspend or prorogue parliament.

He wrote instead what he believed would be his last speech from the throne, a speech which contained a statement as melancholy as the abdication speech of Edward VIII:[29]

> I came into this kingdom, at the desire of the nation, to save it from ruin, and to preserve your religion, your laws and your liberties. And for that end, I have been obliged to maintain a long and burdensome war for this kingdom, which, by the grace of god, and the bravery of this nation, is at present ended in a good peace, under which you may live happily and in quiet, provided you will contribute towards your own security in the manner I have recommended to you, at the opening of the sessions.[30]

They had not, so he would go.

But when he read his speech to the Lord Chancellor, Lord Somers, he pleaded with the King: "This is extravagance, Sir, this is madness. I implore Your Majesty for the sake of your own honour, not to say to anybody else what you have said to me."[31]

Reluctantly, William re-considered his position and accepted Somers' advice.

In 1700 Louis XIV broke his word in the Partition Treaties and allowed the vacant Spanish throne to be taken by the second son of the Dauphin, Phillipe, Duke of Anjou. The Spanish Ambassador fell to his knees and clasping the Duke's hand, said, "The Pyrenees have ceased to exist."

The House of Commons foolishly recognised Phillipe, even trying to impeach the ministers concerned in the partition treaties, Somers, Portland, Halifax and Oxford. Fortunately the House of Lords acquitted them.

With the House of Commons undermining, more through stupidity than treachery, William's balance of power strategy, Louis XIV occupied the Spanish Netherlands.

But when five gentlemen of Kent, fearing invasion, petitioned parliament to provide for the adequate defence of the realm they were arrested.

The brave Daniel Defoe, guarded by sixteen "gentlemen of quality", strode in to the Commons and handed the Speaker his "Legion's Memorial" reminding them they were the elected servants of the people.[32]

The nation demanded, writes historian Bryan Bevan, that "if the King of France would not listen to reason, King William must be asked to declare war on him".[33]

The Lords, differing for the Commons, implored the King to act.

The result was Treaty of Grand Alliance and the War of Spanish Succession (1701-1714).

As a consequence, France's dominance over continental Europe ended, with William's concept of the balance of power recognised in the Treaty of Utrecht.

13.6 The Glorious Revolution and Australia

The principles of the Glorious Revolution are central to the Australian constitutional system for at least three reasons:

First the settlers brought with them the laws of England.

Second, the British soon introduced the Westminster system to Australia, and it became one of the pillars of our nation. This process began before the Eureka Stockade, sometimes incorrectly presented as its cause. By the middle of the 19th century, most of the Australian colonies were self-governing under the Westminster system, in a way in which the colonies of other powers were not.

Third, it is a mistake to think of our Constitution only in terms of the federal Constitution. As Bolingbroke said, a constitution is "that assemblage of laws, institutions and customs, derived from certain fixed principles of reason, directed to certain fixed objects of public good that compose the general system, according to which the community hath agreed to be governed".[34]

Our constitutional system includes the principles in the Bill of Rights, the Act of Settlement as well as our federal and state constitutions.

We should make one caveat: not all parts are entrenched; some significant parts of the constitutional system can be changed by Act of Parliament.

In any event, when Australians agreed, as the preamble to the Constitution Act records, "humbly relying on the blessings of Almighty God, to unite in one indissoluble Federal Commonwealth under the Crown", they did so knowing that golden thread from Magna Carta through the Bill of Rights and the Act of Settlement was fully comprehended in our constitutional settlement.

One of the facile critiques of our Constitution is that it is silent on some matters which are assumed, for example the cabinet and the office of prime minister.

This has no foundation, and may only be advanced to justify some ill thought out change.

The Constitution was never intended as a "stand alone" constitutional primer. It was always intended to complement and not to replace the laws incorporating what were known as the fundamental rights of Englishmen, and to import these fully into the Australian constitutional system. Australia is, as one noted American authority on global affairs wrote, "one of the most democratic and egalitarian societies in the world".[35]

13.7 The Glorious Revolution and the United States

When the American founding fathers set about designing their constitutional model, they did not come to their task in a vacuum.

They had lived in the thirteen most free colonies the world had ever known.

They were and saw themselves as heirs to Blackstone's Fundamental Laws of England, and beneficiaries too of the Glorious Revolution.

James II had tried to remove their representative government.[36] William and Mary had restored it.

It was the belief of the Americans that a subsequent English government was denying them their rights.

It was not so much the Great Proclamation[37] which prevented the colonists taking more Indian land. Nor was it the decision in Somerset's Case concerning a runaway American slave. There Lord Mansfield had found, probably apocryphally, that "the air of England was too pure for a slave to breathe. Let the black go free."[38]

Wise American slave owners knew that this common law ruling would in time spread to America.

To many colonists, these two great concerns were reason enough to try to establish an independent slave-owning state, free to take Indian land. But that alone was not enough. Rather it was the ham-fisted way that the English government unilaterally required the Americans to make a quite fair contribution to their defence against the French.

"No taxation without representation" was their remarkably effective slogan.

Michael Barone argues that the Glorious Revolution was the inspiration for the resulting War of Independence and the formation of the United States of America.

The alternative model was not attractive to the Americans. This was a time when Europe was moving towards absolutism with the great example being in her dominant power, where the Sun King, Louis XIV, was unchallenged.[39]

Absolutism, apparently modern and efficient seemed as much the way of the future as the gullible would later think the Soviet Union, Nazi Germany or Mao's China was.[40]

But out of one corner of Europe, as Barone puts it, an alternative had emerged.

This was a "constitutional monarchy with limits on government, guaranteed rights, relatively benign religious toleration, and free market global capitalism".[41]

This Barone says was a long step forward toward the kind of society we take for granted now. It was "the backdrop for the amazing growth, prosperity, and military success of 18th and 19th century Britain – and for the American Revolution and the even more amazing growth, prosperity, and military success of the United States.[42]

"It changed England from a country in which representative government was threatened to one where it was ingrained, from a nation in which liberties were based on tradition to one in which they were based in part on positive law, from a nation where the place of religion was a matter of continued political dispute and even armed struggle to one where it was settled in a way that generally respected individual choice, from a nation that mostly kept apart from the wars of continental Europe to one that saw its duty as maintaining a balance of power there and around the world."[43]

It was this English and British example of representative government which inspired the founding fathers of the United States and the entire world.[44]

It was copied – with minor variations – in the British colonies, many of which would become major nations.

This improbable revolution, he argues, did much to shape the world as we know it.

Mead writes that many of the values, ideas and attitudes which are thought to be part of "America's unique exceptionalism" actually came from Great Britain.[45]

In particular, he says the ideas of the Glorious Revolution have left "a deep and abiding mark on political culture as well".

As only one example, he points out the Declaration of Independence itself was closely modelled on the Declaration of Rights. The Glorious Revolution also guaranteed liberties.

The "right to bear arms" was very different from the feudal obligation to bear arms. Rather than being an obligation to support the king and his government, it was now "a way for the freeman to protect his property and his liberty". Here we see the clear origin of the Second Amendment in the US Bill of Rights.

Barone also reminds us of the Third Amendment against quartering of troops, the Fourth Amendment against unreasonable searches and seizures, the Fifth Amendment against self-incrimination, and the Eighth Amendment against cruel and unusual punishment.[46]

The Glorious Revolution did not establish religious freedom, but neither did the US Bill of Rights. It also prohibited a federal established church; it is only more recent judicial interpretation which has changed this into mandating the separation of church and state.

And it was not just in the constitution and the law that the Glorious Revolution guided America. It was also in her institutions and even her foreign policy.

The Glorious Revolution had given Britain financial institutions similar to those of the United Provinces, which allowed it to be more effective in government, war and trade than the richer France. This preponderance of sophisticated institutions was continued and developed in America.

13.8 The Glorious Revolution and the world

The Glorious Revolution had influence in two ways. The successful Anglo-Saxon forms of governance have been copied around the world. With the exception of Switzerland and the United States, and only if we disregard their civil wars, only the Westminster system has been successful in providing limited stable government over extended periods, particularly in periods of stress.

Most of the world's successful nations have adapted the principles of the Glorious Revolution. But the Glorious Revolution has had another influence, one on the peace and freedom of the world.

Barone writes that the revolution brought a theme to British foreign policy which the United States inherited when she succeeded as the dominant force in the world.

This was the concept of the balance of power.

Barone sees a line from the Anglo-Dutch alliance against Louis XIV, through the opposition to Napoleon, to that against Imperial Germany and then Hitler. This continued during the Cold War and into today's struggle against terrorism.[47]

Barone wonders: "What kind of world would there be if Britain and then the United States had not gotten into the habit of opposing tyrannical hegemonic powers?"

Whatever the world would have been like, he asserts that Louis XIV, Napoleon, Kaiser Wilhelm, Hitler, Stalin and Osama bin Laden would not have been so constrained, and most may not have been defeated.

Barone concludes that William III and what he terms the improbable revolution of 1688 were indispensable in bringing into being the world we know today.

He ends with these words from Winston Churchill: "His daring and determination and perseverance should be an inspiration to any who are inclined to weariness and flagging resolve in trying times."[48]

Never before, and not since, has there been such a remarkable achievement in such a short time, the discovery of a model of governance which would at one and the same time assure stable government, checks and balances sufficient to prevent continuing and gross abuse of power, and freedoms which would allow a people to grow in a way which had not been seen before.

It was this model which both allowed economic progress and the gradual introduction of democracy, in a way that other governance models promised but never delivered. And this was the basis of both the American system which has been the basis of the rise of that union, and of the Westminster system which has been so widely and successfully adapted in so many countries.

The flame was lit in 1688. The Glorious Revolution must never be forgotten. Not just because history should be taught and understood, but because the lessons which flow from this must be known. As the American philosopher George Santayana famously remarked: "Progress, far from consisting in change, depends on retentiveness. When change is absolute there remains no being to improve and no direction is set for possible improvement: and when experience is not retained, as among savages, infancy is perpetual. Those who cannot remember the past are condemned to repeat it."[49]

Endnotes

1 Conversation with Philip Dwyer, 10 April 2008, author, *Napoleon: The Path to Power 1769-1799*, 2008.

2 Andrew Roberts, *A History of the English-Speaking People Since 1900*, Wedenfeld & Nicholson, London, 2006 at p. 637.

3 *The Declaration of Independence, 1776.* http://www.ushistory.org/declaration/(retrieved 05.05.2013).

4 Walter Russell Mead, *God and Gold*, Alfred A. Knopf, New York, 2007, p.48.

5 http://hdr.undp.org/en/(retrieved 05.05.2013).

6 Mead, op.cit., p. 5.

7 Mead, op.cit., p. 48.

8 A student or graduate of the L'École nationale d'administration (ENA), one of the most prestigious of the French "grandes écoles" from which come the nation's leading civil servants.

9 David S. Landes, *The Wealth and Poverty of Nations: Why Some Are So Rich and Some So Poor*, W.W. Norton, New York, 1998.

10 Thomas Babbington Macaulay, *The History of England*, 1855, Penguin Classics, 1979, p. 51.

11 Michael Barone, *Our First Revolution: The Remarkable British Upheaval That Inspired America's Founding Fathers*, Crown, New York, 2007, p. 225.

12 Barone, op.cit., pp. 226, 221.

13 Letter arguing against the promulgation of the doctrine of Papal infallibility sent to Bishop Mandell Creighton in April 1887.

14 Hernando de Soto, *The Mystery of Capital: Why Capitalism Triumphs in the West and Fails Everywhere Else*, Basic Books, New York, 2000.

15 Fareed Zakaria, *The Future of Freedom: Illiberal Democracy at Home and Abroad*, Norton, 2004.

16 Stephen Castle, "From Prince Andrew, critical words for U.S. on Iraq", *International Herald Tribune*, 4 February 2008. http://www.iht.com/articles/2008/02/04/america/andrew.php, accessed 17 April, 2008. See also Michael Eisenstadt and Eric Mattewson, *US Policy in Post Saddam Iraq*, 2003.

17 Roberts, op. cit., p. 637.

18 William Blackstone, Commentaries on the Law of England, from the Avalon Project at Yale Law School, http://avalon.law.yale.edu/subject_menus/blackstone.asp (full-text), (retrieved 05.05.2013).

19 An Act declaring the Rights and Liberties of the Subject, and settling the Succession of the Crown, 1 Will. & Mar. sess. 2 c. 2.

20 *The Declaration of Independence, 1776*. http://www.ushistory.org/declaration/(retrieved 05.05.2013).

21 Governor-General's Statement of Reasons http://www.ozpolitics.info/guide/topics/dismissal/dismissal-reasons/ accessed 3 May 2008.

22 Barone, op.cit. p. 172.

23 Mead, op. cit., p. 29.

24 It was at the Battle of Aughrim on the 12 July 1791 that many of the Irish Catholic and old English aristocrats, who had been dispossessed of lands to accommodate the plantations under Elizabeth I and Oliver Cromwell, died, and it was this battle which was originally celebrated on 12 July.

25 12 & 13 Wm 3 c.2.

26 Statute of Westminster, 1931 (UK), Preamble.

27 Baron de Montesquieu, *Charles de Secondat, The Spirit of Laws*, 1748, translated by Thomas Nugent, revised by J.V. Prichard. Based on an public domain edition published in 1914 by G. Bell & Sons, Ltd., London. http://www.constitution.org/cm/sol.htm. Rendered into HTML and text by Jon Roland of the Constitution Society (retrieved 03.05.2013).

28 Bryan Bevan, *King William III, Prince of Orange, the First European*, Stacey Rubicon, London, 1997, p. 168.

29 http://www.youtube.com/watch?v=S3qh3OEtTmI retrieved 07.05.2013)

30 Bevan, loc. cit.

31 Bevan, op. cit., p. 169.

32 Bevan, op. cit, p. 174.

33 Bevan, loc. cit.

34 Viscount Bolingbroke, *A Dissertation Upon Parties*, 1735, p. 108.

35 Mead op. cit., p. 118.

36 Barone, op. cit., pp. 236-237.

37 The Proclamation of 1763 was made on 7 October 1763 by King George III at the conclusion of the Seven Years' War. The Proclamation in effect reserved land west of the Appalachian Mountain to the Indians, http://www.ushistory.org/declaration/related/proc63.htm (retrieved 05.05.2013).

38 *R. v. Knowles*, ex parte Somersett (1772) 20 State Tr 1; (1772) Lofft 1.

39 Barone,op. cit.,p. 7.

40 The most celebrated was by Lincoln Steffens who after returning from a visit to Russia in 1921 said "I have seen the future and it works."

41 Barone, loc. cit.

42 Barone, op.cit., p. 8.

43 Ibid., p. 229.

44 Ibid.

45 Mead op. cit., p. 47.

46 Barone, op. cit., p. 232.

47 Ibid., p. 240.

48 Ibid., p. 243.

49 George Santayana, *Life of Reason, Reason in Common Sense*, Scribner New York, 1905, p. 284.

CHAPTER 14

Our unique achievement

This Chapter is based on a paper that was given at an Australia Day Dinner in Melbourne under the auspices of the Australia Day Council (Victoria) Inc. and an article which appeared in Quadrant, *October 2010.*

14.1 Introduction

The arrival of the ships re-enacting the arrival of the First Fleet was the high point of the 1988 celebrations of the Bicentennial of the European settlement of Australia. It took place in front of two million people, something never again surpassed even during the Sydney Olympic Games. Without it there would have been little point in the celebrations in Sydney Harbour on Australia Day 1988. But every effort was made by the Australian government to stop the re-enactment

Notwithstanding the great success of the re-enactment, the official view transmitted to our children and to students in the universities and indeed to the world is that the settlement was a regrettable invasion, that the colony which was established was a gulag and that we should be ashamed of our origins.

This is because the origins of our country are perceived as an embarrassment to the elites who have marched through our institutions and who dominated the 1988 cabinet. They were wrong, and their view contrasts with that of the great bulk of ordinary Australians who are guided as always by their innate common sense, good judgement and decency.

The First Fleet was that extraordinary venture when, under the command of Captain, later Admiral Arthur Phillip, eleven ships sailed from Portsmouth, Hampshire, England, on 13 May 1787 with about 1,487 people to establish the first European colony in Australia.

They did not come alone.

14.2 Freedom

Captain Phillip did not only bring people and provisions – he brought institutions which are with us today and which have made this nation. Those institutions – and the concepts and ideas behind them – are not the property of the Anglo-Saxons of Australia, to the extent that there are still people whose lineage over the last 225 years can be described as pure Anglo-Saxon. Just as in the US, these are their institutions, the concepts and the ideas which belong to all Australians, whenever they or their ancestors came to this land, wherever they came from and whatever their race.

To understand what was being brought here, we should recall the sort of country Britain was when Captain Phillip gave the order to sail. David Landes says, as noted earlier, that the pre-eminence that Britain enjoyed in the industrial revolution resulted from the fact that the British people had "elbow room".[2]

Far from perfect, by comparison with most communities across the Channel, the British were free and fortunate.

Britain, writes Landes, was developing into a precociously modern industrial nation.

The salient feature of a successful society, he writes, is the ability to adapt to new things and ways. And one key area of change was the increasing freedom and security of the people. Yet, he says, the British still call themselves subjects of the Crown, while they have longer than anyone else been citizens.

This was due to that extraordinary constitutional settlement in 1688, the Glorious Revolution, discussed in the previous Chapter. This was a rejection of James II's attempt to direct the constitution towards the absolutist centralist model of government which prevailed on the continent, and especially in the France of Louis XIV. It achieved an "auspicious union of freedom and power".[3]

And this was the constitutional model in its two versions which was to be adopted by democracies across the world.

Alan Atkinson says that in Britain at the end of the American Revolution, two great issues dominated the conversation of polite and ambitious men and women.[4] These were, first, the status of blacks in the Empire, and secondly, penal discipline.

Closely related to this were the issues which drove the Americans to revolt, and resulted in the British establishing a penal colony on this very land.

It is said the victors write history. So when we come to what was in fact very much a civil war, the dominant theme is thought to be "No taxation without representation". Put aside the reasonable claim for some reimbursement of the cost of the successful defence of the colonies against the French, and the error of the British not to involve the colonists in resolving that issue.

But there were two other issues which motivated the American colonists, who were living in the freest colonies the world had ever seen. The first was the Great Proclamation of 1763 by King George III, which reserved all formerly French lands to the West of the thirteen colonies for the Indian tribes and prevented any European expansion.

The other centred on a notorious a case in 1772 concerning a runaway slave, James Somersett.[5] Lord Mansfield is said to have concluded his judgement with the words, "The air of England is too pure for a slave to breathe; let the black go free." Americans, especially in the South, were appalled that Lord Mansfield would by this decision free 15,000 slaves in England, leaving slave-owners with no recourse. Worse, they were outraged that the Imperial Parliament showed no interest in reversing this.[6] They feared of course the precedential value of this in the colonial courts.

It has been said, but nowadays not said too loudly, "The price of freedom from England was bondage for African slaves in America."[7] Beneath the unity of revolution lurked a compromise that could not endure and which would lead to civil war in the next century.[8]

14.3 Sydney and Phillip

Two men stand out in the settlement of Australia. One was the Secretary of State for the Colonies, Thomas Townshend Viscount Sydney.[9] Manning Clark dismisses him for his mediocrity.

Actually his role in establishing the foundations of this country was crucial.

Above all, Sydney was strongly attached to the constitution, "a consideration superior to every other in his mind." He had a reverence for the law and for the consent of the subject.

There is a striking example of the sort of man he was.

This relates to a female convict, one Susannah Holmes. Sentenced to death after being found guilty of theft, she had her sentence commuted to transportation to the American colonies for a term of 14 years. It also relates to Henry Kable, convicted for burglary. His death sentence was also commuted to transportation for fourteen years to America. They were both held at Norwich Castle gaol pending transportation with the First Fleet to New South Wales.

Susannah and Henry entered into a relationship. She gave birth to a son, whom she called Henry. When she was taken to the ship bound for Botany Bay, baby Henry was nine months old. The captain refused to take the child. The gaoler, turnkey John Simpson, saw that Susannah was absolutely devastated. He feared she would take her life.

He did an extraordinary thing. He went off with the child on his lap down to London. He decided he would go to the top. He would see the minister.

He found Lord Sydney on the steps of the Home Office. Instead of sending him away, or turning him over to his advisers – if he had had such people – Lord Sydney listened to his story. And remember, in those days, the TV cameras were not on him and nobody had a mobile phone with a camera. He was not looking for publicity.

Instead of saying Simpson would have to fill out some form and put in a submission which could be considered by some committee in due course, Lord Sydney, who was "greatly affected", immediately "promised that the child should be restored, commending ... Mr. Simpson's spirit and humanity".[10]

As it would today, the story appeared in the media – in several newspapers. It would not have been the result of the efforts of the minister's army of spin doctors. It will astound young people today, but in those days ministers of the Crown did not see the need for such people. The story attracted the attention of one Lady Cadogan. She organised a public subscription.

This produced the grand sum of £20. But if we go back to 1788, using the Retail Price Index this is about £2,060, around A$3,500, today. But using average weekly earnings it is about £24,800, around A$41,359.70.[11]

Whatever it was, it was a small fortune to Susannah. This was used to buy her family – for that is what they had become – a parcel of goods. Our first clergyman, the Rev. Richard Johnson was charged with giving them the parcel on their arrival in New South Wales.

That is not the end of the story of the Kables.

This story tells you something about Lord Sydney. But there is a more important matter concerning the minister.

Lord Sydney, whom too many have glibly dismissed as being of no consequence, took a crucial decision which would have a fundamental effect on the colony. Instead of just establishing it as a military prison, he provided for a civil administration, with courts of law.

Phillip and Sydney came out of the same enlightenment in Britain which was to bring forth William Wilberforce, who was to lead the world's first successful campaign against slavery.

Wilberforce used an image of such power it told a thousand words: a kneeling, powerful black slave, who pleads, "Am I not a Man and a Brother?"

Lord Sydney's enlightened approach reflected very much the views of Captain Arthur Phillip, who was to govern the first colony in the only continent of this world which has never known slavery.

Phillip wrote, before leaving England:

> The laws of this country will, of course be introduced in [New] South Wales, and there is one that I would wish to take place from the moment His Majesty's forces take possession of the country: That there can be no slavery in a free land and consequently no slaves.[12]

In an essay on the subject of our early leaders which was published in the April 2007 edition of *Quadrant*, Dr. Keith Windschuttle wrote:

> The idea that slavery was an affront to humanity that had no place in a free land was part of the original definition of what it meant to be an Australian ... although NSW founder Arthur Phillip's original anti-slavery declaration was once well known to earlier generations of students, historians today rarely mention it.

Like Sydney, Phillip was a humanitarian. As the ship's captain he had to reduce the water ration as supplies dwindled. He reduced his officers' ration – including his own – so that the men would receive a full ration. The navy board had ruled that both soldiers and male convicts should receive the same ration, and women two-thirds. When provisions dwindled in the colony, the ration for most men was reduced to two-thirds. This extended to officers and to the governor. The women's rations were maintained.[13]

What a fortunate conjunction there was in 1788: Great Britain as the colonial power, Lord Sydney as the Colonial Secretary and Captain Arthur Phillip as the Governor.

The result was that Phillip did not come alone. He was able to bring four institutions which would be the foundations of this country: the rule of law, the English language, our Judeo-Christian values, and an institution which would forever ensure leadership beyond politics, the Crown. And from that flowed three marvellous developments.

14.4 The rule of law

Phillip brought the great gift of the rule of law with him. Now the rule of law has, according to Sir Guy Green, two elements.

First, everyone, including and especially the executive arm of government, is subject to the law.

Second, while citizens may do anything not prohibited by the law, the executive government may only do those things authorised by the law.

To speak then of the colony as a gulag or as a primitive ancestor of the gulag is completely erroneous.[14] Of this the distinguished historian Professor Alan Atkinson says, "Nothing could be further from the truth."[15]

To call the colony a gulag is not only a libel on the memory of Phillip and of Sydney; worse it is a libel on the Australian nation.

The Soviet gulags were brutal and lawless concentration camps, especially for political prisoners, who had no rights whatsoever. They were lucky to be alive, if being there could be called a life.

Even under the broadest definition, few of the convicts sent to Australia could be called political prisoners.

So defined, every government in this country, since 1788, has been under the rule of law – every government.

By way of contrast, the rule of law was foreign to the Soviet gulags, indeed to the whole Soviet Union and its once vast empire over Eastern Europe.

The Governor, Captain Phillip, came with a Charter of Justice, which unlike the provisions of the Soviet Constitution, was actually applied.

He came with no lawyers, but a set of law books. Just consider one example.

Remember Henry Kable and Susannah Holmes. At Norwich gaol, Henry, described as "a fine healthy young fellow", had shown not only a "remarkable fondness" for the child but a desperate desire to marry Susannah.

Philip put five of the best behaved women in tents near his own, including Susannah.

Then he gave her permission to marry Henry. And on 10 February 1788, Susannah and Henry and four other couples were married by the Rev. Richard Johnson in the first European wedding ceremony in Australia.[16]

Remember also that the public subscription launched by Lady Cadogan had raised the substantial sum of £20, as noted, worth somewhere between A$3,500 and A$40,000. The first figure is using a Consumer Price Index. The second is based on average weekly earnings. They had bought a parcel of goods which the Rev. Richard Johnson was to give them on their arrival in the penal colony.

But Duncan Sinclair, the Master of the Alexander, the ship which carried the parcel, would only hand over were a few books, claiming the parcel was lost.

On the sworn deposition of Henry Kable, the Judge-Advocate, David Collins, issued a summons to the acting Provost Marshal to bring the Master before the Court on 1 July 1788.

Accordingly, the Master was brought before the Court the next day 2 July at 4:00pm. Justice was delivered expeditiously then.

Three sailors, including the Captain of the Sirius, gave evidence.

This was the Court of Civil Jurisdiction, one of two courts established by The King under Letters Patent, referred to as the First Charter of Justice. (The jurisdiction of this court was transferred to the Supreme Court of New South Wales established in 1814 under the Second Charter of Justice).

Under the law then in force, a convict who had been sentenced to death had no right to sue. This was the law of felony attaint. The Master boasted that he could not be sued by the Kables.

If you go to the law report,[17] you will see that on the summons the plaintiffs' occupation, the words "New Settlers of this place" had been crossed out and nothing put in their place. To have described them as convicts would have ensured they could not sue, and the words "New Settlers" were untrue.

We assume that when Sinclair challenged the prosecution on the ground that the Kables were felons, and thus attainted, the Court must have required him to prove it. As all the convict records had been left behind in England, he could not do so.

In any event the Court found for Kable and ordered Sinclair to make restitution of £15, worth nowadays, somewhere between A$2,500 and A$30,000.

This was the first example of the Australianisation of the common law.

Can those, including Robert Hughes, who say the penal colony was a gulag give a similar example of litigation by prisoners in a Soviet or Nazi gulag, particularly one where the Soviet or Nazi judges upheld the prisoners' assertions?

Of course they cannot.

Incidentally Henry and Susannah had 11 children, and he was a successful businessman. Their descendants celebrate their memory in family reunions, and the hotel *Four Seasons* has a restaurant named Kables after them.

The penal colony of New South Wales, harsh as it was by modern standards, was one of the most successful experiments in criminal rehabilitation the world has ever seen.

It was soon established beyond doubt that everyone, including soldiers, were subject to the same law.[18]

The rate of recidivism, or return to crime, was extraordinarily low, as far as we can tell.

Indeed, from the beginning of the penal colony, the authorities were to insist on the application of the rule of law – at least the criminal law – to all men and women, of all races and colours. That this was to be imperfectly applied, and that there were to be legal restrictions on Aboriginal people, often for paternalistic reasons, is a matter of great regret. But it does not equate to some form of Nazism at the heart of white Australia.

The first prosecution about the killing of an Aborigine was in 1797.[19]

And four years later a convict, John Kirby, became probably the first European sentenced to death for killing an Aborigine after he stabbed a co-operative chief called Burragong, or King Jack.[20]

Perhaps the most remarkable was in the final words of the judge when sentencing the white perpetrators of the massacre of Aboriginal people at Myall Creek in 1838 – over 170 years ago.[21] These words demonstrate that, even then, the principle that the rule of law must in Australian society prevail, whatever the race or colour of the victim or offender, was fully upheld.

There, Mr. Justice Burton declared:

> Prisoners at the bar ... you have been found guilty of the murder of men, women and children.
>
> The circumstances of the murders of which you have been found guilty are of such singular atrocity that I am persuaded that you long ago must have expected what the result would be. This is not the case where a single individual has met his

death by violent means; this is not the case, as has too often stained indelibly the annals of this Colony, where death has ensued from a drunken quarrel; this is not the case, when, as this session the Court has been pained to hear, the blood of a human being and the intoxicating liquor were mingled on the same floor; this is not the case where the life or property of an individual has been attacked, ever so weakly and arms have been resorted to.

No such extenuating circumstances as these, if any consider them extenuating, have taken place. This is not the case of the murder of one individual, but of many – men, women, and children, old men and babes hanging at their mothers' breasts, to the number in all, according to the evidence, probably of thirty individuals, whose bodies on one occasion were murdered – poor defenceless human beings ...

I cannot expect that any words of mine can reach your hearts, but I hope that the grace of God may reach them, for nothing else can reach those hardened hearts which could surround that fatal pile, and slay the fathers, mothers, and the infants ...

I cannot but look at you with commiseration; you were all transported to this Colony, although some of you have since become free; you were removed from a Christian country and placed in a dangerous and tempting situation; you were entirely removed from the benefit of the ordinances of religion; you were one hundred and fifty miles from the nearest Police station on which you could rely for protection – by which you could have been controlled.

I cannot but deplore that you should have been placed in such a situation – that such circumstances should have existed, and above all, that you should have committed such a crime. But this commiseration must not interfere with the stern duty, which as a Judge the law enforces on me, which is to order that you, and each of you, be removed to the place whence you came and thence to a place of public execution, and that at such time as His Excellency, the Governor shall appoint you be hanged by the neck until your bodies be dead, and may the Lord have mercy on your souls.

Let me remind you that this is a judge, in 1838, sentencing to death seven white men for the murder of Aborigines.

What greater evidence of a society under the rule of law for all, and for all races and colours, can there be than these words? And this was in the early 19th century. These words are more than sufficient not only to deny, but to unmask, the unjustified attempt by some to paint our country as a genocidal hell.

14.5 The English language

The benefit that the English language would bring to the new land was not fully understood in 1788.

A language dominates not so much for its quality or the quality of its literature. It is a question of power.

The full realisation of the remarkable vocation of our language came from the extent of the British Empire, and its dominance over France.

In addition, for the very first time in the history of the world, the dominant power was immediately succeeded by another power, its former colony, which spoke the same language.

This was of course the United States. (Admittedly some maintain that we do not speak the same language).

I would not predict which country will surpass the United States. But of the contenders, remember the significant place English enjoys in India.

14.6 Our Judeo-Christian values

The motto of our oldest Australian university is *Sidere mens eadem mutato* (The same mind under a different sky). In many ways this captures the theme of this chapter.

In addition to the rule of law, and our language, our Judeo-Christian values came with the settlement of Australia. They permeate our laws, language, institutions and even our federation.

This does not mean Australia should not welcome those from other religions, nor does it mean that there is any obligation for an Australian to belong to any of these religions, nor indeed any religion.

In fact this openness to others was stressed in the very first sermon preached in this land on Sunday, 3 February 1788.

This first public service was well attended, due no doubt to the direction by the Governor that "no man to be absent on any account whatever".

The service was to begin at 10am under "a great tree" close to the harbour, now the corner of Castlereagh and Hunter Streets.

The Rev. Richard Johnson chose as his text Psalm 116:12:

> What shall I render unto the Lord for all his benefits toward me? I will take the cup of salvation and call upon the name of the Lord.

He began:

> I do not address you as Churchmen or Dissenters, Roman Catholics or Protestants, as Jews or Gentiles ... But I speak to you as mortals and yet immortal ...
>
> The gospel ... proposes a free and gracious pardon to the guilty, cleansing to the polluted, healing to the sick, happiness to the miserable and even life for the dead.

That influence was to continue, although undermined by the so-called Rum Corps.

Over one century later, in the public consultations on the draft of our federal Constitution, more supporting petitions were received than for any other concerning a proposal that the preamble recognise what one delegate called the "invisible hand of providence" in the federation of Australia.

So we find in the preamble a provision which summarises, succinctly, the very pith and substance of that great act of unity.

This is that the people of each of the several states:

> ... humbly relying on the blessing of Almighty God, have agreed to unite in one indissoluble Federal Commonwealth under the Crown ... and under the Constitution hereby established.

This, it should be noted, led to the insertion of the somewhat superfluous clause against the establishment of any religion, section 116.

14.7 Leadership beyond politics: the Crown

The institution which Phillip represented is our oldest. Professor Atkinson says the Crown figured largely in his view of the world. He paid extraordinary attention to our oldest holiday, The King's Birthday.

"Phillip's reconstruction of the Crown within his government, transferring the essence of 18th century monarchy to this vast and remote space, was a remarkable labour of imagination," writes Professor Atkinson.[22]

The Crown has since evolved and been Australianised so much so that our High Court has ruled that the Australian Crown is an institution separate from the British Crown and that allegiance to the British Crown is allegiance to a foreign power.[23]

All that the Australian Crown has in common with the New Zealand Crown, the Canadian Crown or the British Crown is that they are worn by the same person and there the law of succession is identical in each of the sixteen realms.

The Australian Crown is now a significant part of the Australian constitutional system. Providing leadership beyond politics, it is a significant check and balance against the improper exercise of political power.

This is in three ways. First, provided a government retains the confidence of the lower house, it tends to control the house. This control is more evident in Australia. This is unlike the situation in, say, the US. In the Westminster system, the Crown becomes a significant check and balance on this control. It does this as a constitutional guardian through not so much the exercise of but the existence of the reserve powers which former NSW Premier Bob Carr claimed had been destroyed.[24]

Second, the Crown acts as an auditor of the executive. The protocol is that significant government decisions are given effect by advice to the Crown in the Executive Council. The Crown needs to be assured that what is proposed is within power, and that any conditions on the exercise of that power have been fulfilled.

Third, the other state institutions which are outside of the political arena owe their allegiance to the Crown, and not to the government of the day. These include the judiciary, the armed forces, the public service and the police forces.

If the Crown were to be removed from what is according to the Constitution Act, our Federal Commonwealth under the Crown, the result will be that the power of the political class will be considerably increased, unless an alternative institution can be found.

The noted republican, Professor George Williams, agrees the 1999 model had serious flaws.

The place of the Crown is under challenge.

If the Australian people decide to dispense with the Australian Crown, that is their prerogative.

But those who wish to remove it are duty bound to do three things. If they do not they will fail.

First, they must understand the role and function of the Crown. It is surprising how often reformers do not understand what they want to change, or advance spurious reasons for change, for example attaining independence.

Second, they must provide details of exactly what is proposed to replace the institution in all its aspects.

Third, they must, in the words of those great founding fathers, Sir John Quick and Sir Robert Garran, persuade the people in a referendum that the change proposed is "desirable, irresistible and inevitable".[25]

They did not come alone. Captain Phillip brought with him those institutions, concepts and ideas which made this country and are still with us.

There were three principal consequences.

14.8 Self-government

The first consequence of the British settlement in 1788 was that within a surprisingly short period of time, the full panoply of self-government under the Westminster system was exported to five of the six colonial later state capitals, and later to Perth.

The French, the Spanish, the Portuguese did not transmit the parliamentary concept to their colonies, as the British did to their American colonies long before independence, and as they did to Australia.

Why? The reason is that they either could not or would not concede such authority.

With the exception of the Dutch, they did not have parliamentary government concept at home. And the Dutch showed no interest in granting self-government to their colonies.

Parliament, self-government and the Westminster system, the fifth pillar of our nation, came very early to Australia – within one generation of the founding of the penal colony.

Australians quickly adapted these institutions, making them even more democratic and thus, more Australian.

There is one important point.

This had absolutely nothing to do with the Eureka Stockade. There is no need to invent a War of Independence which never occurred.

Initially the power of the colonial governor was restricted by the law and carried out under written instructions from London.

This power was later tempered by an advisory legislative council and executive council. Gradually the legislative council took on an increasingly representative flavour and, within a surprisingly short period, the executive became responsible to that legislature.

This is even more remarkable if we remember that most of the states started as penal colonies.

From 1823 there was to be a gradually increased involvement of the people in the governance of what was now a civil and no longer penal colony.

By 1842, as Professor P.H. Lane points out, we can identify three basic constitutional doctrines applying in New South Wales:

- "No taxation without representation": that is, the newly constituted people's institution was to make laws, including the tax laws.

- "The financial initiative of the crown": that is, the governor must first recommend to the legislature the purpose for which public money was to be appropriated.

- "Parliament controls the expenditure of public money": that is, an appropriation of (most) revenue must be made by the legislature, and in no other manner.

The second *Australian Constitutions Act*, 1850,[26] brought similar reforms to the other colonies (except for the Moreton Bay district – Queensland – which was attached to the New South Wales legislative council until 1859).

This act was extremely important. It empowered the various colonies to draft their own constitutions, although they were still to be approved by the Colonial Office in London before being presented for the Queen's Assent. The New South Wales and Victorian constitutions received Royal Assent on 16 July 1855.

To strike down another myth, the bills were in London well before the Eureka Stockade. Whatever the Eureka Stockade achieved it was not democracy.

The state constitutions were, as Lane puts it, "essentially home grown; even if monitored by the Imperial authorities".

They were never imposed by London. And this was half a century before the federal Constitution. Lane observes that the development of the legislative council in each of the colonies brought about constitutional monarchy in Australia.

A constitutional monarchy, also described as a crowned republic, is a system of government in which the Crown does not exercise absolute power, but only limited power under the Constitution. In particular the crown is advised by its ministers who are answerable, through parliament, to the people.

The state governors today survive as living symbols of the process of evolution to representative and responsible government under the Crown, under which they act as constitutional umpires and auditors.

14.9 Federation

Federation was the second consequence of the British settlement. It was never inevitable. In fact when the British first suggested it the local politicians were outraged. And it was extraordinary; it was different from any other federation.

There were no deaths, no violence, no threats of war.

Sir John Quick and Sir Robert Garran described this great achievement in the following way:

Never before have a group of self-governing, practically independent communities, without external pressure or foreign complications of any kind, deliberately chosen of their own free will to put aside their provincial jealousies and come together as one people, from a simple intellectual and sentimental conviction of the folly of disunion and the advantages of nationhood.

The States of America, or Switzerland, or Germany were drawn together under the shadow of war. Even the Canadian provinces were forced to unite by the neighbourhood of a great foreign power.

But the Australian Commonwealth, the fifth great Federation of the world, came into voluntary being through a deep conviction of national unity.

We may well be proud of the statesmen who constructed a Constitution which – whatever may be its faults and its shortcomings – has proved acceptable to a large majority of the people of five great communities scattered over a continent; and proud of a people who, without the compulsion of war or the fear of conquest, have succeeded in agreeing upon the terms of a binding and indissoluble Social Compact.[27]

Australia is one of the world's oldest continuing democracies. In the United Nations Human Development Index, which measures countries according to their wealth, health and education, Australia invariably comes not only in the top twenty, the top ten, but the top five.

14.10 A good international citizen

There is a third consequence of the British settlement. Australia has been involved in a remarkable way in defending the freedom and liberty of others. In the Second World War, we were one of a handful of countries who fought from the beginning to the end. As a percentage of the population, almost twice as many Australians gave their lives as Americans, 0.57% to 0.32%. In the First World War, it was ten times more Australians as Americans, 1.25% to 0.11%.

This is not to denigrate the great contribution by the United States. It is to compare our contribution with that of another power whose territory was not a theatre of war in the first, and only marginally in the second. It is to give some perspective to our contribution. (A contribution broadly similar to Australia's was made by our ANZAC partner, New Zealand).

14.11 Conclusion

In conclusion, those on the First Fleet did not come alone. What they brought were those considerable and enduring gifts which have made this nation.

These are our heritage. We should neither cast them out, nor ignore them, nor so negligently order our educational system that the young know little about them.

We should not only recall Edmund Burke's wise words; we should also apply them:

> It is with infinite caution that any man ought to venture upon pulling down an edifice which has answered in any tolerable degree for ages the common purposes of society, or on building it up again, without having a model and patterns of approved utility before his eyes.
>
> Society is indeed a contract ... It is a partnership between those who are living, those who are dead, and those who are to be born.[28]

Endnotes

1 Richard J. Tanner, *The First Fleet and the Re-Enactment First Fleet – Some Historical Parallels and Differences*, The Order of Australia Association NSW Branch, 2010. http://www.theorderofaustralia.asn.au/downloads/NSWRJTAddressJan10.pdf   (retrieved 05.05.2013).

2 David S. Landes, *The Wealth and Poverty of Nations: Why Some Are So Rich and Some So Poor*, W.W. Norton, New York, 1998.

3 Thomas Babbington Macaulay, *The History of England*, 1855, Penguin Classics, 1979, p. 51.

4 Alan Atkinson, *The Europeans in Australia*, Volume 1, Source, Naperville, 1997, p. 44.

5 In R v *Knowles*, ex parte Somersett (1772) 20 State Tr 1.

6 Alfred W. Blumrosen & Ruth G. Blumrosen, *Slave Nation*, 2005, p 35.

7 Blumrosen, op.cit., p xiv.

8 Blumrosen, loc.cit.

9 For an excellent biography, see Andrew Tink, *Lord Sydney [The Life and Tines of Tommy Townshend]*, Australian Scholarly Publishing, Melbourne, 2011.

10 Atkinson, op. cit., p. 100.

11 Measuring Worth: http://www.measuringworth.com/ppoweruk/result.php?use%5B%5D=CPI&use%5B%5D=NOMINALEARN&year_early=1788&pound71=20&shilling71=&pence71=&amount=20&year_source=1788&year_result=2010, (retrieved 07.05.2013).

12 Atkinson, op. cit., p. 62..

13 Alan Atkinson, op. cit., p. 105

14 Robert Hughes, *The Fatal Shore*, Harvill, London, 1986, p. 538.

15 Alan Atkinson, op. cit., p. 58.

16 Atkinson, op. cit., pp. 129, 130.

17 *Cable* v. *Sinclair* [1788] NSWKR 7.

18 *Boston* v. *Laycock* [1795] NSWKR 3.

19 R v. *Millar and Bevan* [1797] NSWKR 3.

20 R. v. *Kirby and Thompson* [1820] NSWKR 11.

21 R. v. *Kilmeister* in 1838; http://www.law.mq.edu.au/scnsw/Cases1838-39/html/r_v_kilmeister__no_2___1838.htm, accessed 11 May 2010.

22 Atkinson, op. cit., p. 109.

23 *Sue* v *Hill* [1999] HCA 30; 199 CLR 462; 163 ALR 648; 73 ALJR 1016 (23 June 1999).

24 Tony Stephens, "Whitlam leaves past behind with gifts from high time and low", *Sydney Morning Herald*, 8 November 2005. http://www.smh.com.au/news/national/whitlam-leaves-past-behind-with-gifts-from-high-time-and-low/2005/11/07/1131212008743.html (retrieved 24.04.2013).

25 Sir John Quick and Sir Robert Garran, *The Annotated Constitution of the Australian Commonwealth*, 1901, reprinted by Legal Books in 1976, 1995, p. 988.

26 "An Act for the better Government of Her Majesty's Australian Colonies" (13 & 14 Vic., ch. 59).

27 Quick and Garran, op. cit., pp. 225-6.

28 Edmund Burke, *Reflections on the Revolution in France*, 1790, Oxford, 1993, p. 61.

CHAPTER 15

Our federation – not in safe hands

This Chapter is based on David Flint, "The High Court's workplaces decision: implications for our federal system", National Observer, No. 72, August 2007. The authors thank the editor John Ballantyne for his permission to use this.

15.1 Introduction

The Australian federation was a remarkable achievement. It was the result of the people of the future states agreeing to a compact to form the Commonwealth of Australia. The full details of the proposal were on the table before the people voted.

The Constitution itself was developed by a mainly elected convention, with, for the first time in history, a full record of their discussions. Even today, we know what was in their minds when they decided on the form and details of the federation. And as previously noted, Sir John Quick and Sir Robert Garran remarked that the decision to federate was unusually made without any external pressure or foreign complications.[1] Australians decided to federate through a deep conviction of national unity.

These facts are little known in Australia today. They are only mentioned briefly, if at all, in our schools and universities. This is because these facts contradict the official line pushed by the elites. This is that Australia was a colonial backwater. According to Dr. Lucy Sullivan, the so-called "father of multiculturalism", the late Professor Jerzy Zubrzycki AO CBE, implied in an ABC broadcast in the 1990s that pre-war Australia "lacked a sophisticated science, law, literature, history and system of government..."[2]

This elite denigration of our colonial past supports the contention that the solution to any problem is by handing over full powers to the federal government and parliament, notwithstanding their inability to fulfil their core duties under the Constitution such as defence and border control.

15.2 Our federation under strain

"We need a new vision splendid," argued former Democrat Senator Andrew Murray in 2009.[3] He said that our political and social contract was under serious strain, and not just because the Commonwealth has the money and the states want to spend it. He believes that some of this strain comes from our "creaking Constitution and institutions", and the consequent need to modernise our governance. He also blamed the "centralising tendencies" of the Howard government.

He was critical of any "mere managerial" solution, the principal example of which he says is the action plan proposed by the Business Council of Australia (BCA), which has a focus on efficiency, and which sees no need for radical changes to the powers of the states and the Commonwealth or for any major change to the Constitution.[4]

No reform of the Australian system will be successful, he believes, unless it accommodates revised checks and balances. "I'm talking political economy, a holistic approach," he wrote. "You cannot fix the economic or the social effectively without also fixing political governance. And that means reassessing the Constitution, the separation of powers, a republic, whether the federation should stay, and, if it should, in what form, and the powers that states and the Commonwealth should each have."

He proposed another convention, but this time a standing convention for say, 10 years, with a permanent secretariat and with a budget sufficient to allow for "full engagement and dialogue". This should be supplemented by a "university-based institute for constitutional change, producing discussion papers and fostering public awareness and debate".

These arguments are in the tradition of those who say our Constitution is creaking under the strain, shows its age and is in need of reform. What many really want is a Constitution radically different from that which our founders chose.

In political and media debate, "reform" – as we know only too well – does not necessarily mean improvement. In the Australian constitutional context, "reform" has long been shorthand for centralism, and in recent years has been extended to a vastly increased political role for the judges as well as, and of course, a republic in which the political class increases its powers.

"Reform" often includes the removal of checks and balances, such as the states, the Senate and our oldest institution – and the one above politics – the Australian Crown. In addition, "reform" usually depends on substituting judicial orthodoxy with a degree of adventurism, even where this is disguised, as it was for many decades, from about the twenties to the seventies in a genuflection towards literalism.

The age of our Constitution is used as part of the armoury of the "reformers" who dismiss it as coming from the "horse and buggy" era. They should be reminded that the American Constitution is twice as old as Australia's, and that few Americans would call for a drastic change to it.

Indeed, constitutional longevity in a world where constitutional instability is the norm should be seen as a virtue and not a vice. As John Stone argues, ours is one of the finest – if not the finest – constitutions in the world.[5] The Australian people were more fully involved in the development and adoption of our Constitution than any other people in the modern world. They determined the essence of the new nation in the Constitution's covering clauses when, "humbly relying on the blessings of Almighty God", they agreed, in each of the colonies, "to unite in one indissoluble Federal Commonwealth under the Crown ... and under the Constitution ...".[6]

The intention of the founders, and, most importantly, the people, was very clear. Had the centralist politicians and the judges subsequently kept more to that intention, many if not most of the problems of overlap, of centralisation and of financial irresponsibility by the states would probably have been avoided. That intention was surely that the external affairs and spending powers of the federal government and parliament be limited to the list of powers which the people agreed should be of federal concern. In the meantime, the states should be principally dependent on taxes they raised themselves. The intention was not that the states be reduced to their present mendicant status, but that they should continue as they originally were: self-governing communities now united in a federation where the federal entity had limited enumerated powers.

The problem today is not so much in the Constitution; it is in those who have effectively changed it without seeking the approval of the people, and in the knowledge, it should be noted, that the people would have been most unlikely to agree. The answer is certainly not in the dissolution of the states, the substitution of regions even more dependent on the Commonwealth, in the transfer of even more powers to the Commonwealth, in a vast increase in the power of the judges to govern us through a bill of rights, or in the grafting of some unspecified republic onto our Constitution.

In the meantime, the consequences of the present unsatisfactory situation can be considerably mitigated by sensible working relationships between Canberra and the state capitals. But, above all, what is needed is a return to the principles of the Constitution of our one indissoluble federal Commonwealth under the Crown – principles to which the Australian people have given their consent and which they have so regularly affirmed in a series of referendums.

15.3 Our federation in context

The Australian federation is not some easily disposable appendage, some burden which good sense demands we quickly remove. It is not only part of our history; it remains one of the pillars of our nation. It flows from, and is closely inter-related to, each of the other pillars, discussed in more detail in Chapter 14. Indeed, the federation and its institutions cannot be understood without placing them in the context of those other pillars.

As we have seen, the preamble to the Constitution Act that the British Parliament passed to give effect to our Constitution – with some minor changes – expresses the nature of that compact, and reminds us of the other pillars. As we have seen it recites that the people of the several states, agreed to unite in "an indissoluble Federal Commonwealth under the Crown ... and under the Constitutution".[7]

Those words set out the essence of our federation, which was truly the success story of the 20th century. This is the context of our nation. Just as the United States was formed and still lives under its Constitution, so the Australian nation lives under and still operates under the pillars of our nation which include our constitutional system.

The values that flow from the six pillars of our nation remain relevant today. They are the creeds that Australians have long held and should continue to hold today. Our federation can only be seen as a culmination of history, and in the context of a strong desire and intention to retain the self-governing states as important entities in themselves. This desire to retain the autonomy of the states and their freedom from federal control explains the long delay until 1986 in removing the states from what was mistakenly thought to be an only nominal tutelage of the British ministers in relation to Crown matters.[8]

Under our constitutional system, only two institutions straddle the Commonwealth-state divide. One is the Crown, the other is the High Court. Both are intended to be above politics. While the Crown remains unquestionably above politics, the High Court, or a majority of the Court, has occasionally wandered beyond its role, never more so than in some of their more controversial decisions during the 1990s.

One policy which has dominated the court since 1920, and for which there is no constitutional authority, is centralism, once disguised as an objective exercise in literalist interpretation. This began as long ago as 1920 in the decision of the High Court in the *Engineers' Case*.[9]

According to Professor Geoffrey de Q. Walker, the case inaugurated a method of one-sided interpretation that contradicted the Constitution's plain intention, ignoring the first principles of legal interpretation, and violating the people's wishes as consistently expressed in constitutional referenda, as well as mocking their sovereign power. This, he says, denied the people the advantages of competitive federalism and increased the burden, cost and remoteness of government, more recently pushing the constitutional order to the brink of breakdown.[10]

The Court has continued this trend in the decision in the *WorkChoices Case*.[11] Whether or not we agree with the Howard government's industrial legislation, it is difficult not to be concerned as to the consequences of this decision for the future of the federation. The Court indicated, with Justice Michael Kirby and Justice Ian Callinan dissenting, that the Commonwealth's use of the corporations power is almost without limits. The Court had two decades ago come to a similar conclusion with respect to the external affairs power.[12]

This is dangerous. No one could seriously say that this vast expansion of federal power was the intention of the founders, or that it reflects the wishes of the Australian people. In fact, most of the failed referenda which involved giving more power to Canberra – some even rejected more than once – have been circumvented by High Court decisions which have favoured the Commonwealth.[13]

Professor Greg Craven observed that "the states should be in absolutely no doubt" that this latest decision "is a shipwreck of Titanic proportions. Not since the 1920s has the court struck such a devastating blow against Australian federalism ...".

"How", he asked, "a court can weigh every tiny word of a constitution without grasping the central premise that it was meant to create a genuine federation must baffle historians and psychoanalysts alike." This is, he said, "the greatest constitutional disaster" to befall the states in 80 years.

Reflecting the warning of Justice Kirby in his strong dissent, Professor Craven warned that the federal authorities now have an "open cheque to intervene in almost any area of state power that catches its eye, from higher and private education, through every aspect of health, to such matters as town planning and the environment".[14]

That this should worry conservative constitutionalists is well explained in the dissent of Justice Callinan. P.P. McGuinness warned that this decision could and probably would work both ways. A future government could attempt to regulate prices and incomes, re-regulate the labour market and, if socialism becomes fashionable again, nationalise any sector of the economy. He wrote that the majority had "destroyed our federal system of government". They had effectively abolished any logical or sensible limitation of the federal powers.[15]

Professor Craven said there is not the "least chance that Canberra will use these powers comprehensively to take over such policy nightmares as our health and education systems". Instead, based on long practice, Canberra will employ its new capacity to "cherry-pick politically attractive items and to embarrass uncongenial state governments". In other words, the politicians will, thanks to the High Court, be allowed to behave like politicians.

In handing down its decision on 14 November 2006, the High Court majority said the fact the people may have indicated their objection to a specific change is of "no assistance" to them. That is, the fact the people may have refused to grant some power to the Commonwealth is to be completely ignored. The High Court has turned its back on – or, as Professor Walker says, mocked – the "quasi sovereignty" with which the founders specifically endowed the people.[16]

The result is that the High Court has abdicated much of its role as an important check and balance. As Professor Craven says, we no longer have "even a deeply biased constitutional umpire". The High Court "has given Canberra the key to the constitution".

15.4 Advantages of federalism

Professor Walker observes that for "a framework of government that has created a new nation and given it external security, internal peace, stability, progress and prosperity throughout the most violent, turbulent century in human history", our Constitution has been subjected to an "inordinate" amount of negative comment. He says the chief obstacle to a balanced appraisal today is the failure of the critics to consider the advantages of federalism. He lists ten: the right in the citizen of choice and exit, the possibility of experiment, the accommodation of regional preferences and diversity, participation in government and the countering of elitism, the better protection of liberty, the closer supervision of government, stability, fail-safe design, competition and efficiency, and the resulting competitive edge for the nation.[17]

Professor Walker writes that the debate has hitherto focused exclusively on its disadvantages. More recently, there has been an increasing acceptance of the advantages of federalism. Those advantages were noted in the BCA report.[18] They were stressed in a major report in 2007 by Dr. Anne Twomey and Professor Glenn Withers to the newly formed Council for the Australian Federation, which brings together all of the Australian governments with the exception of the federal government.[19] They argue that by focusing too much on the problems in the operation of the federal system, we forget about the benefits of federation, including checks on power, choice and diversity, customisation of policies, competition (although they do not mention it, unilateral action by the Queensland government led to the abolition of that inequitable tax, death duties, in all states and at the federal level), creativity and co-operation.

The CFAF report drew attention to widespread media coverage of the BCA report which suggested that the cost of inefficiencies in the federal system, or perhaps the federal system itself, cost $9 billion for 2004-2005, or $450 per capita, a conclusion which was highly qualified in the report itself. The authors of the CFAF report preferred to measure the benefits of federation from a comparative OECD study which found that, for the last half century, federations had a 15.1 per cent advantage over unitary states. In addition they measured the benefit of fiscal decentralisation, which ranges between an average of 6.79 per cent, to "federal best-practice", exemplified by Canada, Germany and Switzerland, of 9.72 per cent.

Australia, they conclude, is the most fiscally centralised of the OECD federations, demonstrated by the fact that the states and territories raise only 19 per cent of taxes but are responsible for 40 per cent of public spending. As long ago as at the time of the creation of the United States, it had been realised that such vertical fiscal imbalance is inimical to good government. As a principle, governments should be responsible to the people who elect them for the money they spend. The CFAF report argues that the benefit to Australia from being a federation is already 10 per cent; and that this could be raised significantly by further decentralising our taxation system. The result would be to raise average incomes by $4,188 per annum.

15.5 What can be done?

Both the BCA and the CFAF reports joined in the premiers' call for a constitutional convention. But if one is held, it should not be about that "arid and irrelevant" issue, a republic.[20] Nor should it be distracted by the question of a constitutional bill of rights which bears no relation to the federal issue. The convention should be about the far more relevant issue: how to restore the federation.[21] It could be another task of the convention proposed in Part 3 of this book.

Ideally, this convention could aim to propose amendments to:

* ensure "vertical fiscal balance", so that the states would be responsible for collecting most of their income and answering to their electors as to how they spend it;
* list those powers where state laws are to prevail. The

absence of such a list allowed the High Court to launch, and maintain, its long adventure in forcing centralism on a reluctant nation;

- cap the extent of the external affairs and corporations powers to the other shared powers;

- ensure that minimum bureaucratic overlap occurs in relation to powers the exercise of which are effectively shared; and

- ensure the states are directly involved (and not just consulted) in determining the membership of the High Court. Why not, for example, allow each state chief justice or a nominee to join the bench as "ad hoc" justices in federal disputes?

The success of the constitutional conventions after 1893 was at least in part because they were mainly elected. Only one half of the 1998 Constitutional Convention was elected, and that by a postal system too open to abuse. Many of the nominated members were effectively chosen as almost ex officio members, including the prime minister, the premiers and leading ministers. We argue in Chapter 17 that only the elected delegates should be able to vote. At the same time, prominent constitutional lawyers, political scientists and finance and business experts could be available to give advice, either to the convention as a whole or to individual members, both orally and in writing.

A wholly nominated convention would lack authority and be open to manipulation and bias. It would have as much authority as the endless succession of "summits" which are called to settle some issue and too often to diffuse some debate.

As to procedure, the governments should agree in advance that the principles of the Corowa Plan should apply.[22] This, proposed by Sir John Quick in 1893, ensured that the movement to federation was not bogged down in endless parliamentary debate. When the convention finalises its draft, say in 12 months, it should be made public and sent to all the parliaments for comment. After, say, three months for comment (both parliamentary and public), the convention should have a period, say six months, to consider the comments and to finalise any subsequent changes. Following the Corowa Plan principles, the proposal would then be included in a series of bills for referendums.

The obligation of the federal parliament to do this would be moral rather than legal, the same sort of obligation their predecessors in the states agreed to in the 19th century.

Adopting the Corowa Plan principles would ensure that the conclusions of the convention are put to the people for their decision, and not just ignored or pigeonholed.

There is a clear need to restore the principles and essence of the federal Commonwealth which the Australian people approved and have regularly affirmed.[23] Whether the states are to be restored, or are to be even more emasculated, that decision should be made only by the people in a referendum, and not by circumventing the Constitution, which remains a vision splendid.

Endnotes

1 John Quick and Robert Garran, *Annotated Constitution of the Australian Commonwealth* 1901, reprinted Legal Books, Sydney, 1995 p. 988.

2 Lucy Sullivan, *News Weekly*, 2 March 2013.

3 Andrew Murray, *Strengthening Australia's Democracy, submission on Electoral Reform Green Paper*, 2009. http://www.dpmc.gov.au/consultation/elect_reform/strengthening_democracy/pdfs/24%20-%20Andrew%20Murray.pdf (retrieved 28.02 2013).

4 Business Council of Australia, *Reshaping Australia's Federation: A New Contract for Federal-State Relations*, 2006.

5 ABC Radio National, 13 July 2006.

6 Preamble, *Australian Constitution*.

7 Ibid.

8 Anne Twomey, *The Chameleon Crown: The Queen and her Australian Governors*, Federation Press, Sydney, 2006.

9 *Amalgamated Society of Engineers* v *Adelaide Steamship Co. Ltd*, (1920) 28 CLR 129.

10 "The Seven Pillars of Centralism: Federalism and the Engineers' Case", *Proceedings of the Fourteenth Conference of The Samuel Griffith Society*, 16 June 2002, vol. 14.

11 *New South Wales v Commonwealth* (WorkChoices Case) (2006) 231 ALR 1.

12 *Commonwealth* v *Tasmania* (Tasmanian Dams Case) (1983) 158 CLR 1.

13 David Flint, *The Cane Toad Republic*, Kentown, Wakefield Press, 1999, p. 160.

14 *The Australian*, 17 November 2006.

15 *The Australian*, 15 November 2006.

16 Walker, op.cit., Conclusion.

17 Ibid, see also Greg Craven, "Federalism and the states of reality", *Policy*, Centre for Independent Studies, vol. 21, no. 2, Winter 2005, pp. 3-9.

18 Op. cit, passim.

19 Anne Twomey and Glenn Withers, *Federalist Paper I: Australia's Federal Future, a report for the Council for the Australian Federation*, April 2007.

20 A term used by a republican constitutional lawyer to refer to the Head of State debate: George Winterton, "Who is our Head of State?", *Quadrant*, September 2004, p. 60.

21 See also Queensland Premier Campbell Newman's call: http://www.theaustralian. com.au/national-affairs/federal-bullying-must-end-campbell-newman/story-fn59ni-ix-1226619543944 (retrieved 23.04.2013).

22 Quick and Garran, op. cit., p.153.

23 See Flint, *Twilight of the Elites*, North Melbourne, Freedom Publishing, 2005, Chapter 10, pp. 183-216: "Restoring the Federation".

CHAPTER 16

The ten principles of freedom

This Chapter is based on a longer essay, "Ten Principles of Freedom" published in the National Observer, *Australia, No. 83 (June-August 2010). The authors thank the editor and publishers for permission to use this.*

16.1 Introduction

To be free, and to enjoy that freedom, man must live in an ordered society. We cannot live in a state of anarchy or a state of nature where, as Hobbes famously put it, life would be "solitary, poor, nasty, brutish, and short".[1]

An ordered liberal society allows mankind to lead a full life. This was recognised eloquently by the founding fathers of the United States when, believing that their rights as Englishmen were being denied, they declared: "We hold these truths to be self-evident: that all men are created equal, that they are endowed by their Creator with certain unalienable Rights, that among these are Life, Liberty and the pursuit of Happiness."[2]

For longer than most people, Australians and New Zealanders have lived in liberal societies ordered by democratic institutions whose members are elected under universal suffrage. Most of us would like to see the people of every country enjoy those gifts. So would our governments.

This is true too of the United States. But the United States was the first dominant power to have seriously attempted to impose democratic institutions on foreign countries. On 2 April 1917, President Woodrow Wilson went before a joint session of Congress to seek a Declaration of War against Germany in order that the world be "made safe for

273

democracy". This sort of zeal to convert the world to democracy was more often a view held in liberal rather than conservative circles in the United States – by that we mean "liberal" as the Americans understand the term.

President George W. Bush was an exception. He also decided to make the world safe for democracy, something which had not previously been the ambition of conservative administrations. But no conservative administration had ever known anything like that attack on the territory of the United States known as 9/11.

In March 2003, Deputy Defence Secretary Paul Wolfowitz said that the anticipated incursion into Iraq "would be like wars that you've fought in, a war of liberation, a war to secure peace and freedom not only for ourselves, but for the Iraqi people who have suffered so long under one of the world's most brutal tyrannies".[3]

In 2005, President George W. Bush declared: "Across the generations, we have proclaimed the imperative of self-government, because no one is fit to be a master, and no one deserves to be a slave. All who live in tyranny and hopelessness can know the United States will not ignore your oppression, or excuse your oppressors. When you stand for liberty, we will stand with you."[4]

As Michael Kazin observes, there is nothing conservative about these statements.[5] He says they would have distressed major thinkers on the right – from Edmund Burke at the end of the 18th century – who believed the sudden overthrow of authorities inexorably leads to anarchy and to long periods of war.

Unfortunately, neither President Wilson nor President Bush was successful in advancing his mission. The reason is that freedom cannot be achieved merely by importing a few institutions and decreeing ballot-box democracy. True democracy requires more than just the ballot-box and universal suffrage. These insignia of democracy have to be planted in a fertile field.

During the debate over the Bush Administration's policy to impose democracy across the world, Fareed Zakaria advanced the theory that democracy works best in those societies which have already known "constitutional liberalism".[6] This is the sort of fertile ground in which democracy can succeed.

Constitutional liberalism is a prerequisite essential to democracy and thus to freedom.

The theme of Part 1 of this book is that the principles of constitutional liberalism are being surreptitiously undermined by the powerbrokers and the elites who now govern Australia. And so consequently is our freedom, not only in overt attacks such as those on freedom of speech and of the press and on the right to private property, but also by governments' increasingly detailed and onerous regulation of every facet of our lives.

Before seeking to understand what the essentials of freedom are today, we need to recall the emergence of constitutional liberalism in Britain, the United States and Australia which we discussed in more detail in the first two chapters of this Part.

16.2 The emergence of constitutional liberalism

Australia and New Zealand were fortunate in that the ground was very well prepared for the surprisingly early introduction of democratic institutions and the equally surprisingly early introduction of universal suffrage, including female suffrage.

The elites are filled with such guilt about the settlement of Australia that they are blinded to the extraordinary success this was.[7] The unfortunate consequence is that this is hidden from our children who are given rich helpings of the black armband version of our history.

The young must be told that the early Australasian advances in democracy were the result of the following:

First, the settlers brought with them the common law which assumes all are subject to the same law.

Second, they were societies based on sound civic virtue. They brought with them values more compatible with constitutional liberalism and democracy – that is Judeo-Christian values.

Australia is the only continent not to have known slavery. This was because our founders, Governor Phillip and Lord Sydney, were guided by the Christian gospel in the same way as Wilberforce when he later came to campaign against and eventually overthrow the institution of slavery. "In a new country," Phillip said, "there will be no slavery and hence no slaves."

Third, they were both colonised by the British who, more than any other colonial power, voluntarily exported constitutional liberalism to their colonies, including the American ones. This was because the principles of constitutional liberalism were more developed in Britain than in the other colonial powers, with the exception of the Dutch. (Unfortunately, the Dutch did not export these to their colonies until well after the Second World War).

With the early introduction of the Westminster system into Australia and New Zealand – a process begun in Australia before the Eureka Stockade – the colonies were left to govern themselves, unlike the colonies of other powers.

It would be wrong to think of constitutional liberalism only in terms of those documents referred to as the Australian or New Zealand constitutions. The constitutional system is broader than these. As Bolingbroke said, the constitution is "that assemblage of laws, institutions and customs, derived from certain fixed principles of reason, directed to certain fixed objects of public good that compose the general system, according to which the community hath agreed to be governed".[8]

Our constitutional systems are to be found in that golden thread which goes back through the emergence of responsible government, the English Bill of Rights and the Act of Settlement, back to the Magna Carta. The Magna Carta is especially significant. It was, as Fareed Zarkaria says, the first written limitation on royal authority in Europe.[9]

There are only a handful of countries which have a long

uninterrupted experience of constitutional liberalism and, later, democracy with universal suffrage. They have certain common features which demonstrate to us, in a practical way, what is the essence of freedom.

With the exception of Switzerland, all of these can trace their systems to one particular event which was the most significant single advance in the provision of good government that the world has ever seen the Glorious Revolution of 1688, discussed in detail in the opening Chapter to this Part.[10]

16.3 The essence of freedom

The argument here is that only under constitutional liberalism can democracy flourish. But we cannot assume that once democracy has emerged, we can keep it without effort and without vigilance.

What then is the essence of freedom?

The following are ten principles of constitutional liberalism all or most of which should be in place for democracy to emerge. They must remain in place if democracy is to be maintained.

These are the principles relating to the separation of powers; good, stable and limited government; popular involvement; subsidiarity and, in appropriate cases, federalism; that certain key institutions must be above and beyond politics; civic virtue; private property; rights; and, finally, the sceptical principle.

16.4 Constitutional change and the people

The British have long been seen as offering the classical model for constitutional liberalism without having a so-called written constitution. Those who argue that Britain and New Zealand need a constitution which is in writing usually mean one which is contained in a document which is entrenched. By entrenchment they mean one which cannot be changed by ordinary legislation. Entrenching usually involves the requirement for some special majority in Parliament.

The more democratic version of entrenchment is where the people must approve a bill setting out the proposed changes to the constitution, an important form of direct democracy. In Australia this requires the approval to be given both nationally and in a majority of states. This involves a Swiss-style referendum where the changes are on the table before the people vote.

Australians distinguish such a referendum from a plebiscite, much favoured during the French Revolution and by the Emperors Napoleon I and Napoleon III. It has been used in recent years by devious British politicians, and called a referendum. Most of the British press have let this sleight of hand pass without comment. In this plebiscite, the people are only asked a question, often crafted by spin-doctors and with the details kept secret. If the question is answered favourably, or at times even unfavourably, the details are revealed and then enacted.

A plebiscite is like signing blank cheque, and just as dangerous.

Not having an entrenched constitution worked in Britain for three centuries. There were effective checks and balances on the power of the House of Commons, and an understanding as to how politicians should behave. When the House of Lords refused to pass a budget in 1911, King Edward VII indicated he would create sufficient new peers but only after a second general election which demonstrated public support for the government's position.[11]

But the practice of ensuring there is widespread support for constitutional change is no longer respected by the political class. This is probably related to a general decline in civic virtue in such circles, evidenced by the scandal concerning the expenses of members of parliament revealed before the 2010 election. Thus, in 2003, Britain's then Labour Prime Minister Tony Blair purported to abolish the ancient office of Lord Chancellor by a press release. The handing over of even more power to the European Union, without a promised referendum, is an egregious example. When the EU Constitution was rejected in referendums in the Netherlands and France in 2005, it was replaced by the Treaty of Lisbon which was designed to amend other treaties and was approved by the British parliament without a referendum. It was also approved by all other European parliaments without referendums, except in Ireland.

Apart from constitutional entrenchment, the decline in civic virtue in political circles and the increased power of the parties has led to a re-examination of the very concept of representative democracy, and the introduction of the tools of direct democracy. This is discussed in greater detail in Part 3.

16.5 The separation of powers principle

As we saw in Chapter 13, this can be traced back to the Glorious Revolution of 1688 which introduced the conditions essential for good, limited government.

This principle was fundamental to most of the world's liberal constitutions which provide good government with adequate checks and balances against the abuse of power. Those checks and balances comply with Lord Acton's subsequent warning that "power tends to corrupt, and absolute power corrupts absolutely".

Montesquieu first observed this in England.[12] He found in that separation of the three powers, the executive, the legislature and the judiciary as ensuring political liberty. After his discovery, the legislature and the executive were to come close, as responsible cabinet government replaced what was in many ways an executive monarchy. Most importantly, the judicial power was separate from the other powers..

The separation of the judiciary had, he believed, to be real, and this was certainly the case in England. The dangers of judges holding office at pleasure can be seen in the use of acting judges. With the adoption of laws requiring that judges must retire by a specific age, there has been an increasing reliance in some Australian jurisdictions on commissioning recently retired judges as acting judges.

NSW judges must retire at 72, but can then be appointed as acting judges on a full, or part-time basis until the age of 77. Those acting judges had by early 2010 made up about a fifth of the judges on the Supreme and District courts. Rather than having untenured judges, it would be better if the retirement age were extended to 77 or, better still, removed altogether.

We now have an example of the danger of this practice.[13] As a Land and Environment Court judge, David Lloyd found that the then Minister for Planning, Frank Sartor, was biased when he approved Catherine Hill Bay and Gwandalan land developments by the Rose Group. The developer's contribution to the state of 300 hectares of conservation land, in exchange for the minister's sympathetic consideration of the developments, amounted to a land bribe, the judge ruled. The government then failed to appoint him as an acting judge, notwithstanding the recommendation of the NSW Chief Justice and the problems associated with the shortage of judges.[14]

The principle of the separation of the judicial power and the consequent independence of the judiciary is under threat in two other and more significant ways. First, in some jurisdictions there has been a significant trespass by the judiciary into the legislative terrain, sometimes actually abetted by unwise legislators. Second, there is a tendency in some jurisdictions to establish specialist courts which function under different laws, some inimical to the pursuit of justice.

The first has become most evident in the United States. There the British model of the threefold separation of powers was carried to the American colonies and included in the Constitution of the United States. (It was only after American independence that the British model evolved into the Westminster system as we know it today, where the ministry must enjoy the confidence of the lower house, the House of Commons, thus ending much of the separation between the executive and legislative powers.)

In the second half of the 20th century, the Supreme Court justices of the United States began to trespass more and more into the legislative arena. This is being imitated in other common law jurisdiction, assisted by constitutional or statutory bills of rights. This seriously undermines the separation of powers. Laws are being made by unelected officials without the possibility, or if possible the likelihood, of those laws being repealed by the legislators.

The second area of concern is the establishment of specialist courts. It is no exaggeration that they can sometimes reflect some of the aspects of the Star Chamber of old. There is an Australian example of this. It has been the subject of an adverse decision by a vigilant High Court.[15]

Now it is clear that some of our politicians have a very feudal idea of the law. They think that it is quite proper to apply special, onerous laws to one class of people, in this case employers, large and small. Employers are of course those who make profits by taking risks and who give other people jobs.

Until this decision, NSW employers were subject to an absolute duty of care to their employees. This was enforceable by a summary criminal procedure in an industrial court. There was even an attempt to exclude the supervisory jurisdiction of the Supreme Court and thus the High Court.

Another extraordinary feature of this draconian law was to give unions a good share of the substantial fines collected; a further one was to conduct a criminal trial as if we lived somewhere resembling more the old Soviet Union, rather than under our common law.

In this case, the NSW Industrial Relations Commission had found Graeme Kirk, a hobby farmer, guilty of failing to provide a safe workplace. This related to the case of his experienced part-time farm manager, Graham Palmer, who was killed while moving heavy steel using an all-terrain vehicle in 2001. Mr. Kirk had no farming experience and took no part in running the farm due to ill health. While working on the farm, Mr. Palmer had incorrectly loaded some steel onto a vehicle, and had then cut the corner of a road. The vehicle overturned and he was killed.

The High Court quashed fines totalling $121,000 and said that Mr. Kirk had been "treated very unjustly and in a manner" causing "much harm" and that the prosecution was "absurd". The High Court reminded the politicians that they cannot remove specialist tribunals from the supervision of the courts.

The jurisdiction of the High Court arises from section 73(ii) of the Constitution, which provides for appeals "from all judgments ... of the Supreme Court ... or of any other court ... from which at the establishment of the Commonwealth an appeal lies to the Queen in Council."

A defining characteristic of state supreme courts, the judges ruled, is the power to confine inferior courts and tribunals within the limits of their authority. The politicians can't take this away, even to pay off their clients.

The Court also reminded them there are minimum standards which apply to a criminal trial. And to the credit of the High Court justices, they were unanimous, with Mr. Justice Dyson Heydon wishing to go further in favour of Mr. Kirk.

The decision is a warning to those who would set up Star Chamber-style jurisdictions parallel to the real courts. They clearly offend the separation of powers and the resulting independence of the courts which must in all fundamental respects remain courts of justice.

16.6 The good government principle: stable and limited

Good government must be stable, for reasons which will be obvious, but it must also be limited.

Apart from the idiosyncratic but superb Swiss system,[16] there are two widely known models for stable and limited government. (Since 1958, a third hybrid semi-presidential system has emerged, the French Fifth Republic. Every so often its end is predicted when it falls into some crisis, as in the 2002 presidential election between Jacques Chirac and Jean-Marie Le Pen).

The Westminster system of responsible government is the more modern and, in terms of its successful export beyond the seas, by far the most successful system of government across the world.

The older one is the American presidential system, based on the English constitution as it evolved under King William III and Queen Mary II from 1688 and also on the system of governance of the American colonies where the Governor, although sometimes chosen locally, was appointed by the Crown and not responsible to the colonial assembly.

Paradoxically, it was the American War of Independence which was to see the beginnings of what we recognise as the Westminster system, where the government is responsible to the House of Commons. As noted earlier, following the defeat of the British army at Yorktown, the House of Commons voted that they could "no longer repose confidence in the present ministers." Lord North, the then Prime Minister, resigned.

This was the beginning of the constitutional convention which became firmly established in the middle of the 19th century, that a government must retain the confidence of the House of Commons.

This was the system which the British gave to their settled colonies and other states from the mid-19th century.

Advantages of the Westminster system

The advantages of the Westminster system are that power is not concentrated in one person; it provides greater accountability and is more flexible and responsive to changing situations.

A good example of this arose as a result of the United States' failed invasion of Cuba in 1961, the Bay of Pigs affair.

Within seventy-two hours all the invading troops had been killed, wounded or had surrendered. Richard Bissell, the head of the Directorate for Plans was called to a meeting with President John F. Kennedy about this. President Kennedy admitted that it was his fault that the operation had been a disaster. He explained the constitutional predicament: "In a parliamentary government, I'd have to resign. But in this government I can't, so you and Allen [Dulles, CIA Director] have to go."[17]

Another example of the advantages of the Westminster system is in the continuing accountability of the government to parliament in financial matters. A government denied supply must resign. This was one of the complaints against King James II, that he was "levying money for and to the use of the Crown by pretence of prerogative for other time and in other manner than the same was granted by Parliament". In other words, James was accused of raising taxes without parliamentary approval and ruling without supply.

This is forbidden both under the Westminster system and in the United States, but with different consequences. In the Westminster system, a government which cannot obtain supply must advise a general election or resign.

Thus on 11 November 1975, the Australian Governor-General, Sir John Kerr, withdrew the commission of the then Prime Minister Gough Whitlam for trying to do this, to govern without a grant of supply.

In his reasons Sir John said:[18]

> Because of the principles of responsible government a Prime Minister who cannot obtain supply, including money for carrying on the ordinary services of government, must either advise a general election or resign. If he refuses to do this I have the authority and indeed the duty under the Constitution to withdraw his Commission as Prime Minister.

Soon after the dismissal of Whitlam in 1975, the US Congress failed to grant supply to the Gerald Ford Administration. This led to the partial closure of diplomatic posts around the world, and the termination of various services. An American lady was filmed in Canberra for a television news program saying, "What we need in the US … what we need is a Governor-General."

This occurred again in 1995 and 1996 with a partial shutdown of the United States federal government. When Congress failed to pass a budget bill, the Administration suspended all non-essential services from 14-19 November 1995, and from 16 December 1995-6 January 1996.

The advantage of the Westminster system can also be seen when it is generally agreed it is time for the head of government to go. This can happen speedily, sometimes within days. It is rare that a vote of no confidence is needed when the prime minister's colleagues want him to go. This may be precipitate, as some would say of the forced departure of Britain's Margaret Thatcher in 1990 and of Australia's Kevin Rudd in June 2010.

Contrast this flexibility with the impeachment of the US President (a procedure which comes from ancient England). This is a trial before the Senate where the action, the articles of impeachment, must be approved by the House. The impeachment cannot be founded on poor performance, or a lack of competence or other skills and qualities. Instead the House of Representatives must put the President on trial charged with "treason, bribery, or other high crimes and misdemeanours". The trial must be before the Senate with the Chief Justice presiding, and, to be removed, two-thirds of the senators present must find him or her guilty.[19]

This process leads, as we have seen, to a long paralysis in the government and the nation.

Limited government

Not only should a government be stable, it should be limited. As noted previously, David Landes said of the government of England after the Glorious Revolution that it gave the people "elbow room".[20]

Experience has demonstrated the wisdom of Friedrich Hayek's counsel that much of modern society is far too complex to have decisions made on our behalf by a government, however benevolent.[21]

He warned, we are mistaken if we believe that anyone can have the knowledge necessary to make such decisions as in a government dominated economy.

16.7 Popular involvement principle

The principle of popular involvement requires the legislature should be effective and should properly represent the people. But where the institutions of a representative democracy have been severely compromised, the most appropriate solution is, we believe, to empower the people with the tools of direct democracy as in Switzerland. The example of Switzerland is especially apposite, as it inspired our founding fathers to put the Constitution beyond the control of the politicians acting alone.

The question of grafting the tools of direct democracy onto a representative democracy is discussed in Part 3.

As to the form of a legislature in a representative democracy, the only safe version is one consisting of two houses. The purpose of having an upper house of parliament is to ensure there is a review of all legislative proposals. Given there is no one universally agreed method of election, the upper house should provide representation in a way different from that in the lower house. It is desirable too that the voting system not reinforce the power of the political machines. An example is the appointment of MPs from lists produced by a central party machine.

An upper house is even more desirable under the Westminster system than under the presidential system because of the close identity between the lower house and the executive. It is also especially desirable in a unitary state where there is no division of powers between federal and state legislatures. These two considerations suggest that the restoration of a second house should be high on the agenda.

Elections must be as free from fraud as reasonably possible. Experience indicates that when politicians say measures must be introduced to make voting easier they are either misinformed or they are about to embark on some device designed to enable electoral fraud. These matters were discussed in more detail in Part 1.

16.8 The subsidiarity and federalist principles

For reasons of history and because Australia has such a large land mass, the federalist principle is essential to freedom in Australia. Federalism is part and parcel of the subsidiarity principle, that matters ought to be handled by the smallest, lowest or least centralised competent authority. The corollary is that the central government in a unitary state and the federal government in a federation should only perform those tasks which cannot be performed at a lower level. It also applies to states in a federation. For example, rather than trying to manage public hospitals themselves or through area authorities, why not allow the local community through a board and superintendent and matron to run them?

It is regrettable and perhaps predictable that federalism has few adherents among the Australian political class. Because it is under challenge and has been undermined it is pertinent to concentrate on this. It was good then to see that the Leader of the Opposition, Tony Abbott, has recently changed his views on the advantages of federalism.[22]

As we have argued in this book, the fact that the federation of the Australian states was a truly remarkable achievement is usually ignored or glossed over by the elites, and thus rarely included in the education of our children.[23]

16.9 The principle that certain key institutions must be above and beyond politics

Under a liberal constitution it is accepted that there is a proper place for the conduct of party politics. This is in the legislature and in the formation of the executive government.

At the same time, certain important, indeed crucial, organs must remain above and beyond politics. These are the armed forces, the judiciary, the police, the public or civil service, and the Crown. This also extends to an institution in the public sphere which, with the exception of public broadcasting, is not part of the state, the media.

This concept of a large sphere outside of the political arena is most highly developed under the Westminster system, where the Crown plays a central role.

The proponents of both the Westminster and presidential systems agree that the armed forces should be above politics. This principle is manifested in the proscriptions against both the maintenance of a standing army without parliamentary approval and the quartering of troops. In addition, in the United States, citizens have the right to bear arms. Under the Westminster system, supreme command is vested in the Sovereign or the Governor-General, thus emphasising the non-political role of this office. It is worth noting that the Westminster system has been more successful, at least until recently, in keeping the high command out of the political arena.

Another institution which ought to be beyond politics is the judiciary, which creates the corresponding requirement that the judiciary not participate in politics and the courts not enter into the legislative arena. Again, the Westminster system has been more successful in this. We do find that in some places under the presidential system that the judges are elected or subject to processes which are or have become political, including judicial confirmation. This has been exacerbated by the judges moving into areas previously regarded as the preserve of the legislators.

Another non-political area, at least in the Westminster system, has been the public or civil service. The emergence of a non-partisan public or civil service coincided with the withdrawal of the Crown from political activity and the emergence of the constitutional monarchy as we know it. Walter Bagehot advised the Canadians in 1867 that not only was a non-partisan public service absent in the US, he believed it was impossible. The contrast between the public services of the countries of the Commonwealth and the states of the US remains, even if in Australia in recent years there has been some regrettable weakening of this principle in regard to the higher echelons of the public service.

In the Westminster realms, the Crown remains the central institution providing leadership beyond the political arena. As Viscount James Bryce is reputed to have said, it is not so much the power the Crown wields, but the power it denies to anyone else, which is important. This means that the politicians are required to justify proposals and, in the area of the reserve powers, must accept decisions made by the viceroy in his or her discretion.

In addition, the other institutions outside of the political arena, the judiciary, armed forces, police and public service, do not in the Westminster system owe their allegiance to the politicians, even if chosen through the political process. They owe their allegiance to the Crown which is a trustee for the people. They, as well as the politicians, owe allegiance to the Crown. This is reinforced by their swearing an oath of allegiance.

The making of an oath, such as an oath to tell the truth, the whole truth and nothing but the truth in a court, or an oath of allegiance, should not of course be made lightly. Respect for an oath is integral to that civic virtue which must prevail in a civilised society, apart from any consideration of the effect of a breach on the eternal soul of the delinquent.

It is an indication of the decline in standards in public life that some republican politicians so easily breach their oaths. An egregious example was the decision of the New South Wales republican politicians to abolish the oath they had themselves sworn just before a visit by The Queen.[24]

The republican politicians plan to remove the Crown, but the 1999 proposal to do so in Australia indicates they are not motivated by a desire to improve the governance of the country.

There is another institution which, ideally and when presenting the news, should remain above and beyond politics. This is the media, the fourth estate. As this name indicates, the institution is separate from the other estates in the parliament and is crucial to the maintenance of our freedom. We do not live in a small city-state; we need to be informed. That this institution must be free is essential.

This concept went from Britain to America. The First Amendment to the US Constitution is no more than a statement of the position that the fourth estate enjoyed in England and in America where it was intended only as a restraint on the new federal polity: "Congress shall make no law ... abridging the freedom of speech, or of the press."

Although indulgent, US Supreme Court Justice Hugo Black in 1971 described the role of the press well in *New York Times Co. v. United States*.[25]

> In the First Amendment, the Founding Fathers gave the free press the protection it must have to fulfil its essential role in our democracy. The press was to serve the governed, not the governors. The government's power to censor the press was abolished so that the press would remain forever free to censure the government. The press was protected so that it could bare the secrets of government and inform the people. Only a free and unrestrained press can effectively expose deception in government. And paramount among the responsibilities of a free press is the duty to prevent any part of the government from deceiving the people and sending them off to distant lands to die of foreign fevers and foreign shot and shell. In my view, far from deserving condemnation for their courageous reporting, the *New York Times*, the *Washington Post*, and other newspapers should be commended for serving the purpose that the Founding Fathers saw so clearly. In revealing the workings of government that led to the Vietnam War, the newspapers nobly did precisely that which the Founders hoped and trusted they would do.

This freedom of course gives rise to a moral duty to be responsible. Unfortunately some in the media too readily forget their duty. But the reason why the media are accorded considerable freedom is because of the duty so well described by the London *Times* in 1851:

> The first duty of the press is to obtain the earliest and most correct intelligence of the events of the time, and instantly, by disclosing them, to make them the common property of the nation.

Associated with this is a moral duty to make the reporting of the news clearly distinguishable from comment. As the great editor of the *Manchester Guardian* C.P. Scott declared: "Comment is free, but facts are sacred." The media are of course entirely free to editorialise, the exception being of course public broadcasters such as the ABC and the BBC. It is refreshing then that the former chairman of the ABC recently warned, with particular reference to reporting anthropogenic global warming: "We must ensure that our town square is not a monologue."[26]

Today we see and read too much news which falls into the category of campaign journalism. Too often, rather than reporting, the media wish to be players in the political game.

What does this mean today? The leading Australian Fairfax and ABC journalist David Marr once famously declared that the natural culture of journalism is "a kind of vaguely soft-left enquiry sceptical of authority. I mean, that's just the world out of which journalists come. If they don't come out of that world, they really can't be reporters".

Indeed, he said that any journalists not of this culture should leave the profession. "I mean, if you're not sceptical of authority, find another job. You know, just find another job."[27]

He was absolutely right to say a journalist must be a sceptic – how else can you find the truth? But to say he can come from only one end of the political spectrum is wrong. It leads to issues such as that of Fairfax when it promoted rather than reported Earth Hour, when supporters were to turn off their lights for one hour to reduce their carbon footprint. That is when Sydney's *Sun-Herald* newspaper published photos of Sydney before and during Earth Hour.[28] However, they were not taken on the same day. That is the consequence when the news columns are biased.

There is a particular danger that the gallery may be too close to government or to a particular party. The press should maintain a distance from those exercising power. As earlier noted, British editor and political commentator, Baron Sidney Jacobson, once informed the House of Lords:

> My Lords, Relations between politicians and the Press have deteriorated, are deteriorating, and should on no account be allowed to improve.[29]

16.10 The civic virtue principle

If democracy is to grow and to hold, the ground has to be fertile. The people have to be receptive, having a clear commitment to the performance of their duties as much as of their rights. Their duties include those to their fellow citizens and to the nation. This requires a society to share the same values, that there be a commonality between all people. Ours come from our received Judeo-Christian and democratic values and our commitment the institutions fundamental to our society. This does not mean that belonging to a particular religious denomination is a prerequisite for citizenship. It is the values, not the theological doctrines, which are mandatory. (Of course, many ecclesiastics will argue that the values cannot exist without religion).

The principal civic virtues include active involvement in civil society, that is in philanthropy and pursuits aimed at the public good, in restraint, in being honest and trustworthy, and in observing the principle of reciprocity.

If we do not have a common view of what the essence of being a citizen is and of what our duties and responsibilities to one another and to the nation are, we will of course weaken our society and endanger eventually our democracy.

16.11 The private property principle

That a liberal constitution requires government to be limited is something which socialists have never appreciated. Because much of Western political philosophy in the 19th and 20th centuries was dominated by socialist thought (and still is under the guise of, for example, militant environmentalism), this means that little attention has been given to a principle absolutely essential to any society which is governed under a liberal constitution. This is that the right to private property be protected under the law.

Hernando de Soto has demonstrated that the protection of property rights in a formal property system, and one with adequate records, is crucial to economic development, and that its absence in many Third World countries explains many of their barriers to development.[30]

The Australian Constitution gives the federal parliament the power to make laws for the peace, order and good government of the Commonwealth with respect to the acquisition of property on just terms. We have seen in Australia the adoption of an inter-governmental scheme to satisfy Kyoto Treaty carbon-reduction targets. Funded by the federal government, the states have effectively made land useless to farmers. This is expropriation and, as we have seen, expropriation not on just terms. This is in many ways the thin end of the wedge, a growing predilection for governments to interfere with property rights which offends the private property principle.

This was discussed in greater detail in Part 1.

16.12 Rights principle

Until the latter part of the 20th century, the prevailing view in Australia was that the best guarantee of human rights was through the common law and the system of responsible government.

The American Bill of Rights remained what it was intended to be, a restraint on the powers of Congress to make laws. It was only in the latter part of the 20th century that a judicial *coup d'état* took place and the judges invaded the legislative patch.

But apart from it not being the constitutional intention, legislation by judges, especially legislation effectively amending the Constitution, offends the democratic principle. The judges have no mandate, they are not answerable to the people, and their legislation can only be repealed by the judges.

The results have not been good. The judges' incursions into freedom of speech have effectively given a green light to the most offensive defamation imaginable. Their refusal to accept that the First Amendment was directed to the protection of political speech led them to unleash a torrent of obscene speech (that is speech in the broadest sense) across the United States and therefore the world. In a campaign unjustified by the Constitution, the judges have used the proscription against there being a federal established church as a pretext to drive religion from the public square and from the schools. And then the judges have used separate rights to construct a constitutional right to privacy – a constitutional right unknown to the Founding Fathers. Peering into the penumbrae – the shadows of the Constitution – they have extracted a constitutional right to privacy for women, a right to abortion. By doing that they relieved the often grateful state politicians from doing their duty – that is, to legislate or not in this area.

There is a place for limited specific rights in an entrenched constitution; there is no place for broad generalisations which endow the judges with the discretion to legislate. It is proper to make the power to expropriate conditional on any expropriation being on just terms. A constitutionally entrenched list of broad political rights, and worse, of economic or social rights, places governance in the hands of unelected elites.

It is often argued in Britain, New Zealand and Australia that statutory bills of rights can avoid the excesses of the constitutionally entrenched bill of rights. But, as Professor James Allan warns, "What is happening in Britain is tantamount to having a full-scale US-style or Canadian-style constitutionalised bill of rights."[31]

14.13 The sceptical principle

It is essential that in a democracy, all manner of propositions be subjected to rigorous testing. Unlike dictatorships and primitive societies, a modern liberal democratic society allows the citizenry the privileges of scepticism and opposition.

In the law, in journalism, in trials, in science and in the formulation of public policy, any argument presented has to be subjected to rigorous examination. Without the right, and on occasions the duty, to be sceptical, we could not long remain a democracy under a liberal constitution. We would become the sort of society which insisted that the line handed down from above be instantly received and adopted – Stalinist Russia and Hitler's Germany, being extreme examples.

It is difficult to see how certain professions can be carried on if the practitioners do not employ a healthy degree of scepticism in the exercise of their functions. Among such professions are science, the judiciary and journalism.

Scepticism is not a failing, but a badge of honour. There is currently a theory that we are going through a period of dangerous global warming that is anthropogenic, that is driven primarily by carbon dioxide emissions linked to man's use of fossil fuels. This, it is claimed, requires policies and laws to drastically reduce those emissions.

Paul Monk rightly says that we need to hear the most rigorous challenges to those conclusions.[32] That is because this is the best way known to man to test their accuracy. He declares that this is something fundamental to scientific method, to the practice of liberal politics and the achievement of sound public policy.

One of the most sinister observations by the political class, more suited to Stalin's fraudulent biologist Trofim Lysenko, is that, with respect to anthropogenic global warming, "The science is settled." Those are words more appropriate to a tyrant than to a minister in a democratic government, or worse, a journalist.

In recent years we have seen the development of the "precautionary principle" or "precautionary approach". Principle 15 of the Rio Declaration 1992 states: "In order to protect the environment, the precautionary approach shall be widely applied by States according to their capabilities. Where there are threats of serious or irreversible damage, lack of full scientific certainty shall be not used as a reason for postponing cost-effective measures to prevent environmental degradation."

This principle has found its way into Australian environmental law.[33] Although the national newspaper is much criticised by the elites, *The Australian* has for long argued the precautionary principle with respect to the theory that global warming is mainly caused by man-made CO2 emissions.

If it has a place, the precautionary principle must be applied with common sense and a degree of scepticism in relation to some of the dangers suggested, especially when these are the result of the computer projections of people animated by an agenda.

On one view the precautionary principle merely codifies a very risk-averse version of standard cost-benefit analysis.[34]

As this critic says, central to the precautionary principle is the idea that we can anticipate all of the ramifications of a technology in advance and can tell whether on balance it will be a net benefit or cost to humanity and the environment. That, he says, is complete nonsense. As an example he recalls that when the optical laser was invented, it was dismissed as "an invention looking for a job". No one could imagine a possible use for this interesting phenomenon.

In any event, it would be a folly to apply the principle with unacceptable rigour merely out of a fear that the global warming lobby may be right. The sceptical principle must not be suspended. This is particularly so when we see the extent of the dissimulation, obfuscation, illegal activity, apparent deliberate misrepresentation, use of fear, exaggeration and other examples of impropriety used to require adherence to the theory of anthropogenic global warming.

We can well understand why they fear the sceptical principle. However, it is a principle which must universally apply in science, journalism, the law and public policy.

Endnotes

1 Thomas Hobbes, *Leviathan or The Matter, Forme and Power of a Common-Wealth Ecclesiasticall and Civill*,1651, Penguin, Harmondsworth,1979, Part 1, chap. 3, p. 186.

2 *The Declaration of Independence*. July 4, 1776.

3 Michael Kazin, "What lies beneath: Bush and the liberal idealists", *World Affairs Journal* (American Peace Society, Washington DC), Winter 2008. http://www.worldaffairs-journal.org/article/what-lies-beneath-bush-and-liberal-idealists (retrieved 05.05.2013).

4 Ibid.

5 Ibid.

6 Fareed Zakaria, *The Future of Freedom: Illiberal Democracy at Home and Abroad*, New York, W.W. Norton, 2004.

7 Christopher Akehurst, "Manufactured Guilt", *Spectator Australia*, 2 March 2013.

8 Viscount Bolingbroke, *On Parties* [1735], p. 108.

9 Zakaria, op. cit., p. 38.

10 David Flint, "Three hundred and twenty years of freedom," *Quadrant*, November 2008, pp. 40-47.

11 Simon Heffer, *Power and Place: The Political Consequences of King Edward VII*, Weidenfeld and Nicolson, London, 1998, p. 286.

12 Montesquieu, *Charles de Secondat, Baron de, The Spirit of Laws* [1748], translated by Thomas Nugent, revised by J.V. Prichard. Based on a public domain edition published in 1914 by G. Bell & Sons, Ltd., London. Rendered into html and text by Jon Roland of the Constitution Society. www.constitution.org/cm/sol.html (retrieved 05.05.2013).

13 Joel Gibson, "Judge rejection 'threatens' court independence", *Sydney Morning Herald*, 8 March 2010 www.smh.com.au/nsw/judge-rejection-threatens-court-independence-20100307-pqm0.html (retrieved 24.02.2013.)

14 Ibid.

15 *Kirk v. Industrial Relations Commission*, High Court (Canberra), 3 February 2010. www.austlii.edu.au/au/cases/cth/HCA/2010/1.html (retrieved 07.05.2013).

16 This is the executive council system: James Bryce, *Modern Democracies*, 2 vols, Macmillan, London, 1921, Vol. 2, p. 508 et seq. The unusual feature is that alongside the bicameral legislature and executive council, the people are a separate legislative authority through the referendum and initiative.

17 Richard Bissell, Biography, *Spartacus Educational*. www.spartacus.schoolnet.co.uk/JFK-bissell.htm (retrieved 07.05.2013) This has also been reported as: "If this were the UK, you as the civil servant would continue and I would resign. But it's not." "In the United States, I continue and you resign." www.norepublic.com.au/index.php?option=com_content&task=view&id=1641&Itemid=4 (retrieved 07.05.2013).

18 Sir John Kerr's Statement of Reasons. Following his dismissal of Gough Whitlam on 11 November 1975, the Governor-General released this document outlining his reasons, http://whitlamdismissal.com/documents/kerr-statement.shtml (retrieved 07.05.2013).

19 *US Constitution*, Article II, Section 4.

20 David S. Landes, *The Wealth and Poverty of Nations: Why Some Are So Rich and Some So Poor*, W.W. Norton, New York, 1998.

21 Friedrich August von Hayek, *The Road to Serfdom*, 1944, London, Routledge and Kegan Paul, 1976.

22 http://www.cando.org.au/updates/290-convert-to-federalism-tony-abbott (accessed 23.04.2013)

23 Quick and Garran, op. cit. p. 225.

24 David Flint, "Power grab in NSW", *Australians for Constitutional Monarchy*, 15 March 2006. www.norepublic.com.au/index.php?option=com_content&task=view&id=548&Itemid=4 (retrieved 07.05.2013).

25 *New York Times Co. v. United States*, 403 U.S. 713 [1971].

26 Maurice Newman, Address to ABC staff, *The Australian*, 11 March 2010. www.theaustralian.com.au/business/media/maurice-newman-speech/story-e6frg996-1225839427099 (retrieved 07.05.2013).

27 David Marr, ABC Radio National, *Big Ideas* program, 26 September 2004.

28 ABC TV, *Media Watch*, Episode 7, 2007. www.abc.net.au/mediawatch/transcripts/s1892855.htm (retrieved 07.05.2013).

29 H.L. Deb, 26 January 1978, vol. 388, cc509-71. http://hansard.millbanksystems.com/lords/1978/jan/26/the-press#S5LV0388P0_19780126_HOL_204 (retrieved 01.05.2013).

30 Hernando de Soto, *The Mystery of Capital: Why Capitalism Triumphs in the West and Fails Everywhere Else*, Basic Books, New York, 2000.

31 James Allan, "Charter lobby turns desperate", *The Australian*, 12 March 2010.

32 Paul Monk, "The Open Society and its Friends", *Quadrant*, March 2010. www.quadrant. org.au/magazine/issue/2010/3/the-open-society-and-its-friends (retrieved 01.05.2013)

33 See e.g., *Telstra Corporation Ltd* v *Hornsby Shire Council* (2006) 67 NSWLR 256

34 Ronald Bailey, "Precautionary Tale", *Reason*, April 1999. http://reason.com/archives/1999/04/01/precautionary-tale/2 (retrieved 03.03.2013)

CHAPTER 17

For the sake of our children –
never let this happen again

The theme of this book is that representative democracy has been so compromised by our rulers, the factional powerbrokers and inner-city elites, that government has been mismanaged, the public interest ignored and Australians have lost confidence in the political system.

We have seen the formation of governments whose performance is unacceptable in terms of competence, financial rectitude and honesty, but who are unaccountable except at the quite often confected elections every three or four years. This has led to the adoption of policies and the enactment of laws which are contrary to the common sense, good judgement and the decency of the rank-and-file Australian. These policies are adopted and laws enacted to advance the personal interests of those in power, or an agenda which has never been approved by the people. In brief, these do not pass the "pub test". And sadly, these same policies and laws have been too often retained by successor governments elected to reverse them.

We argue that the democracy which our founders proposed, the people approved and for which Australians fought and died, can only be restored by empowering the rank-and-file Australian. There are examples in the world today of how to successfully empower the people without in any way undermining the stability of government. These include Switzerland, over twenty American states, one US territory, and at least one Canadian province.[1]

17.1 Switzerland

The best example is that of Switzerland, a particularly stable and wealthy country. Switzerland is a federation, probably one of the most decentralised in the world. This has been achieved without the apparent advantages of a single language and central dominant culture – Switzerland has in fact four languages. Nor is she blessed with physical resources. But in terms of the health, wealth and education of its people, law and order and the stability of her institutions, she is one of the world's most successful countries.

By thrift and invention, the Swiss have made pioneering advances in manufacturing, pharmaceuticals and other industries. Once when the country's jobless rate nosed above 1% late in the 20th century, Swiss politicians, straight-faced, talked about the nation's "employment crisis".[2]

All this has been achieved through the introduction of the tools of direct democracy at the federal, cantonal (i.e., state) and local levels so that the people and the politicians work constantly together in the good governance of the country. The politicians are not left, as in Australia, to do what they want to do without regard to the electorate, or hope that some things will be forgotten, between elections.

At the federal level in Switzerland, a petition signed by 50,000 or more voters can refer legislation passed in the previous 100 days to the people for a final decision in a referendum. This happens several times a year. And a petition signed by at least 100,000 people can initiate a proposal for a change to the Constitution.

The very existence of such a system, without it even being activated, is sufficient for the politicians to realise that they are truly accountable between elections and to not regard themselves as the masters with superior intelligence and understanding.[3] Instead, there is a bond – even described as spiritual – between them and the people who are in effect turned into part-time legislators. This does not eliminate the competition of ideas normal to a functioning democracy, in fact it heightens it. It tends to make party and personality small factors, even in the press. They are not concerned so much about who is going to depose whom, and what the politicians have been up to. They have nothing like our disgraceful charade of Question Time and staged debates in our parliaments. What is most relevant in Switzerland is the policy which is being debated.[4] The result is that Switzerland has a continual two-way instruction where the politicians and the people are teaching one another about the best governance of the nation.[5]

In this book, we argue that the people, as a whole, are smarter than our leaders. Unlike Australian politicians, most Swiss leaders actually believe the people are smarter.[6]

Unlike Australia, the politicians, the press, and business leaders take the importance and power of the people into account in everything they do.[7] As a result there is less of a gap between elite and popular opinion in Switzerland than in any other country. When such gaps do occur there is less arrogance and contempt for the people by the politicians, the press and business. And unlike the current situation in Australia, there is less frustration among the people about government. This is because everyone knows that on anything controversial, the people and not the powerbrokers and the elites will have the final say, as they should in any democracy worth the name.[8]

There are consequences. There are apparently remarkably few opinion polls, and when there is lobbying – and there is not much – it is more of the people than the politicians.[9] Members of parliament and the judiciary are not highly paid, have tiny staffs and are willing to concede that they may be wrong.[10]

Readers of this book will be warned by the powerbrokers and the elites of the terrible dangers of similarly empowering the Australian people. There is in fact no such danger – as a whole the Australian people are endowed with common sense, good judgement and decency to a greater level than seems to be the case with our rulers.

But to those who say it will be dangerous and the country will be ruined, the fact is that Switzerland, a wealthy country, enjoys some of the lowest income taxes and consumer taxes in Europe. Over the last 150 years, the Swiss have been less troubled by the wide swings of inflation and deflation seen in the rest of the world. Undoubtedly, the greatest single cause of these successful economic policies that have helped Switzerland grow rapidly over the last century is the existence of the tools of direct democracy.[11]

Switzerland has even provided us with an internal living laboratory which demonstrates the advantages of empowering the people. In several Swiss cantons or states, new government programs must be approved by a referendum before any money can be spent. A Swiss and an American expert decided to test the widespread view that governments will systematically overspend. By scientifically comparing those cantons where governments must seek a mandate for new spending with other cantons over an eighteen year period, they found that mandatory referendums reduced government spending by 19%.[12] It is relevant to note that Swiss cantons are more independent than our states. This is because they are more reliant on their own income than in Australia where the politicians and judges have rearranged matters to give the federal government more control over taxes than in any other federation.

The fact is, the Swiss example demonstrates a better way of governing than leaving it to the powerbrokers and the elites who rule Australia.

Nor does direct democracy mean the adoption of reactionary policies. Gregory A. Fossedal points out that while the attitude of the Swiss on immigration seems to be negative, the votes in various referendums are fundamentally liberal. This indicates that during a referendum, the Swiss carefully consider the arguments for and against the proposition and vote in accordance with what they believe to be the national interest. When they are allowed to, Australians take a similar position. But be warned, readers will be told by the powerbrokers and the elites that Australians are different and cannot be trusted.

It will be said Australians have a terrible record when it comes to referendums. This is just not true. When it comes to these, Australians have a very good record. In fact most of the referendums on which they are allowed to vote have been to increase the powers of the federal politicians and the governing class. Australians usually realise this after they read and have heard both sides. They then usually wake up to the fact that the politicians are trying to pull the wool over their eyes. You see the average Australians are too smart – that is why the powerbrokers and elites fear them.

The Swiss system has many virtues, and among these is a complete rejection of the rule of judges. Judges cannot legislate or even rewrite a constitution as they do especially in the United States and to a certain extent in Australia. The validity of laws cannot be tested in the Federal Court. This is because there is no need for the judges to give detailed instructions on constitutional issues. As a federal court official explains: "The Parliament and ultimately the people write the laws and the Constitution, which frees our justices to decide particular cases. There is not a need for detailed instructions from a court on constitutional issues; Switzerland is a democracy."[13] And the criminal justice system, perhaps in combination with other factors, actually works – crime rates are among the lowest in the world.[14]

And just as our Federal politicians are leaving our country defenceless, the Swiss system means that all able-bodied Swiss men are ready to defend their country. With a population of only six million, the Swiss can place 400,000 trained armed and highly skilled troops in the field within 48 hours.

When our founding fathers were drafting the federal Constitution, they sensibly decided that the institutions of responsible government which came from Britain and had been adopted in the states should also be incorporated at the federal level. In deciding on the other federal institutions, those of the United States and Canada were looked at most closely. In relation to amending the Constitution, the Swiss referendum was adopted so that the people had all of the details on the table before they voted. But the people were not given any power to initiate change. Our founding fathers did not expect that the factional powerbrokers and the elites would so arrange matters and even make laws to ensure that the institutions of representative democracy would be compromised. They did not expect that judges, following the pattern established in the United States, would seize not only legislative power but also the power to amend the Constitution by interpretations having no basis in its wording or original intention.

This must now be reversed. We believe that the only way to restore our democracy is to empower the people – as the Swiss people are empowered – without in any way making government unstable. The only way to reform our institutions and our politicians is to make the politicians accountable on every day, of every week and of every month. Just as Australians are in their jobs and professions. And just as the Swiss politicians are.

There will be opposition to this. It will disenfranchise the factional powerbrokers who will lose their power. It will also disenfranchise the elites who will no longer be able to force their agenda surreptitiously onto a reluctant nation. They will have to argue it before the people and persuade them. As they should in a democracy.

17.2 United States

About 200 million Americans, or 70% of the population, now live in either a city or a state where at least one of the tools of direct democracy is available.[15] We shall say more about the United States when we come to the specific tools of direct democracy but there is one aspect which ought to be mentioned now.[16]

This is that we have in the United States a living laboratory which allows us to compare those states where the citizens have access to the tools of direct democracy with those who do not. There has long been a massive amount of relevant data available, both economic and about people's opinions, to make findings on this. But until low-cost computing became generally available it was not practicable to analyse this data.

Then ten years ago, Professor John G. Matsusaka found himself in the position to do precisely this. He is well qualified as a Ph.D. in economics from the University of Chicago and Charles F. Sexton Chair in American Enterprise in the Marshall School of Business, Gould School of Law, and Department of Political Science at the University of Southern California, as well is being the President of the Initiative and Referendum Institute at USC. He has held visiting appointments at the Hoover Institution at Stanford University, UCLA, Caltech, and the University of Chicago.

He analysed the vast amount of data on the effect of the initiative and came to three significant conclusions.[17]

First, over the last three decades the initiative has had a significant impact on state and local governments. States with the initiative spend and tax less than states without the initiative, they decentralise spending from state to local government, and they raise more money from user fees and less from taxes.

Second, opinion surveys show a majority of people support each of these policy changes: less spending, more local disbursement of funds and greater reliance on user fees compared with broad-based taxes.

Third, the initiative process does not allow special interests to distort policies away from what the public wants. The initiative appears to promote the interests of the many, rather than the few.

So we have the Swiss example, which is federal and state, and the American laboratory where states with direct democracy coexist with states which do not have this, all providing clear evidence of the advantages of the people being empowered and the politicians being made more accountable.

17.3 Direct democracy in Australia

The introduction of direct democracy into Australia at the federal and state levels requires constitutional change. This must be approached carefully. Above all the people should be properly informed before they vote.

To this end, we suggest a process based on the precedent set by our founding fathers. We summarise this at the end of this Chapter, under "Process."

As to the interest in direct democracy in Australia, we should go back to the late 19th century movement to unite the six colonies.

In 1891, at the Constitutional Convention in Sydney, the South Australian Premier Charles Cameron Kingston brought a draft of a federal Constitution which had been printed by the South Australian government printer. The draft included the following clause:[18]

> No Bill passed by both Houses of the Federal Parliament shall be assented to by the Governor-General until after a referendum, if a referendum shall be duly demanded before assent declared.
>
> A referendum may be demanded in respect of any Bill passed by both Houses of the Federal Parliament at any time within three calendar months after the passing thereof.
>
> A referendum may be demanded by –
>
> I. One-third of the total number of members of either House of the Federal Parliament: or
>
> II. Resolution of both Houses of any two local [State] Legislatures: or
>
> III. Twenty-thousand persons entitled to vote at the election of members to serve in the National Assembly [Senate and House of Representatives].

The Convention appointed a constitutional committee to undertake

the task of preparing a draft Constitution. A subcommittee of four –
Charles Kingston, Sir Samuel Griffith, Edmund Barton and Andrew
Inglis Clark – completed the process on board the *SS Lucinda* on the
Hawkesbury River from 27 to 29 March. We must assume that Charles
Kingston's draft, including the provision for a referendum triggered in
one of three ways including a petition from 20,000 voters, was discussed
there. It must have been rejected. It did not appear in the constitutional
committee's draft bill and there was no mention of it in the records of the
plenary session of the convention itself. We do know that the delegates
had the American, Canadian and Swiss constitutions before them along
with much of the relevant literature, so it is reasonable to assume that
they would have been aware of the Swiss use of direct democracy.[19]

Joseph Poprzeczny says that there were about a dozen references to
Switzerland in the debates, but the only relevant comment at the full
session was that by the Victorian delegate, Alfred Deakin:[20]

> ... There are many like myself, who would be perfectly
> prepared, if we were bound to change our present
> constitutions altogether, to adopt the Swiss system, with its
> co-ordinate houses, its elective ministry, and its referendum,
> by which the electors themselves were made masters of the
> situation; but while we would be prepared to consider a
> proposal of that kind, the Swiss relation of the two chambers
> has no analogy whatever to a constitution such as ours, in
> which it is proposed to retain responsible government, and
> in which the government must be responsible to the people's
> chamber.

The most encouraging development was when the Australian Labor
Party emerged at the national level in 1900, its platform included a call
for the initiative and referendum for constitutional change to be included
in the Constitution. On the conservative side, direct democracy has never
been endorsed at the national level. Occasionally, state parliamentary
parties have given some support to the concept. Both Labor and

conservative parties have demonstrated an opportunistic approach to direct democracy, backing it while in opposition, but not supporting it on gaining office, or as Joseph Poprzeczny says, even on the prospect of doing so.[21]

There have been a number of attempts to introduce direct democracy into Australia, and without exception all have been snuffed out by the politicians. Sometimes an alternative was offered as some sort of palliative, the latest being the introduction of the transparently cosmetic "Kitchen Cabinet" process referred to in Chapter 12.

Support by individual serving politicians has been rare. Former Howard government minister, Peter Reith, was an exception, as were Liberal then independent South Australian MP and Speaker Peter Lewis and New South Wales then Federal MP, Ted Mack. Those in office today who support the concept include the Christian Democrat, the Rev. Fred Nile, in the New South Wales parliament. Democratic Labor Party Senator John Madigan and Katter's Australia Party Leader, Bob Katter, are supporters in the federal parliament.

Ted Mack actually introduced direct democracy to North Sydney Council when he was Mayor. An extraordinarily principled politician who was opposed to politicians' generous mainly taxpayer-funded superannuation, he resigned from the New South Wales parliament just before he was eligible for superannuation and later repeated this when he resigned from the federal parliament. He was elected as a Real Republic delegate to the 1998 Constitutional Convention where he opposed the Keating-Turnbull model. Based on votes gained in the Convention election, he was appointed with former Brisbane Mayor Clem Jones and eight delegates from Australians for Constitutional Monarchy to the official Vote No Committee during the 1999 referendum campaign.

Those in the universities have not shown much interest in direct democracy, with the exception of the late Patrick O'Brien, Emeritus Professor Martyn Webb and, especially, Emeritus Professor Geoffrey de Q. Walker. Professor Walker's book, *Initiative and Referendum: The People's*

Law, is probably the most significant literary contribution to the debate.[22] Professor George Williams and Geraldine Chin have also undertaken valuable work in the area and, in the media, Joseph Poprzeczny's contribution and interest have kept the issue alive in recent times.

17.4 Process

The proposal that tools of direct democracy be introduced would, we believe, constitute a significant improvement in the governance of Australia. It would empower the people and make the politicians accountable to them not only in elections every three or four years, but on every day, of every week and of every month.

The decision to include these tools in our constitutional system should not be undertaken lightly. The decision on this should be made by the people once they are fully informed as to what is being proposed.

We believe that the best way to achieve this is by following the precedent established by our predecessors in uniting our country, the Corowa plan or process.

It should be recalled that the first serious attempt to federate our nation failed. The first national Australasian convention met in Sydney in 1891 and after debate the draft constitution was then referred to the colonial parliaments. There the bill was torn apart and the process broke down hopelessly. The New South Wales anti-federation leader John Robertson boasted that "Federation is as dead as Julius Caesar".

But although progress towards federation was stifled by the politicians, the Australian people began to be interested in the concept. The process had awakened a federal spirit throughout the colonies. Branches of the Australian Natives' Association and Federation Leagues were established and a conference of these was held in Corowa in 1893. There were many enthusiastic speeches, but just as the conference was about to conclude, Dr., later Sir, John Quick from Bendigo proposed a motion which was enthusiastically adopted. The motion was so significant it is now known as the Corowa Plan. This Plan, and Quick's meticulous campaign for its success, was to ensure that within seven years federation would be achieved. We should remember that our founding fathers did not have access to modern means of communication, and the process included having the Constitution approved in two referendums in five states.[23] Then the bill had to be taken to London to seek ministerial support for its passage through the British Parliament before Royal Assent could be given by Queen Victoria. Then with a successful vote in Western Australia, The Queen proclaimed the federation to take effect at the beginning of the new century.

The resolution adopted at Corowa reads:

> That in the opinion of this Conference the Legislature of each Australasian colony should pass an Act providing for the election of representatives to attend a statutory convention or congress to consider and adopt a bill to establish a Federal Constitution for Australia and upon the adoption of such bill or measure it be submitted by some process of referendum to the verdict of each colony.

The Corowa Plan proposed that each of the six Australian parliaments legislate to provide the election of delegates to a national convention, and that once the convention agreed on a federal Constitution, this be submitted to the people for acceptance or rejection. If accepted by majorities in two or more colonies, it was to be forwarded to London to be passed into law.

This was modified subsequently to provide for an adjournment of 30 to 60 days after the adoption of the draft Constitution to allow for consultation and for comments from the various parliaments. After that a final version would be settled and submitted to the people of each colony state in separate referendums.

This Corowa Plan not only achieved federation, it was a wonderful gift from our forefathers to show us how to solve any future problems of governance. That time has come. The Corowa Plan of 1893 shows us, in the second decade of the 21st century, how to resolve our present difficulties.

17.5 A new Corowa Plan

We propose that the restoration of the institutions of our democracy, the empowerment of the people and the accountability of our politicians be considered by a constitutional convention. The convention would have the specific task of preparing referendums for the introduction of the tools of direct democracy at the federal, state, territory and local government levels.

We propose that it be agreed that after consultation and comment, each referendum the convention finally proposes be put directly to the people and not debated again in parliament.

The convention would consist of 100 voting delegates elected by the people on a state wide and territory wide basis. This would be in approximately the same proportion as each state and territory is represented in the two houses of the federal parliament.

In addition we propose that there be 60 ex officio and appointed delegates. The 1998 convention also consisted of elected, ex officio and appointed delegates. We propose on this occasion that only the elected delegates be entitled to vote. We believe that the proposals on direct democracy come from the delegates elected for this purpose, but that they should be assisted by the views and experience of the other delegates.

The 60 non-voting delegates would include 30 ex officio parliamentary delegates. There would eight federal delegates, three from each state and two from each territory including the prime minister, premiers, chief ministers, and leaders of the opposition or their alternates.

The other 30 would be experts and community representatives not otherwise represented at the convention. Each premier would choose two, the prime minister four, and the remainder would be chosen by the elected delegates.

Delegates would not be paid but be reimbursed for minimal expenses such as economy airfares etc. It is envisaged that much of the detailed work would be undertaken by an elected drafting committee and other committees meeting and communicating through modern inexpensive methods.

Committees could also be established of all delegates from each state or territory to develop proposals specific to their state or territory and to local government areas.

The proposals would prescribe minimum percentages of voters for petitions to trigger a Citizens' Recall, a Citizens' Veto and a Citizens' Initiative, as well as other methods of empowering the people.

The percentages would be designed not to be too low as to trigger proposals which could not possibly pass, nor so high as to stop campaigns which have a reasonable prospect of success. There would be no need for the percentages to be uniform between the different tools; in fact there would appear to be good arguments for these to vary.

The convention would propose percentages to be attained at both a national and, if thought appropriate, at a state level. This would be to avoid the prescribed percentage being obtained only in the most populous states. Thus for a petition for a Citizens' Veto on federal legislation, the minimum percentage to trigger a vote could be required to be achieved both nationally and in, say, three states. Similarly for the vote to be successful, the convention might require a national majority and a majority in three states.

The convention would be required to produce draft proposals within an agreed time for consultation with and comment by the public and the parliaments. (In the Corowa Plan the convention was to adjourn for 30 to 60 days for this purpose at a time when communication was not as easy as today).

In summary, we propose the restoration of the institutions of our democracy, the empowerment of the people and the accountability of our politicians be considered by a constitutional convention whose ultimate task would be to prepare referendums on the introduction of the tools of direct democracy at the federal, state, territory and local government levels.

Endnotes

1 Thomas E. Cronin, *Direct Democracy, The Politics of Initiative, Referendum, And Recall*, Harvard University Press, Cambridge, 1999; Nick Cowen, *Total Recall*, Civitas, Lansing, 2008; Gregory A. Fossedal, *Direct Democracy in Switzerland*, Transaction Publishers, New Brunswick, 2002, p. ix. At the time of publication the author was the Chairman of the Alexis de Tocqueville Institution, a think tank based in Washington DC and President of the Democratic Century Fund. The foreword is by Alfred R. Berkeley III, then President s of the NASDAQ stock market. The preface is by Richard Holbrooke, US Ambassador to the United Nations and Assistant Secretary of State in the Clinton administration.

2 Fossedal, op. cit. p. 5.

3 Ibid., p. 81.

4 Ibid., p. 81.

5 Ibid, pp. 75-86 1X.3.

6 Ibid., p. 115.

7 Ibid., p. 109.

8 Ibid.,p.80.

9 Ibid., p.109.

10 Ibid., p. 82.

11 Ibid., p. 105.

12 R.P. Feld and John G. Matsusaka, "Budget Referendums and Government Spending: Evidence from Swiss Cantons", *Initiative & Referendum Institute at the University of Southern California*, 2002. http://iandrinstitute.org/New%20IRI%20Website%20 Info/I&R%20Research%20and%20History/I&R%20Studies/Feld%20and%20 Matsusaka%20-%20Fiscal%20Evidence%20from%20Swiss%20Cantons%20IRI. pdf (retrieved 18.04.2013).

13 Ibid., p. 70.

14 Ibid., pp. 155, 159.

15 Dane M. Waters, *Initiative and Referendum Almanac*, Carolina Academic Press, Durham, 2003.

16 John G. Matsusaka, *For the Many or the Few: The Initiative, Public Policy, and American Democracy*, University of Chicago Press, Chicago, 2004, Chapter 1.

17 Ibid.

18 John M. Williams, *The Australian Constitution: A Documentary History*, Melbourne University Press, Melbourne, 2004, pp. 126-7; Joseph Poprzeczny, "Australia – a democracy or just another ballotocracy?", *National Observer*, No. 76, Autumn 2008, pp. 7-32. http://www.nationalobserver.net/pdf/2008_australia_-_a_democracy_or_just_anoher_ballotocracy.pdf (retrieved 05.05.2013).

19 Sir John Quick and Sir Robert Garran, *The Annotated Constitution of the Australian Commonwealth*, 1901 reprinted, Legal Books, Sydney, 1976, 1995, p. 130.

20 Constitutional Convention, Sydney, Debates, 8 April 1891, pp. 709-10.

21 Op. cit., pp. 14-15; George Williams and Geraldine Chin, "The Failure of Citizens' Initiated Referenda Proposals in Australia", *Australian Journal of Political Science*, Vol. 35, No. 1, 2000.

22 Geoffrey de Q. Walker, *Initiative and Referendum: The People's Law*, Centre for Independent Studies, Sydney, 1987.

23 The Western Australian referendum was not held until 31 July 1900, after Royal Assent was given to the *Commonwealth of Australia Constitution Act*, 1900. The vote in the referendum allowed Queen Victoria to declare from Balmoral in her Royal Proclamation fixing the establishment of the Commonwealth of Australia on 1 January 1901 that she was "satisified that the people of Western Australia have agreed to join" the Federation, and that Western Australia would be an Original State.

CHAPTER 18

Recall them to an early election

18.1 Introduction

A recall election allows electors to remove and replace a public official before the end of his or her term of office.

In a system where the executive government is vested in one official, for example, the governor of one of the United States, a successful recall election could result in a change of government. This would necessarily involve sending at least the lower house to an election. Experience indicates that electorates do not exercise the power frivolously and only recall governments which have very much lost their support.

The usual process for a recall election begins with the collection of the signatures of a certain number or percentage of voters. This must be done during a prescribed period of time. In most jurisdictions, the petitioners are not required to specify a ground of recall. If the requisite number of signatures is obtained, voters are asked whether the official in question should be recalled and an election take place. If a majority is cast in favour of recall, the election takes place immediately or on a later date.

18.2 Switzerland

Recall elections are not available at the federal level in Switzerland, but have existed since the late 19th century in some of the country's 26 cantons or states. They remain in Bern, Schaffhausen, Solothurn, Ticino, Thurgau and Uri.

They were introduced into Switzerland with other tools of direct democracy, including the referendum to veto legislation and the initiative.

The number of signatures to trigger a recall petition varies between cantons and ranges from 30,000 (or only 4%), down to as low as 1000, or even 600.

Despite the very low number of signatures required to trigger a recall election, the process has been rarely used, and no Swiss legislature has ever been recalled.

This is probably because there is the ready availability of the referendum to veto legislation and the initiative. In addition, there is the fact that governments tend to be formed with representatives from all of the major parties. At the federal level, there are certain understandings or conventions. For example, it is thought desirable to have one person on the seven member executive council representing one of the three national languages, Italian and French and Swiss.[1] Then each of the three largest provinces – Zurich, Bern and Fribourg – normally has one member. But no canton has two members.

Thus Swiss politics seems to be more about good government and the policies being adopted, and these being in a court with the common sense, good judgement and decency of the Swiss people, rather than a "winner takes all" mentality, as in Australia.

18.3 The United States

Recall elections were introduced into America in the early 20th century as part of the progressive movement. Recall elections are available in 19 American states and in the District of Columbia. In at least 29 states – some sources say as high as 36 – recall elections may be held at the local government level.[2] Most recall elections are held at the city council or school board level.

The methods by which the recall is exercised vary in a significant number of ways. This is a living demonstration of the refusal of Americans to fall for the pressure so fashionable in Australia, to harmonise and make uniform everything across the country. The Americans, being federalists, understand that variation is important. They realise that quite often one national model and way of doing everything is not necessarily the answer. By trial and error and competition, better solutions can often be found.

Two governors have been successfully recalled. This is more than recalling an Australian premier or first minister; it means that the government of the state was thereby recalled. These were Governor Lyn Frazier of North Dakota in 1921 and Governor Gray Davis of California in 2003, which was followed by the election of Arnold Schwarzenegger.

After the scandal concerning the former Governor Rod Blagojevich, who was found guilty of corruption which included attempting to sell the former Senate seat of President Obama for Illinois, voters adopted a referendum amending the state constitution to allow the recall of officials.

The most recent example of a recall election was in 2012, where the Governor of Wisconsin, Scott Walker, was returned with a higher majority.

The states have different forms of recall elections. In some cases specific grounds indicating the alleged misconduct are required. In some states, the grounds can be challenged in court. In other states, no specific grounds are required.

In six states, the election for a successor is held simultaneously with the recall.

In the remaining 13 states, the ballot paper contains only the question of whether or not the official should be recalled. If there is a majority for the yes case, either the office is declared vacant and a special election held, or an appointment is made for the remainder of the term from the same party.

Petitions for recall understandably require more signatures than the other tools of direct democracy. Kansas requires 40%, Louisiana 33.13% while several states require 25%. California has the lowest requirement which is 12%.

18.4 Canada

Recall elections for individual members of parliament were briefly introduced into Alberta in 1936 by the Premier William Aberhart. The recall was to have been triggered by the signature of two-thirds of the voters in a constituency. He developed the concept when he was in opposition, but found that as premier the first recall petition was being made against him. Worse, there was considerable voter support for it. He then introduced an act for the repeal of the *Legislative Assembly (Recall) Act*, 1936, which was passed.

Australian readers will be interested to know that in 1937 the premier expelled the Lieutenant-Governor John C. Bowen, the equivalent of an Australian Governor, from Government House. In 1996, Premier Bob Carr expelled the Governor of New South Wales from Government House. In addition to the reasons offered at the time, Premier Carr subsequently added the vice-regal reserve powers, including the vice-regal power to dismiss a government for constitutional reasons. At the time of writing, the Governor is being restored to her purpose built home.[3]

Back in Alberta in 1937, the Lieutenant-Governor's official car and support staff were also withdrawn. This followed the Lieutenant Governor's refusal to give Royal Assent to three bills effectively nationalising the banks and requiring newspapers to print government rebuttals to "inaccurate" reports. All three bills were later found to be unconstitutional by the courts.

In 1995, the legislature of British Columbia enacted a right to recall all representatives, including the premier. If 40% of signatures of eligible voters are collected, a vacancy is declared in that seat and a new election held. The former representative may stand.

There have been 22 attempts to recall a representative; none have succeeded but one representative, Paul Reitsma, resigned in 1998 during the count of a recall petition when it seemed possible the 40% would be reached.

18.5 Australia

The recall of members of parliament has from time to time received support from individuals on both sides of the political spectrum. Among the major parties, only the Australian Labor Party has endorsed it. Among political parties today, the recall is supported by the Christian Democrats, the Democratic Labor Party, Family First and Katter's Australian Party.

After discussion for some years, recall elections became part of the policy platform of the Labor Party in 1924, until, as previously noted, they were removed in 1963 on the motion of Mr. Don Dunstan, subsequently Premier of South Australia.[4]

Recall elections were later raised in the aftermath of the dismissal of the Whitlam government in 1975.[5]

The exercise of this reserve power of the Crown would always be controversial. Although it was the product of two politicians unwilling to compromise, and who consequently forced Sir John Kerr to act, both politicians tried to shift the blame onto the Crown. Mr. Whitlam did so immediately; Opposition Leader Mr. Fraser did so years later when he converted to republicanism.

Many in the media joined them in their attempts to rewrite history. A Canadian constitutional scholar has asked whether the Crown could easily absorb another such crisis, "however justifiable the Governor's decisions might be from a purely legal point of view".[6] Could this imperil the future exercise of this reserve power? Is it a wasting asset?

Hence the argument that had the recall election been available in 1975, the opposition would have spent their efforts collecting signatures for a petition, rather than denying supply.

The legitimacy of its use, successful or not, would be difficult to challenge. The suggestion was in no way a proposal to remove, amend, codify or reduce the reserve power to withdraw the prime minister's or premier's commission. Under this proposal this reserve power would still exist and would remain available for use against an errant prime minister or premier.

18.6 Australia: New South Wales

"A recall election mechanism would give the public a release valve. It would only prove successful if first, supported by sufficient petitioners, and second, by a majority of electors in any subsequent poll," the then Leader of the Opposition, Barry O'Farrell, argued cogently and passionately in an opinion piece in *The Sydney Morning Herald*, on 11 December 2009, headlined, "We should introduce recall elections."[7]

"It would", Premier O'Farrell said, "put the public back in control."

He continued: "In the words of Abraham Lincoln's Gettysburg Address, it would again ensure in NSW 'that government of the people, by the people, for the people shall not perish from the earth.'"

Referring to the appointment of a new premier as a result of decisions taken by the ruling factional powerbroker in the NSW Labor Party, he said this offered no greater example of all that Lincoln would have found objectionable: government by the factions, ruling "for the benefit of partisan political interest".

He pointed out that the choice of the latest premier had not been made by the voters but by, in former Premier Nathan Rees's words, "the malignant, treacherous and disloyal forces" of the NSW branch of the Australian Labor Party.

Mr. O'Farrell wrote that there was "little doubt" that fixed four-year parliamentary terms in NSW had aided and abetted Labor in its "theft of the state's democratic ideals".

Mr. O'Farrell recalled that it was claimed that fixed parliamentary terms would end "community frustration" with the calling of early elections. It was said these fixed four year terms would give government the certainty needed to get on with "the job of governing".

He said that no one foresaw how a "NSW Labor machine" would be able to "pervert" the new system of fixed terms to protect "maladministration, political inertia and incompetence".

Mr. O'Farrell said that Labor governments delayed acting on such matters as hospital waiting lists until the campaign period before the election.

He reminded readers that six months previously he had argued the introduction of recall elections was one way to improve "the accountability" of the NSW government to the electorate or community.

In his view, recall elections are "democratic, increase accountability, offer a safeguard against abuse and can help restore confidence in, and promote active involvement with, the political process".

He made another point, often overlooked by commentators. "The spectre of being forced to an early election by the public could provide the stimulus needed for government ... to put in a full four-year effort as well as a safeguard against political abuses."

In response to the arguments that recall elections "undermine representative government", are "open to abuse" and "insult hardworking MPs", he said that despite recall provisions existing in the United States for about a century, only two governors have been recalled.

As for the argument about expense, Mr. O'Farrell pointed out that if this were pursued there would not be any elections.

On 3 April 2011, Mr. O'Farrell led the Coalition to victory in the New South Wales election, and on 20 June, 2011, he announced the appointment "of a panel of constitutional experts to advise the NSW government on the possibility of introducing recall elections in NSW". The members were Mr. David Jackson AM, QC (Chairman), Dr. Elaine Thompson and Professor George Williams AO.

All members advised against a recall of individual members of parliament. While finding the issues difficult, the Chairman favoured and Dr. Thompson supported the introduction of the recall process for the whole Legislative Assembly.[8]

Professor Williams did not support the recall, but not because of damage it might do to the Westminster system. He feared the existence of the recall would further restrict the capacity of politicians to make "difficult, long-term decisions". They could be manipulated by "powerful interests". He said he might be persuaded to support the recall if there were a public demand for the change. His colleagues pointed out that the necessary referendum to change the NSW Constitution would establish whether there were such a demand. In their view the referendum, pursuant to section 7B and perhaps also section 7A of the Constitution, should be to incorporate provisions in the Constitution concerning the recall. This should not merely authorise the parliament to enact legislation about this.

Subject to Professor William's reservations, the panel concluded that the only form of the recall which they regarded as feasible was a "citizen initiated recall election" of the whole of the Legislative Assembly. This would be for the general election of the Legislative Assembly which would next have occurred.

This would be accompanied by an election for the seats of the 21 members of the Legislative Council which would otherwise have become vacant at the next general election for the Legislative Assembly.

The panel recommended that the recall not be allowed or initiated during either the first 18 months or the last six months of the term of a Legislative Assembly. The process would begin by an application, supported by 500 signatures, to commence a petition to the New South Wales Electoral Commission. They thought there should be no need to state a ground or reason for the petition.

A petition would then be launched and remain open for 60 days. They proposed the petition could be signed online, subject to verification and auditing.

The panel believed a significant proportion – they suggested 35% – of eligible voters should be required for a petition to be successful. To ensure a reasonable spread across the state, they argued that at least 5% of eligible voters come from at least 50% of electorates.

According to *The Sydney Morning Herald*, Premier O'Farrell received the report at the end of September 2011, but only released it in December after the newspaper's enquiries.[9] A spokesman said the government was considering the findings.[10]

Nothing further was heard until 2GB's Alan Jones reported the Premier's office had informed him that as the panel had recommended against the recall of politicians and the government would be taking no further action on this.

18.7 The way forward

We do not propose that Australia should move from being a stable representative democracy under our constitutional system. What we are proposing is that a convention be held to consider introducing into Australia some of the tools of direct democracy, which have worked so well in Switzerland, and which also exist in some American states and in British Columbia.

This is not a suggestion that we return – if it were possible to return – to the participation by all men (at least all free men) in governing as in ancient Greece. This would be impossible with the size of communities today.

The reason we are advancing this proposal is, we stress, that the institutions of representative democracy in Australia have been compromised by the AAA, the alliance or axis between the factional powerbrokers and the elites.

The result has been the adoption of laws and policies which

contradict the common sense, good judgement and decency of rank-and-file Australians. In brief, these laws and policies just do not pass the "pub test".

We propose that a convention be elected to consider the introduction of the various tools of direct democracy. We stress, as Premier O'Farrell did when he was arguing so strongly for recall elections, that it is not only the use of recall elections which is so important to good government, it is their existence. If those who rule us knew that the people had these tools at their command, it is not that they would put off the difficult decisions of government. Rather it is that they would govern better than they do.

We anticipate that the convention would take the work of the New South Wales enquiry, the submissions made to it, and the rich vein of information which is available in relation to the workings of other systems. They would consider these and then come to a conclusion as to the model which could be put to the Australian people.

As Barry O'Farrell put it, "the right to petition for a recall election would put the public back in control".

Endnotes

1 Gregory A. Fossedal, *Direct democracy in Switzerland*, Transaction Publishers, New Brunswick, 2009, p. 52.

2 National Conference of State Legislatures http://www.ncsl.org/legislatures-elections/elections/recall-of-state-officials.aspx (retrieved 23.03.2013).

3 Return the Governor, *Australians for Constitutional Monarchy*. http://www.norepublic.com.au/index.php?option=com_content&task=blogcategory&id=34&Itemid=38 (retrieved 24.03.2013).

4 Geoffrey de Q. Walker, *Initiative and Referendum: the People's Law*, Centre for Independent Studies, Sydney, 1987, pp. 154-155.

5 David Flint, *Her Majesty at 80: Impeccable Service in an Indispensable Office*, Australians for Constitutional Monarchy, Sydney, 2006, pp. 35-37. http://www.norepublic.com.au/index.php?option=com_content&task=view&id=1024&Itemid=24 (retrieved 24.03.2013).

6 David E. Smith, *The Invisible Crown: The First Principle of Canadian Government*, Toronto University Press, Toronto, 1995, p. 32.

7 http://www.smh.com.au/opinion/politics/we-should-introduce-recall-elections-20091210-km6k.html#ixzz2ORneigD6 (retrieved 24.03.2013).

8 *Recall Elections for New South Wales? Report of the Panel of Constitutional Experts* ("Recall Report"): Mr. David Jackson AM, QC (Chairman), Dr. Elaine Thompson, Professor George Williams AO, Statement M. http://www.dpc.nsw.gov.au/__data/assets/pdf_file/0013/134221/Panel_of_Constitutional_Experts_-_Review_into_Recall_Elections.pdf (retrieved 22.03.2013).

9 Sean Nicolls, "Let voters dump bad government, experts decide", *Sydney Morning Herald*, 14 December 2011. http://www.smh.com.au/nsw/let-voters-dump-bad-government-experts-decide-20111213-1ot83.html

10 Recall report, Section N, par. 21.

CHAPTER 19

Don't like their taxes and their laws? Veto them

19.1 Introduction

Australians are increasingly disillusioned with the present system of government. Ninety percent have a negative view of it, in practice or principle, according to the Australian Constitutional Values 2010 Survey undertaken by Newspoll for Griffith University. Rather than staying as it is, 74.5% would like to see system reformed 20 years from now.[1]

But the options offered for reform were predictable.

The factional powerbrokers and the elites love nothing better than having the voters consider some or other predictable "solution" to the way they have misgoverned the country. Examples include the abolition of the states or local government, or the insertion of another tier of government in the "regions", a project began by the Whitlam government.

These distractions are not real solutions. They ignore three realities. First, the states are not such an obstacle to the will of Canberra. The centralist politicians and judges long ago flouted both the original intention of the Constitution and the wishes of the people whenever they have been consulted in a referendum. They have emasculated the states, making them mere shadows of themselves. Instead of obstacles, the states are more often than not obedient mendicants on the federal government. Occasionally, the state politicians will offer a display of independence for the benefit of the voters; a few exceptions really believe in states' rights.

Second, whatever the elites in the eastern capitals think, the people of each state must agree to their abolition – and they never will.

Third, it is most unlikely the people would agree to a fourth tier of government.

What the respondents were not asked – and are rarely asked – is whether they think our system would be improved by making the politicians more accountable by empowering the people. They were not asked about reviving an idea proposed by one of Australia's great founding fathers in the discussions leading up to the federation of our country.[2] This is to give the people the right to vote on legislation about which a large number may object. In other words, they were not asked whether the people should exercise a veto over their politicians and indeed their judges when they make laws or change the Constitution.

We propose that the fairest way for this to be considered, along with the other tools of direct democracy, is through the election of a constitutional convention dedicated to discussing these proposals and submitting referendums on these to the people for discussion, debate and determination. This process would befit one of the world's oldest continuing democracies but one which, in the estimation of the people, has been captured by the factional powerbrokers and the elites.

An excellent example of precisely the type of legislation which should be referred to the people was offered by the Gillard government in 2010. On several occasions during the election campaign, both the Prime Minister, Julia Gillard, and Treasurer, Wayne Swan, were at pains to assure the voters that the government would not impose a carbon dioxide tax. The Prime Minister famously stated: "There will be no carbon tax under the government I lead."[3] The Treasurer's assurance is almost as well known: "No it's not possible that we're bringing in the carbon tax; that is a hysterically inaccurate claim being made by the Coalition."[4]

The outrage which greeted this breach of promise has stayed with the government. It could not have been done in Switzerland or many American states. The people could have exercised their right of veto.

The people's veto is often referred to in the academic literature as a "referendum". This is in contrast to the "initiative". The initiative is a proposal for the adoption of a law, rather than the repeal or cancellation of a law. It is also referred to as a Citizen's Initiated Referendum, "CIR".

Broadly speaking, the word "referendum" refers to any question that appears on a ballot.[5] The word is well known to Australians because of the provision in our Constitution which requires that a referendum record the approval of the people both nationally and federally for any proposed change to the Constitution.[6]

There are two types of referendums: the legislative referendum, where a legislature refers a measure to the voters for their approval, and the popular referendum, a measure that appears on the ballot paper as a result of a petition by the voters.

In this Chapter we examine the process whereby a number of voters can initiate a petition for a vote about a particular law, bill, or administrative act which they invite a number of voters to sign. In addition, a vote could be requested on whether a treaty be ratified or about a ruling by activist judges which has legislative effect. This process requires a prescribed number or percentage of voters to sign a petition within a specified period after the passing of the bill or other instrument.

Once the prescribed number or percentage of signatures are gathered and verified, a general vote on the bill or law is taken in a referendum. If a majority reject the bill or law, then it does not take effect.

We are not discussing the advisory referendum, usually referred to as a plebiscite in Australia. In this, a question is put to the people to gauge their opinion on some particular issue on which the legislature or the government already has ample legal and constitutional authority to act. The people's vote is not binding and there is no obligation on the legislature or the government to act in accordance with their wishes.

There have been three such plebiscites at the federal level in Australia, two on conscription in 1916 and 1917, and one in 1977 on a national song, often referred mistakenly to as a vote on a national anthem. State plebiscites have taken place on such matters as hotel trading hours, daylight savings and in one instance, the location of a dam.

19.2 Switzerland

The people's veto and the initiative became a regular feature of Switzerland cantons or states after 1830, with the people's veto being introduced at the federal level in 1874.[7] This is often referred to by the Swiss as the "brake pedal" of direct democracy. Just its existence is said to encourage the politicians to consult widely with all interest groups before legislation is introduced.

To trigger the vote, a referendum committee has 100 days following the publication in the *Federal Gazette* of a legislative act or prescribed treaty to collect 50,000 signatures on a petition, have them validated by the communes and submit them to the Federal Chancellery. Alternatively eight cantons may call for a vote.[8] The vote is taken through an optional referendum, and is decided by a majority of those voting.[9]

It is worth recalling the context. The Swiss people must already be consulted in a mandatory referendum on not only any change to the Constitution, but also any proposal that Switzerland join a collective security organisation, such as NATO, or a supranational community, such as the European Union. These mandatory referendums have to be approved both nationally and also in a majority of the 26 cantons.[10]

It is also possible to initiate a referendum at the cantonal and the communal level. These often have a greater scope than federal referendums. Consequently the Swiss may vote several times a year on various proposals, some referred by the authorities and some on the initiative of concerned citizens.

19.3 New Zealand

There is a prominent movement in New Zealand which is campaigning for the introduction of the people's veto, the "100 days – Claiming Back

New Zealand Movement".[11] The movement is headed by the noted author and founder of the New Zealand think tank the Summersounds Symposium, Amy Brooke. She has just published a book explaining the proposal.[12]

The immediate cause for the formation of the movement was the consequence of a plebiscite or referendum held under the *Citizens Initiated Referenda Act 1993* (NZ). This legislation provides that if 10% of the voters sign a petition over a 12 month period, a vote shall be taken on a question to be settled by the Clerk of the House of Representatives.

A petition for a plebiscite or referendum was launched in February 2007 in response to a private member's bill, the *Crimes (Substituted Section 59) Amendment* Bill, which would remove parental correction as a defence for assault against children. The question was, "Should a smack as part of good parental correction be a criminal offence in New Zealand?" The result was that 87.40% voted No and 11.98% voted yes.

Amy Brooke and her colleagues were understandably shocked when the *Crimes (Substituted Section 59) Amendment* Bill was passed – against the wishes of the people – by the single house parliament in 2009 with the support of the Labour Prime Minister, Helen Clark, and the National Party leader, John Key. Another private member's bill legalising smacking gained no support from the major parties.

The 100 days – Claiming Back New Zealand Movement was critical, declaring: "Not one of the major parties' so-called constituent MPs stood up to be counted and to represent the views of their constituents although polls showed that New Zealanders were well over 85% opposed to this ominous and intrusive legislation."

"It's time now to claim back this country," they said. "The Swiss claimed that right 160 years ago, when they realised that they no longer had a democracy."

The movement proposes that when any legislation is passed by parliament, a 100 days scrutiny period or moratorium must follow to enable the country to examine the implications of what is being proposed. And if, as in Switzerland, 50,000 voters sign a petition calling for a referendum during those 100 days, a vote by the people is to determine the issue.

19.4 Australia

As we have seen in Chapter 17, one of our founding fathers and South Australian Premier, Charles Cameron Kingston, brought a draft federal Constitution to the 1891 Federal Convention which have introduced the veto into Australia.[13]

In its early days, the Australian Labor Party supported the introduction of the veto, as well as the initiative and later the recall.[14] Legislation was introduced four times from 1915 for this purpose in Queensland, but never enacted because of upper house objections and unacceptable amendments. When Edward Theodore became Premier, the proposal was abandoned, Theodore holding the people in low esteem as "fickle and irresponsible".[15]

Nevertheless, the initiative and referendum became part of the Federal Labor platform in 1908, joined in 1912 by the recall. W.M. Hughes was given leave to introduce an *Initiative and Referendum Bill* in 1914 but with the war this did not proceed. Despite some interest from the individual legislators, a few academics and one journalist, no Australian jurisdiction has ever introduced the veto or indeed the initiative or the recall. As mentioned previously, the provisions for direct democracy were removed from the platform in 1963.

19.5 USA

Inspired by the initiative and referendum mechanisms in Switzerland, and with growing dissatisfaction with the way in which powerful business interests were accumulating wealth and exercising political influence against the interests of farmers and small business people, a progressive movement developed in the United States in the late 19th century.[16] A major part of their reform agenda was the introduction of the tools of direct democracy. In 1897, South Dakota was the first state to do this, followed in 1900 by Utah and in 1902 by Oregon. Other states followed, especially along the West coast and the Midwest. In the East, only Massachusetts, Maine and Maryland followed. As a result, a number of the progressive measures were adopted relating to working hours, pensions and environmental matters. One initiative was to begin the direct election of American senators rather than their indirect selection by the state legislature. Then in the second half of the 20th century, more states adopted some of the tools of direct democracy – Alaska, Wyoming, Illinois, Florida and Mississippi.

Now 24 states offer voters access to the people's veto or popular referendum to approve or repeal an act of the legislature. If the legislature passes a law that voters do not approve of, they may gather signatures to demand a popular vote on the law. Generally, there is a 90-day period after the law is passed during which the petitioning must take place. Once enough signatures are gathered and verified, the new law appears on a ballot for a popular vote. During the time between passage and the popular vote, the law may not take effect. If voters approve of the law, it takes effect as scheduled. If voters reject the law, it is voided and does not take effect. Most of the 24 states also allow voters to initiate referendums about proposed or citizen initiated laws.

The percentage of voters needed to sign which will trigger a vote on legislation ranges from 3% in Maryland to 15% in Wyoming, with 5% in California. Some exempt certain legislation. For example, Colorado exempts "laws necessary for the immediate preservation of the public peace, health, or safety, and appropriations for the support and maintenance of the departments of state and state institutions, against any act or item, section, or part of any act of the general assembly ...".[17]

Eleven states exempt certain appropriations funds. Of these, Wyoming exempts appropriations and dedications of revenue and Montana and two other states exempt all appropriations bills. Montana's provides that the people may approve or reject by referendum any act of the legislature "except an appropriation of money".[18]

Montana's Constitution also provides that while a petition signed by at least 5% of the qualified electors in each of at least one-third of the legislative representative districts will trigger a referendum, only a petition signed by at least 15% of the qualified electors in a majority of the legislative representative districts will suspend the law until the vote.[19]

19.6 Arguments for the people's veto

In summary the argument here is that the institutions of representative democracy in Australia have been seriously compromised by what are the most powerful political parties among comparable democracies.[20]

This has led to the people being ruled in the interests of an axis between factional powerbrokers and the inner city elites. A series of laws and policies have been adopted which too often do not pass the "pub test". That is they are not laws and policies which are consistent with the common sense, good judgement and decency of rank-and-file Australians.

On one view the politicians are there to do our bidding and to apply the mandate which the people have accorded them. The other view was famously argued by Edmund Burke, that "your representative owes you, not his industry only, but his judgement; and he betrays, instead of serving you, if he sacrifices it to your opinion".[21]

The plain fact is we have neither. The politicians are not doing our bidding nor are they exercising their judgement. Rather, most politicians resemble "two sets of whipped dogs who follow their masters".[22]

Professor Walker pointed out even in 1987 that the position is far worse in Australia than in the United States, or other Westminster countries including Britain, Canada and New Zealand.[23] Few in 2013 would disagree with the proposition that the situation has deteriorated since then. Debate had long declined in Australian parliaments; they have been replaced by an embarrassing charade.

Just as *Pravda* and the Australian Communist Party newspaper, *Tribune*, argued in favour of whatever was the latest line coming out of Moscow, so Australian politicians will endorse almost anything which is the current line handed down by the powerbrokers. We saw this example in March 2013 when the government introduced legislation to gag the press with an ultimatum that the package be passed in days.[24] Labor politicians came out to defend the bills and the ultimatum, retreating to an embarrassed silence when the government, realising the game was up, abandoned all of the contentious parts of the package.

Imagine the impact of the existence of power for the people to veto legislation, introduce their own and recall governments without the power even being exercised.

19.7 Case against the people's veto

The main argument against the veto and initiative is that it would undermine the Westminster system of responsible government where the government is formed on the floor of the lower house and is responsible to parliament. This necessarily involves the development of a party system which is at its strongest in Australia, so strong that the present concentration is against the public interest. We rail against concentration of power in the private sector – although we are not as effective in Australia as we should be.[25] Why do we tolerate this concentration of political power by these shadowy forces?

One particular argument against the people's veto is that wealthy interests and the media would wield undue influence. Professor Walker has marshalled considerable evidence to suggest that money and the media do not necessarily win campaigns. A superb example was the conclusion that the amount of news coverage and comment unfavourable to President Reagan in his presidential campaigns exceeded favourable coverage by a ratio of 22:1.[26]

In the 1999 Australian republic referendum, the Australian Republican Movement (ARM) was so much better funded than Australians for

Constitutional Monarchy (ACM) that only the ARM could afford television advertising, which turned out to be extensive. (Later in the campaign, there was separate publicly funded advertising for the official Vote Yes and Vote No Committees). In addition, most of the mainstream media campaigned in favour of the Yes case, not only in opinion and comment, but also in the news. Nevertheless, the No case prevailed nationally, in all states, and 72% of federal electorates.

It is an unacceptable argument to say voters are not competent to judge proposals and that they would not vote for necessary but hard measures. Much is made of the voting record in federal referendums, ignoring the fact that these to have been mainly held to grant additional powers to the federal parliament, or to the federal government. When the Australian people have considered something worth voting for they have done so, as they did in 1967 in relation to Aboriginal matters. At the same time they refused to do what most of the politicians wanted – to break the nexus between the House of Representatives and the Senate. They were no doubt persuaded that this provision in the Constitution stopped the politicians from vastly increasing the size of the House and that if this occurred, the smaller states would be disadvantaged and not only in a joint sitting.

Another example of the sophistication of the Australian people was when they rejected the proposal in 1951 by the popular Menzies government to ban the Communist Party. The vote was scheduled after much of Eastern Europe had fallen under Soviet influence, after the communists had tried to take over Greece, after they had had taken over China, were advancing in Indochina and Malaya, when Australian troops were fighting the communists in Korea, and when the Australian Communist Party clearly took its orders from and was funded by Moscow. It was not that the Australian people were in any way influenced by the communists, who were a failure electorally. It was that the Australian people did not believe that membership of a party should be forbidden, at least outside of a general war.

But there are those in Australian society who do not regard the opinions of the rank-and-file with respect. The former Foreign Minister Senator Gareth Evans is on record as putting the proposition that the politicians and the elites know better than the people. He claimed "it is just no longer possible, if indeed it ever was possible, for the people to be aware of all the factors that are necessary to sensibly determine an issue".[27]

Switzerland is an excellent example of the use of direct democracy not only to maintain lower taxes but provide adequate taxation for the purposes of sound government. Over the last 150 years, suspicious both of high taxation and of a granting vast powers to a central bank, she has been less troubled by the wild swings of inflation and deflation experienced in almost every other country.[28] Switzerland has refused to join the European Union, although surrounded by that entity, and not fallen prey to the dangers of the Eurozone.

19.8 Treaties and judge-made laws

In any Australian people's veto, laws, whether by parliament, the executive, or the judiciary should also be included. So should treaties. In Switzerland the most important treaties must be referred to the people for approval; other important treaties may be the subject of a petition for a referendum. Treaties are of particular significance. First they may be entered into by the executive with parliamentary approval not necessary. Legislation is required where the rights and duties of Australians are affected, although the High Court has attempted to circumvent this.[29] Worse, the High Court has effectively ruled that entry into a treaty in itself extends the powers of the federal parliament.[30]

The power of the courts to make law is subject to the power of parliament to change any such ruling. Should not the people enjoy the same power as the politicians?

One field where parliament cannot correct the High Court is in its interpretations of the Constitution. The High Court has at times followed the lead of the Supreme Court of the United States in not so much interpreting the Constitution as amending it contrary to the original meaning and the wishes of the people as expressed in referendums. The result has been that the federal parliament and government have garnished the income of the states, and entered into fields beyond their competence and capability.

Surely the people ought to be able, through their veto, to restore the original meaning of the Constitution which they have consistently maintained when allowed to via referendums.

These matters are worthy of careful consideration in the proposed convention to be elected by the people.

19.9 The process

Under our proposal, the detailed model for a people's veto would be the task of the elected convention. The convention would have to consider the number of signatures necessary to trigger a referendum. Should it be a precise number such as 50,000 in Switzerland and as proposed in New Zealand, or perhaps larger to have regard to the Australian population? Should it be a percentage and if so what should be the precise figure? Usually the number of the exercise of people's veto is lower than that for a recall. As we have seen, this ranges in the US between 3% and 15% with most over 5% or 10%.

In relation to the federal exercise of people's veto, should a certain number of state parliaments also be entitled to call for a referendum? In Switzerland eight cantons can initiate this. Under the Australian Kingston proposal any two state parliaments could, provided both houses so resolved. (This was before Queensland abolished its Legislative Council).

The question will arise as to whether certain matters should be excluded from the veto. None are excluded in Switzerland. The most common areas excluded in America are appropriations, that is, provision by the legislature allocating taxation revenue to a specific purpose.

Presumably only recent legislation should be the subject of a people's veto. In Switzerland this is 90 days, under the Kingston proposal before federation in Australia it was three calendar months, and under the New Zealand proposal is 100 days (hence the elegantly named "100 days – Claiming Back New Zealand Movement").

The petition will have to be initiated and registered, presumably with the Australian Electoral Commission and there should be a minimum number of persons proposing the petition for the signature collection to begin.

What period should be allowed for the collecting of signatures? Professor Walker suggests that the usual period is five months – clearly it should not be too short.[31]

There would need to be provision against abuses as well as an audit of a percentage of signatures.

These days, with modern technology, the question will arise as to whether signatures should be permitted online. If so, what security should be applied?

Australians are used to a yes/no booklet being prepared by parliament and circulated by the Australian Electoral Commission to all voters. But in relation to a people's veto, presumably the proposers will draft the argument in favour of a yes vote, with opponents in parliament preparing the no case.

When would the vote be held? Should a possible number of occasions throughout the year be specified for this? The Swiss vote every three months on referred questions, if this is needed.

Delaying voting until the election would save money but would seem to be unreasonable if sufficient Australians wanted to vote on the issue. Take the case of the carbon dioxide tax introduced by the Gillard government. Surely voters would have expected to be able to vote on that as soon as possible and not wait until the next election.

Should voting be compulsory? Given the frequency of referendums this may be unduly demanding. Remember that compulsory voting principally serves the interests of the political parties, saving them the problem of most parties in nearly all countries of getting out their supporters to vote. Why should Australia's political parties have it so easy?

Should the costs of the campaign be left to those involved, or should there be some public funding? It would seem unfair if the no case were funded by the government and the yes case had to be self-funded. Perhaps both should be left to private funding.

There will be suggestions that there should be limits on advertising expenditure; this may be unconstitutional. Instead, there will need to be a consideration as to what disclosure of campaign funding should be made.

There will also be questions as to whether payment to signature collectors should be allowed. If it is suggested this be banned there may be constitutional issues. Naturally it would not be appropriate for those signing a petition to be paid for their signature

What majority should be required? Should it be a majority of those voting? Or should there have been an absolute majority of those voting, which would take into account those who vote informally?

Should the majority be spread across the country? For example, should there have to be a national majority and a majority in, say, at least one state other than the two most populous states.

As can be seen, there are number of matters needing to be settled in a model provision for a people's veto. To reiterate, this would be best discussed at a convention elected for the purpose and we stress that in our view delegates should not be paid and should communicate by the most modern methods.

Endnotes

1 http://www.griffith.edu.au/__data/assets/pdf_file/0019/207064/Constitution-al-Values-Survey-March-2010-Results-1.pdf (retrieved 30/03.2013).

2 See Chapter 17.

3 http://www.youtube.com/watch?v=ApCwoj35d3M (retrieved 30/03.2013).

4 http://www.youtube.com/watch?feature=player_embedded&v=P2i3XC-_eA0 (retrieved 30/03.2013).

5 *National Conference of State Legislatures*. http://www.ncsl.org/legislatures-elections/elections/initiative-referendum-and-recall-overview.aspx (retrieved 19.04.2013).

6 *Constitution*, s. 128.

7 Geoffrey de Q. Walker, *Initiative and Referendum: The People's Law,*, Centre for Independent Studies, Sydney, 1987, p. 15.

8 This must be a treaty of 15 years duration or more, one to enter into an international organisation or one changing Swiss law to accord with a multilateral unification of law: *Swiss Constitution*, Article 141, Optional Referendum.

9 *Swiss Constitution*, Article 141, Optional Referendum.

10 *Swiss Constitution*, Article 140, Mandatory Referendum.

11 http://100daystodemocracy.wordpress.com; see also http://www.amybrooke.co.nz/ (retrieved 30/03.2013) It was this movement which was the immediate inspiration for the authors' interest in the citizen's veto is a splendid tool of direct democracy.

12 Amy Brooke, *The 100 Days – Claiming Back New Zealand – What has gone wrong and how we can control our politicians,* Howling At The Moon Publishing, Auckland, 2013.

13 John M. Williams, *The Australian Constitution: A Documentary History,* Melbourne University Press, Melbourne, 2004, pp. 126-7; *Joseph Poprzeczny,* "Australia — a democracy or just another ballotocracy?", *National Observer,* No. 76, Autumn 2008, pages 7–32. http://www.nationalobserver.net/pdf/2008_australia_-_a_democracy_or_just_another_ballotocracy.pdf (retrieved 05.05.2013) .

14 Walker, op.cit., pp. 20-21.

15 Ibid.

16 Thomas E. Cronin, *Direct Democracy: the Politics of Initiative, Referendum, and Recall,* 1999, Harvard University Press, Cambridge, pp. 38-60; Nick Cowen, *Total Recall: How Direct Democracy Can Improve Britain,* 2008, Civitas, London, pp. 11-25.

17 *Colorado Constitution*, Article V, Section 1(3).

18 *Montana Constitution*, Article III, Section 5(1).

19 Ibid., Section 5(2).

20 Walker, op. cit., sets out in Chapters 2-4 detailed arguments for and against the veto and the initiative.

21 Russell Kirk, *Edmund Burke, A Genius Reconsidered*, Intercollegiate Studies Institute, Wilmington, 1997, pp. 82-3.

22 Walker, op. cit., p. 31, citing Prof. C.J. Hughes of the University of Leicester.

23 Ibid.

24 Media Reform Bills Package: *Broadcasting Legislation Amendment (Convergence Review and Other Measures) Bill* 2013, *Broadcasting Legislation Amendment (News Media Diversity) Bill* 2013, *News Media (Self-regulation) (Consequential Amendments) Bill* 2013, *News Media (Self-regulation) Bill* 2013, *Public Interest Media Advocate Bill* 2013, *Television Licence Fees Amendment Bill* 2013.

25 Supra, Chapter 5, "Why do they hate our farmers?"

26 Walker, op. cit., pp. 87-93.

27 Hansard, Senate debates, 1 March 1979, 409; Walker, op. cit., p. 80.

28 Gregory A. Fossedal, *Direct Democracy in Switzerland*, 2002, Transaction Publishers, New Brunswick, 2002, p. 105.

29 *Minister for Immigration and Ethnic Affairs* v *Teoh* (1995) 183 CLR 273; see Chapter 6.

30 See Chapter 6.

31 Walker, op. cit., p. 135.

CHAPTER 20

Make laws the people want

20.1 Introduction

The Citizens' Initiative, or as it is usually described, the Citizens' Initiative Referendum, is a procedure which enables a prescribed number of voters, through a petition, to call for a referendum on whether a proposed law should be adopted.

There are two kinds, the constitutional initiative and the legislative initiative. The constitutional initiative is found in Switzerland at the federal level, in the Swiss Cantons and in eighteen American states. The legislative initiative exists in Swiss Cantons (or states) and twenty-three American states.

There are two forms of the legislative initiative. These are the direct and indirect initiatives. Under the direct initiative, a petition with the prescribed number of signatures goes straight to the ballot. Under the indirect initiative, the legislature has a specified time to enact the proposed measure. But if the legislature refuses to act, or fails to do so, the measure then goes to the voters. This was the form proposed in the *Popular Initiative and Referendum Bill* introduced into the Queensland parliament several times between 1915 and 1919. It was never enacted.

20.2 Switzerland

The Swiss make wide use of the constitutional initiative, with sometimes several initiatives a year.[1] This is probably because there is no provision for a legislative initiative at the federal level. Under this, a referendum is triggered by a petition of 100,000 voters or by eight cantons or states.

There is a period of 18 months to collect the requisite number of signatures. This runs from the official publication of the call or demand for an initiative proposing a revision of the Constitution.[2] This may take the form of a general proposal or of a specific draft of the provisions actually proposed.[3]

If the federal assembly is in agreement with an initiative in the form of the general proposal, it drafts the bill on the basis of the initiative and submits it to the vote of the people and the cantons.[4]

But if the federal assembly rejects the initiative, it must submit it to a vote of the people; and the people decide whether the initiative is to be adopted. If they vote in favour, the federal assembly drafts the corresponding bill.[5]

Where the initiative is in the form of a specific draft, this is submitted to the vote of the people and the cantons. The federal parliament either recommends the initiative for adoption or rejection. If it wishes, it may simultaneously present a counterproposal.[6]

One of the most controversial Citizen's Initiative Referendums in recent years was the proposal to add subsection (3) to Article 72 of the Swiss Constitution on the subject of Church and State. It was self-explanatory reading simply "(3) The building of minarets is prohibited." The argument of the initiators was that the minaret was not a religious symbol, but indicated a place where Islamic law is established. Notwithstanding the opposition from the broad-based coalition government, the majority of politicians and leading churches, this was passed by a majority of 57.5% of the voters, with only four Cantons voting against the proposal.

This has led to threats of legal action, including recourse to the European Court of Human Rights claiming a breach of the European Convention on Human Rights. The federal parliament has a reserve power to declare an initiative invalid in whole or in part for reasons including the "violation of the mandatory rules of international law".[7]

These are what are called the "peremptory norms" of international law. They are binding without a state having to accept them under a treaty, and include such matters as the rules against crimes against humanity, genocide, slavery and torture. Proposals are now being made that the parliament also have the power to reject petitions in breach of obligations Switzerland may have accepted under international law, such as those under the European Convention on Human Rights. Any such proposal would have to be approved in a referendum.

Certainly, the Swiss have the greatest opportunity of any people to participate in their government, with the additional fact that able-bodied males must serve in the army. Apart from frequently voting, the Swiss are unusually active in local councils which handle matters normally dealt with in other countries by the higher bureaucracy. For example, the grant of citizenship to immigrants is considered and determined at the local council level, and local councils are typically large and voluntary.

The statistics on voting are revealing.[8] From 1848 to 2010, 562 issues have been put to a popular vote and the number of votes has significantly increased in recent decades. Between 1991 and 2000, 106 items were put to a vote. At a typical ballot, the voters will be called on to determine between one and four federal issues. The vote on 18 May 2003 was a record when the voters were called on to decide nine issues, eight of which were result of initiatives from the public.

This does not mean that the Swiss do not exercise great care and discretion in relation to initiatives. Their judgement has been demonstrably good and their country is very well governed, perhaps the best governed in the world. While a large number of initiatives are put, 90% fail. And it is important to stress that the existence of popular participation, including the tools of direct democracy, have created a political class significantly different from that in Australia. Parties tend to form coalitions, and issues are decided on their merits, not because of loyalty to a particular factional powerbroker or to the party itself.

The politicians are not well paid, are often part-time and understand the need for regular consultation. Rather than regarding themselves as the masters who are better informed and better able to take decisions, they accept the need to work with and learn from the people. According to one account assembly member see themselves as teachers who need to learn from the whole nation of citizens.[9]

"No teacher who holds his pupils in contempt will succeed, or even stay long in the job ... a teacher with any wisdom soon realises he has much to learn from his pupils. Instruction is no longer one-way – particularly when the classroom is an intelligent one like the Swiss people, and the teacher a humble, part-time instructor who thinks himself a citizen, not a sovereign."[10]

The Swiss have certainly developed a superior form of government.

20.3 United States

Twenty-five American states allow their voters to initiate legislation, with sixteen of these allowing the petition to go straight to a ballot under the direct initiative. Two states impose more onerous requirements for a direct initiative but allow petitions with fewer signatures to be referred to the legislature as an indirect initiative. Seven use the indirect initiative process under which the petition goes first to the legislature, which can decide to adopt it and to present their version of the law for the people's consideration.

The number of signatures varies from 2% of the resident population in North Dakota (13,452 in 2012), to a high of 15% of the total number of votes cast in the preceding election in Wyoming (28,624 in 2012), although most are in the range of 5-10%.[11] Some states require a geographical spread over their counties. Eighteen states also allow voters to initiate amendments to the constitution and 16 allow the proposal to be placed directly on the ballot. Typically states will require slightly more signatures than for a legislative initiative, generally in the range of 8-12%.

Florida mirrors the Swiss experience. There is no provision

for legislative initiatives in that state, only constitutional initiatives. Consequently Florida has more constitutional initiatives than most states.

The period to collect signatures ranges from 64 days in Massachusetts through to an unlimited period in Arkansas, Ohio and Oregon.

20.4 Australia

Australia urgently needs a radical reform of her government. We have the most powerful and oligopolistic political parties in the democratic world with an extraordinary concentration of power in the hands of the factional powerbrokers of the parties. Their alliance or axis with the inner city elites has ensured that an agenda has been adopted which is too often alien to rank-and-file Australians. From past experiences, Australians have found that too much of such an agenda continues in important aspects, no matter what the result is of particular elections.

Australians have long been fobbed off by all manner of supposed reforms to the governance of the nation, including longer terms (four years instead of three, with an extraordinary eight years for upper house members), fixed terms, a politicians' republic, more centralisation, abolition of the states, and even measures such as community cabinets.

We explored these in more detail in Chapter 12.

The only solution is to empower the people and thus make the politicians truly accountable on every day, of every week, of every month and every of every year. This will result in a change in the quality of government but also in the quality of the politicians – that is the Swiss experience. To achieve this, the people should be empowered with the tools of direct democracy. To ensure that this is properly considered we propose an elected unpaid convention to be dedicated to the task of drawing up the proposals for consideration in a series of referendums.

As to the arguments for and against the citizens' initiative, as well as the process, these are much the same as we have already discussed in relation to the citizen's veto. There will be an argument that the signature requirements for an initiative should be higher than for the people's veto.

But as readers will see, the difference prescribed for constitutional and legislative initiatives in the United States is only marginal.

It might be argued that Australians are reluctant to vote often. But those interested in the future of their country are hardly going to regard themselves as being harassed if they are called on to vote three or four times a year. In fact true citizens would be delighted to be involved in decision-making. Of course this should be voluntary; compulsory voting exists to make the tasks of the concentrated oligopolistic major parties easier, dispensing with the usual burden for democratic parties of interesting people sufficiently to come out to vote.

There is one particular area where somewhat different considerations may apply. This is in relation to initiatives proposing amendments to the Constitution. The 1900 Constitution was a superb document, but like everything else created by humans, it has its weaknesses.[12] One is the fact that only the Commonwealth parliament, or possibly one House (probably not the Senate), may propose amendments to the Constitution. This power of initiation should have at least been extended to, say, two of the state parliaments.

It would be consistent with the argument of this book that this power be extended to the people. This means that the initiators would have to propose precise amendments to the Constitution. Given the importance of what they might propose, it is reasonable to expect both a larger number of signatures and some reasonable geographic distribution. This should not necessarily be from a majority of states, but most of the signatures should not come from the most populous states. The details of the proposal are best left to discussion within the convention which is proposed to represent all parts of the Commonwealth, the membership of which is weighted, it will be recalled, according to the distribution of the parliamentary seats as set out in the Constitution.

Endnotes

1 Swiss Constitution, Articles 138 and 139.

2 Normally the initiative demand will be for a partial revision.

3 Article 139(2).

4 Article 139(4).

5 Ibid.

6 Article 139(5).

7 Article 139(3).

8 http://www.swissinfo.ch/eng/specials/switzerland_for_the_record/world_records/The_ Swiss_vote_more_than_any_other_country.html?cid=8483932 (retrieved 02.04.2013).

9 Gregory A. Fosssedal, *Direct Democracy in Switzerland*, 2002, Transaction Publishers, New Brunswick, 2002, p. 85.

10 Loc. cit.

11 National Conference of State Legislatures. http://www.ncsl.org/legislatures-elections/ elections/recall-of-state-officials.aspx (retrieved 23.03.2013).

12 In the event of a disagreement between the houses, which is repeated after an interval of three months, the Governor-General may submit the proposed law to the electors. It would be likely that the Governor-General would act on the advice of the government rather than regarding this as a discretionary power.

CHAPTER 21

Political candidates chosen for merit, not loyalty to the factional powerbrokers

21.1 Australian democracy: how one person decides who will represent 100,000

Australians are rightly proud of their democratic heritage. The six colonies that preceded federation were such pioneers in extending the vote that others agitating for democratic reform around the world looked to us for inspiration. In 1902 Australia was the second nation (behind our Kiwi cousins) to pass legislation giving all women the right to vote and throughout our history Australia has fought to defend the democratic rights of others around the world.

How have we arrived at a situation where political candidates are rarely chosen on merit, but for loyalty to some often faceless party boss, some factional powerbroker? In any other part of Australian life this would be a scandal. There would be demands for reform.

Our robust democratic heritage has, however, produced complacency. We have rested on our laurels and fallen behind world's "best-practice" democracy. The Australian people are not to blame – they are perhaps more interested in politics than ever. The fault rests with our two major political brands – the Australian Labor Party and the Liberal Party. Australians will readily embrace direct democracy reforms including the need to get past the gatekeepers of our political system – the major parties. Without the parties adopting the elementary principles of an open, transparent and democratic order, it is unlikely they would agree to empower the people and make the politicians truly accountable to them.

Recent evidence shows that Liberal and Labor will continue to ignore these reforms until they have democratised themselves.

Democratised political parties will take political power away from the few – the factional powerbrokers – and give it to the broad membership. The two key functions of a political party in need of reform are, first, the candidate selection process and, second, the method of electing party "executives" who act as the "board of directors" for the state party organisations. Australia's political gatekeepers will no doubt need to be unshackled from their current conflict of interest before they can be expected to agree with reforms to empower the Australian people and make the politicians truly accountable.

The internal workings of our major parties are presently ruled by factions, who manipulate antiquated party structures resulting in real decision-making power being held by very few. It is a comparable state of affairs to the House of Commons in the United Kingdom before the Great Reform Act of 1832. Prior to this milestone, the UK appeared at face value to be somewhat democratic – but the system was thoroughly corrupt. Whole cities like Manchester were denied even one member of parliament while "rotten boroughs" consisting of as few as 11 voters enjoyed two representatives in the House of Commons.

The reforms of 1832 were hard fought – vested interests seldom relinquish their privileges with equanimity. Those who benefitted from the corrupt system delayed and obfuscated at every step. Days of riot across Britain by the common people fuelled fears of a French style revolution and only that finally caused the power clique to "blink". While 1832 did not give a vote to everyone it did break the back of vested interests and made universal suffrage inevitable. Democratic empowerment of the people lit the fuse for the great leaps forward of the Victorian era.

If Labor and Liberal were commercial entities they would rank among the most powerful brands in Australia. Every election millions of people vote for a candidate about whom they have little knowledge or interest as individuals – instead they chose the Labor or Liberal "brand". The first goal of an aspiring parliamentary candidate is not to impress the electorate but to win the right to wear the Labor or Liberal brand on election day.

21.2 The preselection rort

The internal fights within the party organisations that attract negative press coverage, all boil down to one thing – who gets to wear that brand on election day because that brand is the ticket to a parliamentary career. What follows is a summary of how to become a parliamentarian under the current factionalised structure in either party.

First you apply to join the local branch of a party by filling out a simple form and paying a nominal membership fee. It is likely your membership will be accepted but sincere applicants can be rejected by the local branch because of a mere suspicion they are a spy from a competing faction.

Once membership is confirmed the aspiring MP will quickly have to decide which faction to join. With momentary exceptions that prove the rule, political parties coalesce around two factions. This isn't necessarily a bad thing – robust parties are strengthened by internal debate about ideas – but today's labels left and right conceal the struggle to maintain power around strong personalities with little coherence in terms of competing world views.

The factions are fiefdoms built on loyalty to the factional bosses, the powerbrokers. Many of those most heavily involved in factions have no sincere interest in politics, being neither right nor left. Rather they are in politics because (a) they need a job and (b) politics makes them be and feel important. The more hard work someone does for a faction (i.e., stacking in new members, rorting loopholes, cajoling others to "follow the ticket" in internal ballots, etc), the more credit is built up in their "factional bank account". Once they have sufficient credit aspiring parliamentarians will receive the blessing (and the votes) of the faction to nominate for preselection. This is a purely "transactional" model of leadership where the currency that pays the bills is an exchange of favours.

There may now be a period of apprenticeship. Labor offers placement in the unions as an official, a position once filled by rank-and-file workers in the relevant industry. These positions are now in the gift of the powerbrokers and awarded to graduates – often in law – who are in their allegiance. This is no longer because of some "light on the hill", rather it is the wealth and power which flows from this position, the seat in parliament, perhaps a ministry, the early retirement on generous superannuation paid by the taxpayers, the resulting "jobs for the boys" and the rivers of gold flowing from the consultancies in, say, coal seam gas mining or renewable energy.

Now to find a seat. It matters not that the aspiring candidate has no connection with a particular seat. The citizens within the seat do not matter; what matters is winning preselection. This is where the party decides who its candidate will be for the upcoming local, state or federal election.

Let us imagine that within a certain seat there are 700 resident financial members of the party. The vast majority have no say about who their candidate will be for the next election. The ordinary members are expected to work hard for and donate time and money to a candidate but are not expected to have an opinion about candidate selection. The candidate will be chosen by around 100 party members who are almost entirely factionally owned. The greatest factional crime would be to go into a preselection with an open mind. Preselectors are chosen precisely for their proven reliability in following factional direction.

The 100 delegates to the preselection meet in a community hall for up to ten hours, even though in many cases the result is preordained long before the meeting begins. The prospective candidates (often up to 20) give a short speech before the 100 preselectors and then answer some questions, but rarely does it matter what they say. It doesn't really matter either if the candidate doesn't present any achievements of note; what matters is which faction "has the numbers." To win preselection someone needs to win just 50% of the preselectors plus one. So if there are 100 preselectors just 51 people will decide which candidate will get to wear the Liberal or Labor brand on election day. As few as 51 people can decide who will represent 100,000 Australians in Canberra.

This has been the experience of the Labor Party for several decades. Since the 1980s it has also been the story of the Liberal Party across much of Australia. It explains why so few high calibre people remain in political parties. Many join, hoping to make a substantial contribution to public life, but soon lose interest. Australian parliaments are filled with individuals who have never held a job outside of politics. They are people who want to be entrusted with the power to spend other people's money, but have never contributed to the pool of taxpayer money themselves.

These politicians cling desperately to their status and cash because most of them know they will have difficulty finding employment in the real world. They know the faction put them into parliament and so the faction can just as easily remove them, so they obey neither their conscience nor the will of the electors; rather, they obey the faction. Obeying the faction within parliament means employing factional staff and supporting the faction's candidate for the position of parliamentary leader. This is in addition to the standard dues of factional membership.

What does this mean come election time? In a safe seat the MP is normally the loyal agent and servant of the faction. He or she will need to develop the skills of an actor in dealing with constituents, but at the same time speaking in parliament when allowed, asking questions according to precise instructions, barracking and interjecting as expected, and voting precisely as instructed.

21.3 Americans pioneer the solution – democracy

The solution is to open up the candidate selection process so that hundreds (not dozens) of people have a vote. The factions are furiously busy to arrange 51 out of 100 to robotically vote for their candidate; it is simply beyond their power to manipulate a ballot of several hundred. The best chance for merit to prevail is achieved by handing the decision to a larger group less capable of manipulation.

There are two simple mechanisms to democratise candidate selection – plebiscites and primaries. A plebiscite occurs when every local member of a party is entitled to vote for their parliamentary candidate. A "primary" occurs when the party invites supporters from among the general public to select candidates. It is to be preferred because supporters cannot be expelled by the powerbrokers, as members can.

Other nations around the world have already democratised their political parties. Prior to 1912 powerful factions controlled the two great parties of the United States – the Republicans and Democrats. The term "smoke filled rooms" originates from the way these factions used to choose political candidates. The 1912 presidential election was the first to begin taking power away from the factions and giving it to the party supporters through primaries, with Oregon being the pioneering state. Fifty-six years followed with only 11 other states adopting primaries until the 1968 Democratic Convention in Chicago.

Street riots in Chicago were caused in part by the unfair candidate selection process and this convinced the Democrats that every state should hold primaries to select their candidate for president. The Republicans soon followed and in 2012 around 20 million Americans participated in the 2012 Republican primaries. The United States accommodates an amazing diversity of opinion but no one advocates a return to the former factionalised system. There are conservative and liberal (that is small 'l') wings of the Democrats and Republicans but these are based on sincere philosophical differences – which is precisely what you want in a political party.

In recent years France has embraced primaries to choose its national leaders and in the UK both the Conservative and Labor Parties have adopted plebiscites to select their candidates for parliament and their parliamentary leaders. Some will say – as does one of the authors – that the election of the leader by the membership is, if not in compatible with the Westminster system, in fact inappropriate as well as a pointless and unhealthy gesture. A prime minister or a premier is not an executive president. He or she is *primus inter pares* – first among equals. The appropriate electorate is the parliamentary party or caucus. They are better judges in deciding who should chair the cabinet. Asked in 2012 why he opposed the direct election of leaders, one of the authors replied that he had two reasons: "My reasons are ... Kevin Rudd and Malcolm Turnbull."

The Canadian equivalent of the ALP today is the New Democratic Party (NDP). In the Canadian election of 2001 the NDP was almost annihilated and in response embraced internal democratic reform. Those reforms are credited with the NDP's rejuvenation. Across Europe political parties of the left and right have embraced democratic reform as have those in Chile, Uruguay, Columbia, South Korea, Taiwan and even Armenia.

In the democratising of our major parties, there is a particular problem with organisations affiliated to any party which receives the massive legal and financial benefits awarded them by their representatives in parliament. Take the Labor Party. Their affiliated unions are often now headed, not by workers, but by ambitious professional executives from the universities. It is difficult to see how delegates chosen by these executives would receive, directly or indirectly, a large bloc of votes in any democratic primary, except as individual members of the party. And what role should they have in the management in addition to their role as individual members? Bloc voting by affiliates is a serious issue which the convention would need to examine.

21.4 Promising signs

So Australia is now the laggard, but there are encouraging signs. While the media take more interest in Labor's advocates of democracy, it is the Liberal Party that is actually further advanced. Howard government Minister David Kemp retired from parliament in 2004 and in 2007 became president of the Victorian Liberal Party. After three years campaigning within the party David Kemp oversaw the replacement of preselections with plebiscites (a form of primary, limited to party members). The Victorian Liberal Party secretariat previously employed four full-time staff to manage crippling factional disputes. Now those four have been replaced by one part-time staff member. The party's membership had been in slow decline but the introduction of plebiscites has seen a steady increase in membership of the Party. This ought not to surprise us since there is now a good reason to join.

The South Australian Liberal Party has embraced plebiscites and the founding constitution of the Liberal-National Party of Queensland also began with plebiscites. The NSW Liberal Party is certainly one of Australia's most important political entities. Its factionalism has been more intense and destructive than in any other division of the Party since the 1960s. In 2011 an ordinary but courageous branch member, John Ruddick, campaigned for party president on a platform of "Smash the Factions" advocating top to bottom democratisation. Mr. Ruddick advocated democratising the Senate and the Upper House candidate selection process – a step other state divisions of the Liberal Party have not yet taken. This campaign lit the spark of a democratisation debate within the division. Although he only received 9% of the vote for party president in 2011, Mr. Ruddick ran again on the same reform agenda in 2012 and secured 38% of the vote.

The Labor Party's John Faulkner, Bruce Hawker and Sam Dastyari among others have called publicly for ALP primaries and for the membership as a whole to choose the parliamentary leader. These calls have received praise from the media and even parliamentary leaders but real reform is yet to materialise. Mr. Hawker wrote recently in *The Sydney Morning Herald*, that "by taking power from the few and giving it to the many Labor can reform itself and guarantee its long-term future".[1]

The genie is out of the bottle. Now that the broad memberships of the Liberal and Labor parties are becoming aware of their options, it is inevitable they will demand democratic reform. Shortly before the fall of South African apartheid, Archbishop Desmond Tutu told the leaders of the old regime: "You may have all this power, but you have already lost. Come: join the winning side."[2] The Archbishop was so confident because he knew that a system could not survive if it denied a vote to 80% of the people.

The same can be said to the factional bosses who run the ALP and some divisions of the Liberal Party.

As Victor Hugo wrote, "An invading army can be resisted, but not an idea whose time has come."[3] The 1980s in Australia are remembered principally as an era of positive economic reform. There are rational grounds to expect that this decade will be recalled as a time of positive political reform when our major parties gave their power away and the Australian people felt the refreshing breeze of direct democracy.

21.5 The parties must become open, transparent and democratic

If there is one thing that our politicians love to do, it is to lecture the rest of us on how we must behave – that we must be open, transparent, democratic, non-discriminatory, compete fairly, not engage in unfair combinations, not engage in oligopolistic monopolistic practices, etc. Not only do they lecture us, they also pass legislation and establish agencies to ensure that we do as they say. They sometimes tell companies and people dealing with them that they must follow certain guidelines, for example about employing staff according to gender and majority status.

But as we have already seen, it is a case of doing what we say, not what we do. (In the same way we must wait for our superannuation until we are 55).

There is one exemption from this: the political parties to which they belong and who instruct them on what to say and how to vote. Not only do they regard the parties as exempt from being open, transparent and democratic, they have passed special legal protection to allow them to continue in these activities, at least one of which is illegal if it were followed by other citizens.

Remember their pincer operation: privileged statutory access to the electoral rolls on the one side and special exemptions from the privacy laws so that otherwise illicit databases can be established on you, their constituents. Then they can design campaigns to persuade you that your representative and his or her political party have your best interests at heart.[4] Remember that applications to make a postal vote are sent out from politicians' offices to be returned to them. What is done with them will not of course be at all affected by what is on the database. Nobody would be tempted to put aside the application if it were established that you were not inclined to vote for that candidate, would they?

Then there's the distinct advantage the political parties enjoy of having the name of the party on the ballot papers, and filing their preferences with the electoral commission concerning Senate votes above the line.

Then there is the generous funding by the taxpayers of election campaigns which our politicians have legislated to create, giving them a great advantage over other candidates.

Politicians also have offices and loyal staff chosen by them attached to them. There are numerous advantages for sitting politicians and for the parties who have endorsed them. Remember too the protection given to those powerbrokers who are trade union officials from the standards of financial propriety applicable to say, company directors.

Why aren't conditions applicable to them similar to those which apply to every other organisation and business? Is it not time to break up the tight oligopoly and the unacceptable practices of the major parties in order that the preselection of our politicians and the management of the parties are open, transparent and democratic?

The major parties should be warned. Australians may not put up with their scandalous behaviour for much longer.

Endnotes

1 Bruce, Hawker, "Power to the people: how Labor can reinvent itself", *The Sydney Morning Herald*, 5 January 2013. http://www.smh.com.au/opinion/power-to-the-people-how-labor-can-reinvent-itself-20130104-2c8s9.html#ixzz2PHcIodR0 (retrieved 02.04.2013).

2 "Dalai Lama honours Tintin and Tutu", *BBC News*, 2 June 2006. http://en.wikiquote.org/wiki/Desmond_Tutu (retrieved 02.04.2013).

3 *Histoire d'un Crime* (The History of a Crime). Written 1852, published 1877. http://en.wikiquote.org/wiki/Victor_Hugo (retrieved 02.04.2013).

4 See Chapter 10 concerning the exemption for politicians.

CHAPTER 22

Citizen judges

22.1 Introduction

It is crucial in a democracy that the activities of government be subject to investigation. The point is to expose not only maladministration and corruption, but also, through the existence of such investigative systems, to discourage both. There is a significant weakness in this. Although the ultimate responsibility of government in our democracy lies with the people, they have no role in any such investigations. One exception is where an investigation is followed by a prosecution before a judge and jury.

The position is different in the United States. In the reform and restoration of our institutions we suggest that there be a place for those who would in effect be citizen judges.

Governments under the Westminster system are constitutionally responsible to parliament, so we would expect parliaments to fulfil their duty to ensure that government is efficient, effective and clean. So, parliamentary committees are constantly investigating government, but this is weakened by the rigidity of our two party system, which has become the plaything of the factional powerbrokers. When the committee is headed by someone genuinely independent, it will be resisted if it seems too effective.[1]

From time to time specific and powerful enquiries, such as royal commissions, will be established into specific issues and events. To be effective, such bodies must be led by independent and qualified people, and have the power to compel the production of documents and the

361

attendance of witnesses to give evidence. In addition, the proceedings need to be protected, or "privileged". This means that actions for defamation should not be available or readily available against what is said there or published in a report. In addition actions for breach of confidence in relation to documents produced should not be available. Royal commissions and parliamentary enquiries will normally enjoy these powers and be protected, that is, privileged.

A government will at times establish an enquiry lacking in any powers whatsoever. This will be done for cosmetic reasons so that it can be argued that the government has done something. But by giving it no powers, the government can be sure that little of an embarrassing nature will be revealed. Thus when there were allegations that around $5 billion dollars had been lost in the management of the Rudd government's $16.5 billion Building the Education Revolution, the federal government appointed a task force under Brad Orgill to conduct an enquiry. But it had no powers to compel the giving of evidence or the production of documents and could in no way protect people speaking to it from, say, defamation actions. It revealed losses of $1.5 billion but investigative reporters believed that several billion dollars had been wasted.[2]

22.2 Royal commissions

Royal commissions – and other judicial enquiries however named – have long enjoyed an important place in Australia, casting light into issues shrouded in darkness. Invariably presided over by a distinguished lawyer, unhindered by the rules of evidence which seem these days to be too often designed to keep the jury in the dark, a royal commission can, as we have seen, compel witnesses to appear and give sworn testimony and produce documents, as well as protect those who come before it.

The Australian Law Reform Commission has given two reasons for retaining the description "royal commission" for such judicial enquiries.[3] First, this term is very well known, which means that it is a clear way to communicate to the public the extraordinary nature of such an enquiry.

Second, the title "royal commission" is helpful in that it indicates how the highest form of public enquiry is established – namely by the governor-general of Australia or the governor of a state. The Law Reform Commission declared that it is appropriate that "the Australian head of state should continue to be responsible for establishing the highest form of public enquiry in Australia."

In recent years, to their credit, both the Brumby government in Victoria with respect to the Victorian bush fires and the Queensland Bligh government with respect to the Brisbane floods have appointed royal commissions. It should be stressed that the great advantage of royal commissions is not only in the findings but in the public availability of the evidence given under oath and the documents produced. However they can only be established by the executive.

22.3 Standing commissions

There is a growing practice of establishing standing bodies which have strong investigative powers. They usually have wide powers to inform themselves both in calling for the production of documents and for witnesses to give evidence before them. They have a standing brief, for example, to investigate corruption.

The danger is that with an overzealous agenda, with public hearings where the rules of evidence do not apply and where erroneous and unjustified findings are made, they can do substantial and unjustified damage.[4] We have separately argued that the rules of evidence in criminal cases are too strict.[5] We do not say that there should be no rules of evidence and in any event in cases heard before the courts the accused is entitled to cross-examine, and it is very well known that a finding of guilt can only be made where it is beyond reasonable doubt.

22.4 Grand juries

Both the grand jury of 24, and the petit (or petty jury) of 12 with which we are well accustomed, came to the United States with British colonisation. While grand juries are mentioned in the Magna Carta, their first mention was in legislation of the time of Henry II, the *Assize of Clarendon* in 1166. Their task was to report on all crimes or breaches of the King's Peace. Gradually their role was to decide on whether there was sufficient evidence for a prosecution to be brought before one of the visiting assize judges from the Court of King's Bench in London. They came to the ancient Assize Towns under the King's Commissions of *oyer et terminer* (to hear and determine) and general gaol delivery. On such a visit, the grand jury would receive a number of bills of indictment for their consideration. If after hearing the witnesses, a majority thought there was a sufficient case to go to trial, the words "a true bill" were endorsed on the back of the bill. If not, the words "not a true bill" (or *ignoramus*) were endorsed instead and the bill was said to be ignored or thrown out.

By the Victorian era, committal proceedings were taking place before a magistrate to determine whether the Crown had established a *prima facie* case.[6] If a *prima facie* case were established the accused would be committed for trial before a judge and jury. Once committal proceedings became the normal way of dealing with criminal cases, the grand juries were on the way out. They were abolished in England in 1933.

That old English institution not only survives in the United States, it thrives, the founding fathers believing it was an institution which should be preserved. They saw merit in citizens being able themselves to check government excesses.[7] Under the Fifth Amendment, which is part of the Bill of Rights, "No person shall be held to answer for a capital, or otherwise infamous crime, unless on a presentment or indictment of a grand jury, except in cases arising in the land or naval forces, or in the Militia, when in actual service in time of War or public danger ...".

A grand jury is frequently convened to deal with corruption and organised crime. It consists of between 16 to 23 individuals chosen randomly from registered voters in the electoral district where the grand jury is convened. The purpose of the grand jury remains as it was in England. The role of the grand jury is not to judge the accused but to decide whether a prosecution is recommended. Normally they will do this on evidence presented by a prosecutor. Their verdict is, as it was in old England, either a "true bill" or "no true bill".

Rather than being chaired by a judge, the grand jury elects its own foreman or, as the office is styled now, a foreperson. The prosecutor may be present in the room and as the only lawyer there, gains certain authority from that status. An over ambitious prosecutor can sometimes use the forum to launch intrusive investigations. But it should be noted that the grand jury meets in secret, so the reputation of anyone investigated is not usually affected unless a prosecution follows.

There have been times when strong jurors have ignored prosecutors and launched their own enquiries, especially where they suspected corruption in government and powerful organised crime. These so-called "runaway" grand juries were more common in the past. But, as we have said, the grand jury meets in secret and minimal damage can be caused to reputations.

While a federal grand jury is selected at random, the methods chosen in the states vary. In some states a jury commissioner is appointed by the judge with the task of finding suitable candidates. This may limit the selection to like minds, occupations and strata in society and has been criticised.

22.5 Australia

The grand jury came to some of the Australian colonies just as it was declining in England. It disappeared in most but continued to exist until recently, at least on paper, in Victoria under section 354 of the *Crimes Act*, 1958. Under this any person in specified circumstances could apply to the Full Court of the Supreme Court with an affidavit disclosing an indictable offence. The applicant could seek an order to the Juries Commissioner to summon a grand jury of not less than twenty three to attend and "to enquire present do and execute all things which on the part of the Queen shall then and there be commanded of them ...".

But after some unsuccessful attempts in recent years to convene grand juries, especially one relating to Prime Minister Julia Gillard, the section was repealed in 2009.

22.6 Increasing corruption: a place for citizen judges.

We have a range of institutions which may commence investigations into such matters as corruption and organised crime. Parliamentary investigations will necessarily be politically oriented. Standing bodies such as the New South Wales ICAC will necessarily have an already established workload and agenda, sometimes reflecting the tastes and interests of those in charge. The problem and difficulty with royal commissions and other judicial enquiries is that they can only be instituted by the Crown acting on the advice of the government of the day. There is a gap, a democratic deficit. And that is the ordinary citizens are in no way involved in this investigation. A democracy should have the benefit of that involvement.

In the United States there is considerable scope for citizen judges sitting on grand juries. To an extent their role has in more recent years been reduced by the pressure of the American establishment. But there are moves in the US to restore to the grand jury greater but reasonable autonomy to investigate organised crime and corruption.

In Australia we live under one of the most concentrated and corrupting forms of political power among comparable democracies. The factional powerbrokers who run the major political parties exercise enormous authority and control. We argue that there is an alliance or axis between those powerbrokers and the elites the result being that an agenda which quite often would not pass the "pub test" is adopted and enforced.

In the meantime there is a growing concern about the role of the factional powerbrokers, particularly in relation to the vast wealth which is being acquired as a result of mining across the country, including mining on prime agricultural land, urban land and in water catchment areas. In addition, because of lax federal laws some have access to trade union funds and superannuation funds. All of this potential for massive corruption and abuse of power cries out for greater investigative powers in Australia so that the people may be properly informed as to what is going on, and crime and corruption kept to a minimum.

We believe there is a place for citizen judges and that this matter should be considered by the convention which we believe should be elected with a brief to consider the referendums on which the Australian people should vote about the proposed introduction of the tools of direct democracy.

Endnotes

1 Note the 2010-2011 enquiry into the NSW government's $5.3 billion power station sale by a Legislative Council Committee chaired by the Rev. Fred Nile, http://www.onlineopinion.com.au/view.asp?article=11443 (retrieved 05.04.2013).

2 http://www.theaustralian.com.au/national-affairs/ber-waste-tops-15b/story-fn59ni-ix-1226090622303 (retrieved 05.04.2013).

3 Australian Law Reform Commission, *Royal Commissions and official enquiries*, 2010- 2012. http://www.alrc.gov.au/enquiries/royal-commissions-and-official-enquiries (retrieved 07.05.2013).

4 The most notorious instance was that of Premier Nick Greiner of New South Wales who was forced to resign in 1992 as a result of an unfavourable ICAC finding of corrupt conduct. This was subsequently found to be wrong in law by the New South Wales Court of Appeal, but it was impossible to restore Mr. Greiner to office.

5 See Chapter 2.

6 This means that if the facts alleged by the Crown were true, an offence would have been committed.

7 S. Brenner, "The Voice of the Community: A Case for Grand Jury Independence", *Virginia Journal of Social Policy and the Law* 67, 1995. http://campus.udayton.edu/~grandjur/recent/lawrev.htm (retrieved 05.04.2013); Doyle Charles, *The Federal Grand Jury*, Nova Science Publishers Inc, New York, 2008.

CHAPTER 23

A call to arms

It is sad to reflect on the unfortunate fact that Australia, in the 21st century, lives under what must be the most corrupted system of government among the handful of countries which can claim to be the world's oldest continuing democracies. Our institutions have been compromised and we are now – contrary to the constitutional intention – the world's most centralised federation. The result is that the quality of government has significantly declined, and that the ability of our people to realise their full potential is limited by government waste, interference and control.

It is of crucial importance that we correct this. To do this we need to appreciate how serious the problem is, the great value of what we have inherited, and what solutions the experience of other countries offer.

Accordingly this book opens with an attempt to demonstrate how this unfortunate state of affairs developed and its consequences.

We especially made a point of recalling what is no longer being taught to the young – our history. The point is that when Australians decided to come together as one people, we were already an advanced democracy. Much of this was through making our own those superb gifts which came from the British – the rule of law, the English language, our oldest institution, the Australian Crown, our Judeo-Christian values and responsible government under the Westminster system.

It is important to remember that federation was achieved not by the decisions being taken by the politicians, although the politicians of that time were often men of great quality chosen by the people, not preselected for their allegiance to some shady powerbroker. Once the people set their minds on the union of this country in 1893, with the co-operation of the imperial power, they achieved this in a remarkably short period of time. And when we did come together, we continued to be an exciting laboratory of new ideas empowering the people.

What was not realised at federation was that our representative democracy would fall under the control of the factional powerbrokers that would form an alliance of convenience with the elites who had marched through and occupied so many key institutions. They were not to know that with the assistance of activist judges and international organisations an agenda could be imposed which just does not pass the "pub test".

This has led to elections where the people are called on to choose between candidates too often selected not for merit but for their allegiance to a factional and at times corrupt powerbrokers, elections whereby the electors are compelled to sign a blank cheque in favour of a government which, even if it turns out to be seriously incompetent, deceitful and massively wasteful, will be beyond any proper control for three or four years.

The answer is not in the endless series of false solutions proposed, usually by the politicians and the elites, to improve this corrupted system – fixed terms, longer terms, new methods of voting, abolishing one tier of government, introducing a new tier of government, imposing a politicians' republic, and even that embarrassing charade, community cabinets, and so on.

Not one of the above when introduced has improved government. And, be assured, none ever can.

The only solution is that, while retaining our representative democracy, we make our politicians accountable not just every three or four years in elections worthy, in many aspects, of a guided democracy.

We must make our politicians accountable as rank-and-file Australians are – on every day, of every week, of every month and of every year.

This can be done by introducing into Australia those tools of direct democracy which have worked so well in Switzerland and in over 20 American states.

As our federation was achieved though a peoples' convention, so we propose that a convention – of unpaid delegates – be elected with the task of working out a series of proposals to be considered by the people in referendum.

We propose that this would be to introduce into Australia the right of Australians to vote on:

- whether to recall a government to a new election,
- whether to repeal a new piece of legislation, such as tax, or cancel a treaty, and,
- whether to vote on new legislation.

These votes would be triggered by an appropriate number of Australians signing a petition calling for a vote.

The convention would also consider whether machinery should be established for citizens themselves to initiate enquiries into corruption and crime without a government having to establish a royal commission as in the United States which has retained that wonderful old English institution, the grand jury.

In addition the convention would consider whether the major political parties, so generously funded by the taxpayer, and so privileged under the law, should not by way of return; do what they should long ago have done. This is what they must surely do as the 21st century progresses, make their parties – and especially their preselections – open, transparent and above all democratic.

We realise that such a convention will only be held if the politicians decide to allow it. And the politicians will only allow it if there is enormous pressure from the public.

The fact is the fate of our country, and of this and future generations, is in our hands. If there is enough pressure it will happen.

We ask that you help us in achieving this by recording your support on our site, www.cando.org.au, or sending the information on the following form to CANdo – Australia's Voice, GPO Box 4379, Sydney, NSW 2001.

David Flint

Jai Martinkovits

You may follow David Flint on Twitter at **@profdavidflint** and Jai Martinkovits at **@jaimartinkovits**

Title...

Christian name...

Surname...

Honours...

Email..

Phone (including Area Code)..

Mobile phone...

Street (Including number)..

....

City/Town/Suburb... State............................

Post code...

Bibliography

Australian Law Reform Commission, *Royal Commissions and official enquiries*, 2010-2012. http://www.alrc.gov.au/enquiries/royal-commissions-and-official-enquiries (retrieved 16.02.2013)

Barone, Michael, *Our First Revolution: The Remarkable British Upheaval That Inspired America's Founding Fathers*, Crown, New York, 2007

Bevan, Bryan, *King William III. Prince of Orange, the Frst European*, Stacey Rubicon, London, 1997

Blackstone, William, *Commentaries on the Law of England*, from the Avalon Project at Yale Law School, http://avalon.law.yale.edu/subject_menus/blackstone.asp (retrieved 05.05.2013)

Blumrosen, Alfred W. &. Blumrosen, Ruth G., *Slave Nation*, Source books, Naperville, 2005

Bolingbroke, Viscount, *A Dissertation Upon Parties*, 1735

Brenner, S., "The Voice of the Community: A Case for Grand Jury Independence", *Virginia Journal of Social Policy and the Law* 67, 1995

Brooke, Amy, *The 100 Days – Claiming Back New Zealand – What has gone wrong and how we can control our politicians*, Howling At The Moon Publishing, Auckland, 2013

Brown, Bob, *The 3rd Annual Green Oration*, 23 March 2012. Bob Brown http://greensmps.org.au/content/news-stories/bob-brown-delivers-3rd-annual-green-oration (retrieved 1.01.2013)

Bryce, James, *Modern Democracies*, 2 vols, Macmillan, London, 1921, Vol. 2

Burke, Edmund, *Reflections on the Revolution in France*, 1790, Oxford, 1993

Burke, Edmund, *Speech at his arrival at Bristol*, 3 November, 1774

Business Council of Australia, *Reshaping Australia's Federation: A New Contract for Federal-State Relations*, 2006

Carling, Robert, "Self-sustaining Leviathan", *Centre for Independent Studies*, 19 October 2012. http://www.cis.org.au/publications/ideasthecentre/article/4585-self-sustaining-leviathan (retrieved 19.01.2013)

Carlyle, Thomas, 19 May 1840, "Lecture V: The Hero as Man of Letters. Johnson, Rousseau, Burns", *On Heroes, Hero-Worship, & the Heroic in History. Six Lectures. Reported with emendations and additions*, Dent, 1908. http://www.gutenberg.org/files/20585/20585-h/20585-h.htm (retrieved 12.02.2013)

Cater, Nick, *The Lucky Culture*, Collins, Pymble, 2013

Consultative Group on Constitutional Change, *Resolving deadlocks: the public response*, Commonwealth of Australia, Canberra, 2004. http://pandora.nla.gov.au/pan/79623/20080117-2207/dpmc.gov.au/conschange/report/docs/report.pdf (retrieved 16.02.2013)

Cowen, Nick, *Total Recall*, Civitas, Lansing, 2008

Cronin, Thomas E., *Direct Democracy, The Politics of Initiative, Referendum, And Recall*, Harvard University Press, Cambridge, 1999

Cuneen, Margaret, *Sir Ninian Stephen Lecture*, University of Newcastle, 2005. http://www.smh.com.au/news/national/margaret-cunneens-lectu re/2005/09/23/1126982234942.html

David S. Landes, *The Wealth and Poverty of Nations: Why Some Are So Rich and Some So Poor*, W.W. Norton, London, 1998

Department of Immigration and Citizenship, *Settlement Outcomes for New Arrivals*, 2010 http://www.immi.gov.au/media/publications/research/_pdf/settlement-outcomes-new-arrivals.pdf (retrieved 2.08.2012)

Director of Military Prosecutions, *Annual Report*, Canberra, 2011

Doyle, Charles, *The Federal Grand Jury*, Nova Science Publishers Inc, New York 2008

Electoral Reform, a Discussion Paper, Department of Justice and Attorney-General, January 2013

Fareed Zakaria, *The Future of Freedom: Illiberal Democracy at Home and Abroad*, W.W. Norton, New York, 2004

Faulkner, John, *Political Integrity: The Parliament, the Public Service, and the Parties*, speech to the *Integrity in Government Conference*, University of Melbourne Law School, 4 December 2012. http://www.senatorjohnfaulkner.com.au/file.php?file=/news/QCRMVHXKFO/index.html (retrieved 21/12/2012)

Feld, R.P. and Matsusaka, John G., "Budget Referendums and Government

Spending:Evidence from Swiss Cantons", *Initiative & Referendum Institute at the University of Southern California*, 2002. http://iandrinstitute.org/New%20 IRI%20Website%20Info/I&R%20Research%20and%20History/I&R%20 Studies/Feld%20and%20Matsusaka%20-%20Fiscal%20Evidence%20 from%20Swiss%20Cantons%20IRI.pdf (retrieved 18.04.2013)

Finlay, Lorraine, "The Attack on Property Rights", *Proceedings of the Twenty-second Conference of The Samuel Griffith Society*, 2010. http://samuelgriffith.org.au/ docs/vol22/vol22chap3.pdf (retrieved 8.01.2013)

Flint, David, "Three hundred and twenty years of freedom", *Quadrant*, November 2008, pp. 40-47

Flint, David, *The Twilight of the Elites*, Freedom Publishing, North Melbourne, 2003

Flint, David, *Her Majesty at 80: Impeccable Service in an Indispensable Office*, Australians for Constitutional Monarchy, Sydney, 2006. http://www.norepublic.com. au/index.php?option=com_content&task=view&id=1024&Itemid=24 (retrieved 24.03.2013)

Flint, David, *Malice in Media Land*, Freedom Publishing, North Melbourne, 2005, pp. 56-60

Flint, David, *The Cane Toad Republic*, Wakefield Press, Kentown, 1999

Fossedal, Gregory A., *Direct Democracy in Switzerland*, Transaction Publishers, New Brunswick, 2002

Freedom House, *Combined Average Ratings – Independent Countries*, 2011

Friedrich, Carl J., *The New Belief in The Common Man*, Little, Brown and Company, Boston, 1942

Hamilton, A., Madison, J. and Jay, J., *The Federalist Papers*, J. and A. McLean, New York, 1788. http://www.gutenberg.org/ebooks/1404 (retrieved 15.02.2013) 1788

Hayek, Friedrich August von, *The Road to Serfdom*, 1944, Routledge, London, 1976; Chicago, University of Chicago Press, 2007

Heffer, Simon, *Power and Place: The Political Consequences of King Edward VII*, Weidenfeld and Nicolson, London, 1998

Hobbes, Thomas, *Leviathan or The Matter, Forme and Power of a Common-Wealth Ecclesiasticall and Civill*, 1651, Penguin, Harmondsworth, 1979

Hughes Robert, *The Fatal Shore*, Harvill, London, 1986

Howard, John, Sir Paul Hasluck Foundation Inaugural Lecture, *Quadrant*, December 2012. http://www.quadrant.org.au/magazine/issue/2012/12/the-importance-of-knowing-where-we-came-from (retrieved 04.05.2013)

Kirk, Russell, *Edmund Burke, A Genius Reconsidered*, Intercollegiate Studies Institute, Wilmington, 1997

Landes, David S., *The Wealth and Poverty of Nations: Why Some Are So Rich and Some So Poor*, W.W. Norton, New York, 1998

Lasch, Christopher, *The Revolt of the Elites*, W.W. Norton, New York, 1995

Leeser, Julian, "WorkChoices: Did The States Run Dead?", Samuel Griffth Society, Vol. 19, Chapter 1, 2007. http://www.samuelgriffith.org.au/papers/html/volume19/v19chap1.html (retrieved 06.05.2013)

Macaulay, Thomas Babbington, *The History of England*, 1855, Penguin Classics, 1979

Matsusaka, John G., *For the Many or the Few: The Initiative, Public Policy, and American Democracy*, University of Chicago Press, Chicago, 2004

McLean, Ian W., *Why Australia Prospered*, Princeton University Press, Princeton, 2012

Mead, Walter Russell, *God and Gold*, Alfred A. Knopf, New York, 2007

Michael Kazin, "What lies beneath: Bush and the liberal idealists", *World Affairs*, American Peace Society, Washington DC, Winter 2008. http://www.worldaffairsjournal.org/article/what-lies-beneath-bush-and-liberal-idealists (retrieved 05.05.2013)

Milton, John, *Areopagitica: A speech of Mr. John Milton for the Liberty of Unlicensed Printing to the Parliament of England*, 1644

Molan, Jim, "Why our defence forces face terminal decline", *Quadrant*, March 2013, pp. 8-15. http://www.quadrant.org.au/magazine/issue/2013/3/why-our-defence-forces-face-terminal-decline (retrieved 04.05.2013)

Monk, Paul, "The Open Society and its Friends", *Quadrant*, March 2010. www.quadrant.org.au/magazine/issue/2010/3/the-open-society-and-its-friends (retrieved 01.05.2013)

Montesquieu, Baron de, Charles de Secondat, *The Spirit of Laws*, 1748, translated by Thomas Nugent, revised by J.V. Prichard. Based on an public domain edition published in 1914 by G. Bell & Sons, Ltd., London. http://www.constitution.org/cm/sol.htm (retrieved 05.05.2013)

Morris, Dick and McGann, Eileen, *Here come the Black Helicopters: UN Global Governance and the loss of Freedom*, Broadside Books, Northampton, 2012

Murray, Andrew, *Strengthening Australia's Democracy, submission on Electoral Reform Green Paper*, 2009. http://www.dpmc.gov.au/consultation/elect_reform/strengthening_democracy/pdfs/24%20-%20Andrew%20Murray.pdf (retrieved 28.02 2013)

Newman, Gerry, *Research Report 3 – Analysis of Declaration Voting*, Australian Electoral Commission, 2004, updated 2011. http://www.aec.gov.au/About_AEC/Publications/Strategy_Research_Analysis/paper3/(retrieved 29.12.2012)

North, Douglass C., Wallis, John Joseph & Weingast, Barry R., "A Conceptual Framework for Interpreting Recorded Human History", *NBER Working Paper*, No. 12795, December 2006

Poprzeczny, Joseph, "Australia – A democracy or just another ballotocracy", *National Observer*, No. 76, Autumn 2008, pp. 7-32. http://www.nationalobserver.net/pdf/2008_australia_-_a_democracy_or_just_anoher_ballotocracy.pdf (retrieved 05.05.2013)

Priest, Tim, "The rise of Middle Eastern crime in Australia", *Quadrant*, January-February 2004, pp. 9-16

Priest, Tim and Basham, Richard, *To Protect and To Serve: The Untold Truth about the New South Wales Police Service*, New Holland, Sydney, 2003

Quick, John and Garran, Robert, *The Annotated Constitution of the Australian Commonwealth*, 1901, reprinted by Legal Books, Sydney, 1976, 1995

Recall Elections for New South Wales? Report of the Panel of Constitutional Experts ("Recall Report"): Mr. David Jackson AM, QC (Chairman), Dr. Elaine Thompson, Professor George Williams AO, Statement M. http://www.dpc.nsw.gov.au/__data/assets/pdf_file/0013/134221/Panel_of_Constitutional_Experts_-_Review_into_Recall_Elections.pdf (retrieved 22.03.2013)

Report on the Manipulation of the Oil-for-Food Programme (27 October 2005). http://www.iic-offp.org/story27oct05.htm (retrieved 28.04.2013)

Roberts, Andrew, *A History of the English-Speaking People Since 1900*, Wedenfeld & Nicholson, London, 2006

Bennett, S., *The Politics of Constitutional Amendment*, Research paper, no. 11, 2002-03, Department of the Parliamentary Library, June 2003. http://www.aph. gov.au/library/pubs/rp/2002-03/03RP11.pdf (05.05.2013)

Secondat, Charles de, Baron de Montesquieu, *The Spirit of Laws*, 1748, translated by Thomas Nugent, revised by J.V. Prichard, G. Bell & Sons, Ltd., London, 1914, rendered into html and text by Jon Roland of the Constitution Society. www.constitution.org/cm/sol.htm

Smith, David E., *The Invisible Crown: The First Principle of Canadian Government*, Toronto University Press, Toronto, 1995

Smith, Sir David, *Head of State*, McLeay Press, Paddington, 2005

Soto, Hernando de, *The Mystery of Capital: Why Capitalism Triumphs in the West and Fails Everywhere Else*, New York, Basic Books, 2000

Spencer, Peter, *Land and Sea-Property: The Institute of Secure Property – the most important human right*, Lecture, Cairns, 27 April 2010. http://sosnews.org/pdf/peter-spencer-cairns.pdf (retrieved 07.04.2013)

Staley, Louise, *Reshaping the Landscape: The quiet erosion of property rights in Western Australia*, Institute of Public Affairs & Mankal Economic Education Foundation, *Project Western Australia*, Discussion Paper, December 2007

Tanner, Richard J., *The First Fleet and the Re-Enactment First Fleet – Some Historical Parallels and Differences*, The Order of Australia Association NSW Branch, 2010. http://www.theorderofaustralia.asn.au/downloads/NSWRJTAddressJan10.pdf (retrieved 05.05.2013)

Tink, Andrew, *Lord Sydney [The Life and Times of Tommy Townshend]*, Australian Scholarly Publishing, Melbourne, 2011

Twomey, Anne and Withers, Glenn, *Federalist Paper I: Australia's Federal Future, a report for the Council for the Australian Federation*, April 2007. http://www.caf. gov.au/Documents/AustraliasFederalFuture.pdf.(retrieved 05.05.2013)

Twomey, Anne, *The Chameleon Crown: The Queen and her Australian Governors*, Federation Press, Sydney, 2006

Walker, Geoffrey de Q., *Initiative and Referendum: The People's Law*, Centre for Independent Studies, Sydney, 1987

Waters, Dane M., *Initiative and Referendum Almanac*, Carolina Academic Press, Durham, 2003

Weldon, Sheldon S., *Democracy Incorporated: Managed Democracy and the Specter of Inverted Totalitarianism*, Princeton University Press, Princeton, 2008

Williams, George, and Chin, Geraldine, "The Failure of Citizens' Initiated Referenda Proposals in Australia", *Australian Journal of Political Science*, Vol. 35, No. 1, 2000

Williams, John M, *The Australian Constitution: A Documentary History*, Melbourne University Press, Melbourne, 2004

Zakaria, Fareed, *The Future of Freedom: Illiberal Democracy at Home and Abroad*, W.W. Norton, New York, 2004

Index

More publications by David Flint

"The Control of Foreign Investment in Australia", with G. Twite, in
Australian Micro-Economic Policies and Cases (1980)

"Foreign Investment and the New International Economic Order" in
Permanent Sovereignty over Natural Resources in International Law (1984)

The Law of Foreign Investment in Australia (1985)

"Monetary Law Developments in the 1990s" in
The Right to Development in International Law (1992)

Business Law of the European Community with Gabriel Moens (1993)

Australia in Press Law and Practice (1993)

"Lapdog, Watchdog or Junkyard Dog? The Media's Role in Australia's
Monarchy/Republic Debate"
in *The Australian Constitutional Monarchy* (1994)

"Economic Development, Foreign Investment and the Law, Issues of
Private Sector Constitutional and Legislative Safeguards for Foreign Direct
Investment: A Comparative Review Utilising Australia and China", with
Robert Pritchard and Thomas Chiu, in *Involvement, Foreign Investment and the Rule
of Law in a New Era* (1995)

"Freedom of Speech and Media Regulation" in *India in Asian Laws
Through Australian Eyes* (1997)

Foreign Investment with Thomas Chiu (1998)

The Australian Constitution in No Case Papers (1998)

"The courts and the media; what reforms are needed and why?"
in *The Courts and the Media* (1999)

"Australian republicanism, sovereignty and the States" in *Restructuring Australia:
Regionalism, republicanism and reform of the nation-state* (2004)

*Australian defamation law reform in Defamation and
Freedom of the Press* (2004)

"A Successful Conservative Party Ready to Rebuild" in
Liberals and Power (2007)

"Monarchy or Republic" in *The Howard Era* (2009)

www.ingramcontent.com/pod-product-compliance
Lightning Source LLC
Chambersburg PA
CBHW020332270326
41926CB00007B/145